GLOBALIZING THE
COMMUNITY COLLEGE

GLOBALIZING THE COMMUNITY COLLEGE
STRATEGIES FOR CHANGE IN THE TWENTY-FIRST CENTURY

John S. Levin

palgrave

GLOBALIZING THE COMMUNITY COLLEGE
© John S. Levin, 2001
Softcover reprint of the hardcover 1st edition 2001 978-0-312-23906-0

All rights reserved. No part of this book may be used or reproduced in any manner whatsoever without written permission except in the case of brief quotations embodied in critical articles or reviews.

First published 2001 by
PALGRAVE™
175 Fifth Avenue, New York, N.Y. 10010 and
Houndmills, Basingstoke, Hampshire RG21 6XS.
Companies and representatives throughout the world

PALGRAVE is the new global publishing imprint of St. Martin's Press LLC Scholarly and Reference Division and Palgrave Publishers Ltd (formerly Macmillan Press Ltd).

ISBN 978-1-349-38679-6   ISBN 978-0-312-29283-6 (eBook)
DOI 10.1057/9780312292836

Library of Congress Cataloging-in-Publication Data
Levin, John S.
Globalizing the community college : strategies for change in the twenty-first century / John S. Levin.—1st ed.
    p. cm.
Includes bibliographical references and index.

   1. Community colleges—United States. 2. Community colleges—Canada. I. Title.
LB2328.15.U6 L48 2001
378.1'543—dc21
                                                           2001018509

A catalogue record for this book is available from the British Library.

Design by Letra Libre, Inc.

First edition: April 2001
10 9 8 7 6 5 4 3 2 1

TABLE OF CONTENTS

Preface		ix
Introduction		xvii
1.	Globalization and the Community College	1
2.	The Cases: Seven Colleges in Two Nations	19
3.	The Domains of Globalization: The Economic Domain	39
4.	The Cultural Domain	63
5.	The Information Domain	81
6.	The Domain of Politics	99
7.	The Process of Globalization	121
8.	What Remains Behind: The Community College in the Twenty-First Century	159
Appendix		183
Notes		195
Bibliography		229
Index		245

Of all the paths . . . there is, at any given moment, a *best path* . . . to find this path and walk in it, is the one needful thing.

—Thomas Carlyle, *Past and Present*

Education—comprehensive liberal education—is the one thing needful and the one effective end.

—Charles Dickens, *Speeches of Charles Dickens*

Success as measured by economic output bears no close relationship to human achievement. The most ardent artistic effort is now devoted not to the arts but to promoting the sale of goods and services. And so also most of our scientific effort. Darwin's successors now concentrate heavily on getting new products for the market.

—John K. Galbraith, "For Richer, for Poorer"

PREFACE

My connection to community colleges began in 1970, when I was enticed away from a youthful ambition for life as a university professor of English. I began to teach literature at a community college, Douglas College, in British Columbia, Canada, and soon forgot the university track, choosing instead to immerse myself in curriculum and instruction, and later in administration, at community colleges. I was a founding member of two community colleges and a participant at a third when it was undergoing a radical change from a focus upon distance education and open learning to traditional, classroom-based education. I was present at two of these colleges when they formalized collective bargaining and when government legislation altered these institutions from community- to government-funded. I lived through a severe recession in the 1980s and through changes in the government in power. I observed countless students whose parents had never seen beyond the twelfth grade and whose homes had no books. I encountered hundreds of students who had left high school years earlier, returning to school in their thirties or forties or fifties, or even sixties and seventies. I watched these students as they finished reading *Wuthering Heights,* completed a biology lab on the cell, or walked out of a philosophy class disturbed by the ethical implications of capital punishment. They were, in the exclamation of Dickens's Joe Gargery, "astonished." Their teachers were largely enthusiasts, not hidebound pedants as Carlyle claims his teachers were. Others at the institution—librarians, counselors, administrators, and support staff—seemed to be true believers: they acted as if the institution and what occurred within it mattered. For over two decades, this environment was my professional home. We used to say we were married to the college, so I assume our association was more than a professional one.

Now, as I address the topic of the community college, this connection sits, so to speak, on my shoulder as I write. My relationship to the community college is personal, and I have, in reflecting upon and writing about the institution, endeavored to maintain verisimilitude, based upon both empirical evidence and some collective understanding of the institution held by practitioners. I strive to be faithful to the past as well as to the empirically validated present.

Yet, it is unlikely that many, if any, within the community college readily think of their institution as enmeshed with globalization, one of the principal threads and themes of this book. Globalization as I present the phenomenon is a scholarly concern. As a scholarly matter, globalization is both a concept and a process. Conceptually, globalization suggests the drawing together of disparate locations and the compression of time. As a process, globalization intensifies social and political relationships and heightens economic competition. Unlike earlier forms of globalization, such as nineteenth-century imperialism, the form of globalization in the past two decades has been propelled by electronic technology and the movement of people, specifically migration. The concept and the process provide me with a channel to follow in my examination of the community college as it has developed over the past decade. Thus, in one sense, globalization is a heuristic, an avenue for uncovering organizational behaviors: it is an amalgam of a process that blends external pressures upon the institution and institutional responses to these pressures. Globalization leads to the ways in which organizational players react to forces greater than themselves and the ways in which these forces play out in their organization.

My scholarly interest in community colleges over the past decade and a half has emphasized organizational behaviors, with the goal of understanding the actions and interactions of organizational members. In the first part of this period, I addressed the ways in which key organizational members, particularly institutional leaders, acted and brought about or contributed to organizational change. In the latter part of this period, I turned to examine those influences upon organizational behaviors, such as government actions in legislation that affect community colleges. Globalization as a topic developed from my earlier explorations into the North America Free Trade Agreement (NAFTA) and its implications for higher education in Canada, Mexico, and the United States. I was fortunate to be a participant in several trilateral meetings on higher education, and I was awarded a research grant from the Canadian Embassy in Washington, D.C. to study NAFTA and its effects upon community colleges. I soon began to see NAFTA as part of a much larger phenomenon. I was also influenced by the work of my colleagues, Sheila Slaughter and Larry Leslie, whose early drafts of their book, *Academic Capitalism,* I read and to whom I offered limited advice on their treatment of Canadian higher education. I was curious as to whether the concept of academic capitalism, applied by Sheila and Larry to research universities, had applicability to community colleges. Eventually, I concluded that while similar forces were at work for both research universities and community colleges, such as a relative decrease in resource allocations from the state to institutions and a relative rise in user costs (for example, tuition fees), there were several fundamental differences between these institutions. These differences suggested that academic capitalism did not apply to community colleges. Some of these differences have to do with the research mission of universities and the connection of research to industry and government. Some of the distinctions between community colleges and research universities pertain to the relative autonomy of university professors compared to community college faculty, and some concern governance and management of these institutions, particularly regarding the legal basis of institutional authority. Nonetheless, I was stimulated to locate a concept that corresponded to academic capitalism for community colleges.

One of the distinctions between Slaughter and Leslie's analysis of research universities and mine for community colleges concerns their emphasis upon economics—upon finances specifically. While they seem to characterize institutional behaviors in universities as economically determined, I see institutional behaviors in community colleges as less singularly propelled. While Slaughter and Leslie view globalization, which to them is also a powerful external force, as solely economic in nature, I view globalization as more multifaceted, including culture and technology as well as economics.

Globalization with its multiple meanings and its multidimensional characteristics, including the altering of temporal and spatial relations, became a useful tool as I first applied the concept to organizational behaviors within community colleges. Its utility as a multifaceted concept paralleled the multipurpose nature of the community college and the complex and unclear identity of the institution.

All too often, the community college is viewed entirely as an educational institution, part of the education structure and hierarchy. Although this is not altogether an inaccurate perception, it is a diminution of the functions and actions of community colleges. Community colleges are more than educational institutions; yet, they are defined as such and compared to other postsecondary educational institutions. The enormous power of the perception and practice of stratification in the U.S. has had an identifying effect upon community colleges as the least prestigious and the lowest-quality postsecondary institution. Stratification employed in this way has been deleterious to the historical development of the institution and has likely biased actions directed toward students from community colleges, such as outcomes of their performance as transfer students at universities. For example, at my university, transfer students are unequally treated in the distribution of financial awards, in part because many of these awards are distributed well before the university admits the transfer student to the institution. Many of the community college transfer students are doubly disadvantaged: first, because of their economic backgrounds, which are inferior to those of native university students; and second, because they are often unable to secure appropriate financial assistance, either because they are at the back of the line for scholarships and bursaries or because they are part-time students and do not qualify for assistance.

Comparisons between universities and community colleges belie the complex identity of the community college as a multipurpose institution fulfilling a number of cultural, economic, political, and social goals. In small communities, the community college serves as a cultural and social center as well as the only postsecondary institution within commuting distance. For many students in either large or small communities, the community college is the only public educational institution that will accept them for college-level studies given their high school academic performance. Furthermore, of the many types of postsecondary institutions facing students who are unprepared for college-level studies, the community college is the only institution whose legal and social mandate is remedial education. In acting upon a plethora of intended goals and in responding to the cultural, economic, educational, political, and social needs of its community or communities, the community college is highly susceptible to economic, political, and social forces.

The multipurpose character of community colleges aside, they have as educational institutions received both unequal and misunderstood attention, again diminishing their acknowledged impact on postsecondary education and training. First, the size of their student populations is if not misperceived then ignored. In the United States in the period from 1993 to 1994, community college student enrollments constituted 35 percent of all college and university enrollments and 39 percent of all undergraduate enrollments. Similarly in Canada, the figure was 38.5 percent of all enrollments and 42 percent of undergraduate enrollments. Second, community colleges are viewed disparagingly, particularly in the United States, as junior colleges or vocational institutions, suggesting an inferior institution to colleges and universities, which are perceived as senior and academic.

To view the community college as only an educational institution is to miss or misunderstand the interactions and relationships between the institution and its milieu; its environment, such as state government, social agencies, cultural and political institutions; and the economy, locally, nationally, and globally. To view the community college through globalization as a concept and as a process is to uncover organizational behaviors and an institutional identity that is not as readily evident when the community college is approached through a narrow lens, which is typical of educational research on the institution. As a conceptual framework, globalization enhances our understanding of organizational behaviors and institutional identity, touching on such topics as organizational change, leadership, education, and work.

To call the community college a globalized institution is not to say that it serves or responds to a global constituency or that it has global purposes. The community college has become a globalized institution because it has been affected by global forces, by the actions of intermediaries who have responded to global forces, and by the interpretations of organizational members to both global forces and to the responses of intermediaries. Globalization as a process finds an outlet within the community college in which economic, cultural, and technological behaviors are advanced along lines consistent with and supportive of globalization.

My use of globalization aids me in explaining what happens in community colleges—that is, the behaviors of organizational members and the actions of the organization. It also leads me to understand institutional identity—that is, the various meanings attributed to organizational action by both community college constituents and stakeholders.

My scholarly interest in community colleges was borne out of my work with John Dennison, now professor emeritus at the University of British Columbia and formerly, as John likes to point out, *the professor* of the University of British Columbia when he was the sole higher education scholar at that institution. He was also, according to campus lore, a member at some point in his career of almost every campus committee or body. John's contributions to Canadian higher education are immense. He charted the first path for scholarship on the community college, a path on which everyone, especially me, are but followers of John. In my work since 1993, as exemplified in this book, I have left that path, lighting out for larger territory than that surveyed by John. I have researched community colleges in both Canada and the United States. My judgment is that the value of the teacher can be seen in the independence and innovation of the student. If my present work exhibits independent and innovative thinking, then the credit goes to John.

Before John, my wife Lee Levin, the author Lee Stewart, helped me bridge the gap between practice and scholarship by pushing me toward doctoral work at mid-career. Lee's own work, including her narrative style in the historical analysis of the experience of women at university, *"It's Up to You": Women at UBC in the Early Years* (UBC Press, 1990), inspired me, not competitively but as an exemplar of scholarship that yields new knowledge in the field of higher education. Also motivating was *Lee's Complaint,* as I called it, a diatribe against the ills of social science research—its presentism. This complaint made me ever mindful of historical context in my study of organizations.

Once I leapt into the scholarly world of a research university, I was aided and abetted by my colleagues at the Center for the Study of Higher Education: Larry Leslie, Gary Rhoades, Sheila Slaughter, and Doug Woodard. Larry, Gary, and Sheila always gave me pointed and useful criticism of whatever work I was courageous enough to ask them to peruse. Doug was supportive of what I was doing, always encouraging me to do more, and this gave me confidence to reach a little higher. I say this because without such an environment and without the expertise that surrounded me, I would not have ventured beyond the traditional or customary approach to the study of community colleges. I was also supported in my study of community colleges by numerous students who looked to me to guide them, and I made myself work harder for them. These include, among others, Angie Fairchilds, Sue Kater, Ken Meier, Maxine Mott, and Christie Roe.

I am indebted to several institutions for this book. First, the Social Sciences and Humanities Research Council of Canada supported the research investigation that is the backbone of this book. Second, the University of Arizona granted me a sabbatical leave in the fall of 1999 so that I could actually have time to write. Third, and last, seven community colleges in two countries—the United States and Canada—agreed to participate in my research investigation and assisted me in the collection of data. All of these institutions made this book possible.

My personal and professional experiences no doubt played a considerable role in how I address the community college in this book. From childhood, I had an aversion to autocratic authority figures, probably the result of my misdemeanors and punishments at a private school where I endured—barely for a year. In later life, during my administrative career at a community college, my Dickensian past was replaced by a Kafkaesque present, and I was, along with other administrative colleagues, victimized by a tyrannical chief executive officer. Those and other similar experiences have impressed upon me the value of kindness, fairness, and justice. While I seek to uncover what we might call truth, I do so without malice or caprice and in the spirit of good faith. I try to be fair to my subject. I seek neither to vaunt over nor to condemn the institution of the community college.

My perception of the community college during the present period of globalization is rooted in an English Victorian past and guided by writers such as Charles Dickens and Thomas Hardy, who seem to be astonishingly relevant to the intersection of globalization and education. Their world was undergoing paradigmatic alteration as a consequence of industrialization just as ours is changing with the emergence of electronic communications. Hardy projects the agrarian and rural response; Dickens, the comerial and urban. They sensitize us both to the potential of dehumanizing qualities of advanced industrialism and materialism and to the values that sustain our humanity during turbulent times, personal and social. My link to these and other writers, such as D. H. Lawrence and Emily Brontë, was awakened during my analysis of organizational behaviors and institutional change. They adjusted my vision to the tensions between progress and continuity in personal, social, and institutional dynamics.

INTRODUCTION

In the latter part of the 1990s, professionals at one of the largest higher education institutions in the United States began not only to question the purposes of their work but also to act upon raising consciousness about a spiritual and emotional void in a learning organization. At Maricopa Community College District in Arizona, professional staff began an underground movement to discover or recover meaning for administrative and instructional work at their institution. This movement, neither a formal institutional activity nor one publicly acknowledged as operational, even within the institution, was referred to as "the authenticity project." It was supported personally by the institution's chief executive officer and its participants included respected administrators, faculty, and other professional staff. As one of the premier community college systems in the world, an institution synonymous with the concept of educational innovation and led by one of the best known higher education leaders in the nation, Maricopa Community College District with its ten colleges was facing an organizational existential crisis. In its preeminent position among U.S. community colleges, with unparalleled resources and annual revenues in excess of $500 million, this institution was suitably positioned to serve its community for global competition. Yet, economic security, measures of institutional effectiveness, and reputation were not enough to stave off discontent among organizational members, who apparently discovered a void at the center of their professional lives. "The authenticity project" initiated a self-reflective process and suggested that the role of leaders might be directed more profitably to the facilitation of human development, self-knowledge, and personal engagement of organizational members with each other for the well-being of the institution's community as well as for the maintenance of institutional performance.

What gave rise to these behaviors and to these longings for more than job achievement is of particular interest, yet puzzling because of the emphasis in community colleges in recent decades on the same or similar outcomes attained by Maricopa Community College District. It is as if the institution had captured the traditional ideals of the community college—access for all, responsiveness to community needs, pipeline to further education and employment opportunities, emphasis upon teaching and learning—and found the prize wanting. Although Maricopa Community College District is not one of the institutions examined in this book, "the authenticity project" serves to illustrate what is acknowledged as missing or lost as colleges respond to the demands of globalization. In the pursuit of innovative approaches or simply survival tactics to respond to their various communities and stakeholders, as well as to maintain their reputational image, community colleges have lost the humanistically meaningful part of their mission while attaining economic and political goals.

Although part of the educational structure, the community college is a unique component. As an institution, the community college is both responsive to external demands and adaptable in meeting those demands. In the 1990s, these demands came most forcefully from both the private sector and government, and they were economically oriented demands. While all of higher education internationally experienced rising levels of economic objectives from government, business, industry, students, and the public in general, community colleges were poignant examples of the instrumentality of higher education.

Community colleges became more overtly connected to the marketplace and to the ideologies of a neoliberal state. Organizational behaviors resembled those of private business and industry, pursuing competitive grants, relying more and more on the private sector for revenues, privatizing services and education, securing contracts with both the private and public sectors, and simply "economizing"—that is, letting financial rationales take precedence over others. The institution's mission now encompassed the acquisition of resources and the prudent ministering of its own financial resources. Colleges expanded their traditional mission by enlarging workforce training and by emphasizing skills development. This resulted in a more overt concentration upon private sector interests and reflected changing priorities for student learning.

In the 1990s, then, community colleges faced new and more forceful pressures. The most pronounced of these was globalization. While the global economy played a dominant role in institutional behaviors and actions, other global flows such as culture and information technology affected institutions. Community colleges changed in significant fashion, following globalizing patterns including an emphasis upon competitive, workplace skills in education and the speeding up of processes in work. A pattern was established beginning in the 1980s and institutionalized in the

1990s toward a more corporate and businesslike approach to education along with the use of new technologies for both instruction and work.

To indicate the consequences of globalization in community colleges not only nationally but also internationally, I focus upon seven community colleges in two nations—the United States and Canada—as concrete examples of both the globalizing pattern and the significant alteration to the institutions. The colleges examined, although varying in their responses to external pressures, reflected the globalizing process in their actions and reinforced globalization in their internal operations and organizational behaviors. The reflection and reinforcement were evident in the changing managerial ideology at colleges, with emphasis upon education and training as commodities, the actions to align the institution with the marketplace, and the drive in operations for economic efficiency. College managers relied upon new technologies to propel change in both work and education. College programming changed to meet perceived marketplace employment and work-force requirements. Largely as a consequence of government funding constraints, colleges sought new revenue sources, particularly from private citizens through increased fees from international students and from business and industry, as well as higher tuition fees generally. Colleges worked at increasing efficiencies in production. They did not diminish production. Rather, colleges endeavored to expand production with fewer or the same revenues relative to institutional size. In general, money—and not educational objectives—drove production.

Economic ends dominated the mission of community colleges in the 1990s, refashioning traditional missions of access and responsiveness to community educational and training needs so that these became means, not ends. Instead, improving economic conditions of regions and nations, through such activities as work-force training, both to compete in production globally and to attract investors with a competitive economic environment, became a preeminent, articulated concern. Furthermore, by "economizing," by operating institutions more efficiently, colleges imitated the behaviors of businesses or corporations and became participants in the global economy. This was precisely the intent of government policy for community colleges in the two nations.

Community colleges evolved into multifaceted institutions, incorporating the purposes of several organizations into one. They were not only the traditional community colleges, with comprehensive curricula and open access, but also training centers, charter schools, private high schools, language institutes, music conservatories, applied research centers, and businesses. They were simultaneously educational institutions and entrepreneurial businesses. They maintained democratic principles—most notably open access to educational opportunities, a characteristic of "democracy's college"[1]—yet responded more emphatically to corporate and economic interests of the local community. The shift was from community service to private sector interests while preserving and expanding education and training opportunities for community members. Marketplace values and behaviors, including training and retraining of the work force, motivated institutional programming patterns. Finally, priorities for student learning shifted from an emphasis upon individual personal development, career preparation, and educational advancement to skills development and workplace practice.

These alterations marked a significant shift for community colleges toward intensified occupational objectives promoted by a global economy and resource management practices adhered to in the private sectors of business and industry. While contending with enormous culture changes within their communities, as a consequence of immigration patterns and the pervasive information revolution that affected most if not all organizations, community colleges were decidedly instruments of government economic policy at the end of the twentieth century. They were poised to take on the expectations of the state for economic prosperity.

Neglected in this economic preoccupation are education and a balanced recognition of human achievement and worth. Such an awareness is exemplified by those involved in "the authenticity project" at Maricopa Community College District, even though the project is at a consciousness-raising phase. For the community colleges I examine, the means to accomplish the occupational objectives and the expectations of both government and the private sector is a road paved with overworked professionals and support staff. Their organizations are emotionally unhealthy environments in which economic interests outweigh social and personal concerns. They are contentious sites, with struggles over resources, professional status, and the goals of student learning. They are perhaps the starting or the ending points in higher education's reaction to learning for the sole purpose of earning.

Yet, the stirrings of institutional members at the Maricopa Community College District in response to work without meaning, especially personal and even spiritual meaning, suggest that the economic orientation of community colleges may have reached its stretching point. In the fulfillment of ambitions to become an institution of national and international importance or in simply surviving economically, the community college may change yet again, and, like the Maricopa Community College District, may find that all that glitters is not gold.

The Organization of This Book

The book contains eight chapters and an appendix that describes the research underlying the discussion. Chapters one and two establish the foundation for the examination of community colleges and globalization and introduce the seven institutions used for the analysis of institutional alteration.

In chapter one, I present my argument about changed conditions for community colleges and the altered mission and changed structures that stem from organizational response to the globalization process. I introduce the research project that underlies this book and the theoretical perspectives used to examine organizational change. This chapter summarizes the globalization debate and shows connections between globalization and the community college. The second chapter begins with a discussion of research on community colleges, noting the paucity of research on organizational behaviors. I then turn to the seven colleges, the principal focus of my investigation, first by identifying common bonds among the seven institutions and second by discussing each college separately. In this discussion, the social, political, and economic contexts are interwoven with central issues that have faced the colleges in the 1980s and 1990s.

A detailed analysis of the effects of globalization and organizational responses to globalization is presented in chapters three, four, five, and six. The analysis proceeds from a conceptualization of four domains of globalization behaviors—economic, culture, information, and politics.

Chapter three demonstrates that organizational behaviors reflected increasing focus upon the acquisition of revenues or strategies to respond to revenue decline including its threatened decline. The major outcomes of these behaviors included stress upon organizational members to increase production, tension over job security, and frustration over the quality of institutional performance. Chapter four is a detailed discussion of the cultural domain. I focus upon three cultural aspects of globalization: (1) the dominant ideology associated with globalization, (2) the involvement and interactions of people in and with other cultures, and (3) the conceptualization of the world as a single place. I turn to the first two of these cultural aspects and apply them to organizations, specifically to the community college. For the third aspect, I consider potential cultural change as an outcome of the use of electronic technology. In chapter five, I address the third domain of globalization behaviors—information. Information technologies and their accompanying behaviors are evident in both work, especially administrative work, and instruction. For administrative work, I examine the effects of the use of information technologies. In instruction, I consider the expected outcomes of the use of informational technologies. Overall, organizational culture was altered at these institutions: the general support for information technologies and their increasing use was evidence of at least a tacit agreement between labor and management to accept management's goals of greater efficiency and rising productivity.

I discuss the domain of politics in chapter six, concluding the discussion of the domains of globalization. Government policies endeavored to direct community colleges toward economic goals, emphasizing workforce training and state economic competitiveness as outcomes, compelling colleges to improve efficiencies and to become accountable to government and responsive to business and industry. Colleges responded to government policies, neglecting aspects of their mission and thus their communities because their focus and their resources were directed toward government priorities. In responding to government demands for increased productivity, colleges precipitated tensions in labor relations, where management asked for and expected, for example, faculty to teach greater numbers of students and to use technology to support their added responsibilities.

Chapter seven offers a discussion of the process of globalization in all seven of the case study institutions. Community colleges did not eradicate behavioral patterns associated with the preservation of institutional identity, the accommodation of growth, the emphasis upon a comprehensive curriculum, and other traditional patterns. The globalization process accompanied these behavioral patterns and in some cases initiated others, such as marketization. Institutional responses to both global forces and to the responses of intermediaries, such as government, to global forces resulted in considerable alteration to institutional mission and structures at the seven colleges.

Chapter eight, the final chapter, addresses how colleges reflected and reproduced globalization and ultimately changed as institutions. I examine the ways in which these colleges have been altered as a consequence of the globalization process, and I address the implications of what has changed as well as what was retained from the past. I conclude by conceiving a trajectory of institutional change for community colleges in the twenty-first century and suggest that college constituents and influencers can respond to the effects of globalization in beneficial ways. Following chapter eight, an appendix describes in considerable detail the research methods employed for the study that supports this book and its argument.

This is one of the few examinations of community colleges in more than one national jurisdiction, certainly the only extended, book-length discussion of community colleges in more than a single nation. With a dominant theme of globalization coursing its way through the book, the comparative approach of examining community colleges in two nations suggests that the results of organizational behaviors in a global context are neither institution nor nation specific. We see in the process of globalization a borderless world, in which the local is penetrated by a global ideology that is economically motivated, in which the local is affected by the outcomes of conditions in other countries that lead to immigration on a global scale, and in which the local is significantly influenced by the pervasive use of information technologies, shrinking both spatial and temporal experiences. We also learn that public policy, and specifically education policy at the postsecondary level, is consistent with private sector interests, largely shaping citizens into economic entities as either workers or consumers or both.

Moreover, we see that responses by community college professionals and stakeholders[2] to these conditions are contributors to organizational and institutional change. These responses or reactions to global forces, such as the information technology revolution or the global economy, have refashioned the community college, orienting the institution to a global and economic context.

CHAPTER 1

GLOBALIZATION AND THE COMMUNITY COLLEGE

Introduction

The community college in North America has neither history nor image as an institution with a global focus or occupying a global context. Since the 1960s, the institution has been viewed and conceived as a social and educational institution that responds to its local community, offering open access to postsecondary education and providing comprehensive education and training programs to meet the needs of individual students. Its image is based upon its assumed mission: to serve the underserved and to expand access to postsecondary education and training. Historically, community colleges have prided themselves on fulfilling the needs of individual students and serving their local communities.

Yet, in the 1990s, with the rise in public and government emphasis and attention upon a global economy, the community college became not only a more prominent regional and national institution but also an institution that was affected by macrolevel changes in the external environment, even globally stimulated changes. These included government policies to reflect both societal and economic concerns such as the training of a globally competitive work force and private sector demands for an increase in work-based training and specific skill acquisition for workers.

Global forces, particularly economic ones, accompanied and contributed to organizational change in the 1990s, and colleges in response to these forces altered their missions and structures. These alterations in effect moved colleges away from local community social needs toward local market needs and in line with national and international agendas of dominant influencers such as governments and businesses, suggesting a more pronounced economic role for community colleges. This economic role was a consequence of responses to globalization and a perpetuation of a globalizing process. Pressures upon community colleges to fulfill specific roles—from social to educational, and including economic—have influenced the institution since its beginnings.[1]

Originating in the United States, near or at the beginning of the twentieth century, the community college was referred to as a junior college. Not until the end of World War II was there any significant reference to a community college. The Truman Commission of 1947 first formalized the term "community college,"[2] and even so it was not until the 1960s that both the term and the concept of a college that served community needs became standard usage. From the 1960s to the 1980s, rapid expansion of these institutions, both in student numbers and in campuses, underlined the need that community colleges filled: literally hundreds of colleges were established and millions of students were added to previous enrollment levels. In the United States, at the start of the 1960s, there were 390 public community colleges; by 1990, there were 1,281. In 1990, there were close to 5 million students enrolled in community colleges, when in 1960 there were just over 500,000.[3] With growth came change.

Those who worked in community colleges in the late 1960s and early 1970s and continued to work in these institutions at the close of the twentieth century experienced substantial and often dramatic changes. Much of the change in the early 1970s was a function of growth: more students; more programs; more courses; more faculty, support staff, and administrators; and the inevitable formalizing of the bureaucracy. In addition, campuses moved from temporary quarters, where they were located in high schools and in portable buildings, to new sites and new facilities: permanent campuses led to more formalized maturity of these institutions. By the late 1970s, there were other dramatic alterations to institutional life. These included unionization and the institutionalization of developmental and remedial education.[4]

Unionization, and indeed labor-management relations, in community colleges is a largely untold but instructive story. As a hybrid institution growing out of the high school and yet with a college identity, the community college combined the working conditions and employee status of the four-year college and the secondary school. Issues such as academic freedom, governance, and supervision were complicated and potentially contentious at these institutions. As the institution developed into the 1970s, issues were often seen to reflect more of a singular community of interest—either labor or management. To some extent, unionization eroded the former collegial environment of the late 1960s and early 1970s, when college members saw themselves as "one big family." But unionization also accorded faculty and support staff groups a more formal role in institutional affairs and likely more just treatment in their work. As well as the "one big family" sentiment of the pre-unionization period, that same period saw smaller institutions and less complexity in institutional operations.

It was also during the 1970s that the comprehensive mission of the community college reached full bloom. Prior to this period, university transfer, vocational, and community education were the main curricular areas of the institution. With the recognition that both university and occupational programs contained students who were unprepared for college-level work and that there was a large segment of the community in need of developmental education to function in society, colleges inserted programs and courses, commonly referred to as remedial and developmental education.[5] This alteration expanded the mission of the community college and changed internal dynamics among faculty and among program areas. By the close of the 1970s and the early part of the 1980s, college members and observers began to question the wisdom of the expanded mission, both for institutional performance and for the use of resources.

In the 1980s, economic factors took center stage. Public sector funding was more seriously questioned, and education as a whole was under scrutiny as epitomized by the publication *A Nation At Risk*.[6] For higher education, a number of commissions and reports suggested that teaching and learning were not priorities at U. S. colleges. Prominent national stakeholders challenged the slide away from traditional academic skills, and connected this shift to the underperformance of the U.S. economy. George Keller gave colleges and universities a wake-up call in managing these institutions.[7] For community colleges, the message was mixed and confusing.

The "management revolution" sweeping North American business did catch on in community colleges, but aspects of their mission, such as open access, made institutional performance somewhat problematic. Some institutions tried to meld performance with access by implementing standards for remediation.[8] Most institutions were caught up in maintaining enrollments so as not to lose state dollars.

The 1980s can be seen as a gathering place for the accumulation of developments of previous decades. This gathering place had a jumbled appearance, combining a wide collection of programs and educational services and a complicated organization, with a mixture of structures, an array of processes, and stresses over labor, including workloads and performance, as well as the division and coordination of labor.[9] Both education and work became fertile ground for change and for confrontation.

Institutional mission and purpose were challenged.[10] Managing colleges became a prevalent topic and an area of institutional tension.[11]

By the end of the 1980s, community colleges were well-established institutions poised to either continue their largely traditional path begun in the 1960s and 1970s or alter directions in education and their patterns of work. Financial issues began to put pressures upon the institutions, as governments restrained their fiscal allocations in the face of rising costs and with enrollment growth in the 1980s just over 1percent per year nationally.[12] One obvious outcome of these fiscal pressures was the trend toward greater numbers of part-time faculty and relatively fewer numbers of full-time faculty working at these institutions in the period between 1980 and 1990.[13] Nonetheless, pressures in the 1980s were not extreme enough to push community colleges beyond their traditional patterns or to alter their mission and purposes.

A similar narrative pertains to the community colleges of Canada, the other jurisdiction examined in this book. With the inception of community colleges dating just to the 1960s, Canadian institutions have a shorter history, one characterized by considerable diversity among colleges, especially from province to province.[14] In spite of this diversity, there are also large areas of commonality, especially in regards to mission.[15] Their history is more compressed than that of U.S. colleges; and, with the exception of the provinces of Alberta, British Columbia, and Quebec, there was a pronounced emphasis upon job training at public colleges.

By the end of the 1980s, Canadian community colleges were sophisticated public institutions tied to their respective provincial governments and largely funded by those governments. Since the 1960s, they had undergone significant growth both in student enrollments and in institutions, with approximately 125 public community colleges enrolling approximately 500,000 students at the beginning of the 1980s.[16] Perhaps most evident by the end of the 1980s was the more prominent role of federal and provincial governments including their policies and practices directing these institutions, as well as more centralizing tendencies within provincial systems.[17] Nonetheless, public community colleges held to their traditional missions and largely local orientation.

In the decade of the 1990s, however, community colleges in both the United States and Canada faced new and more forceful pressures. The most pronounced of these was globalization. There are four major and distinctive domains of influence with respect to globalization—economics, culture, information, and politics. The behaviors within these domains—those of organizational members and stakeholders—affected both education and work within these institutions. Community colleges changed in significant fashion in the 1990s, and what was altered and what was retained from the past are defining attributes of these institutions, as well as signals of their purposes and functioning in the twenty-first century. For the early decades of the twenty-first century, the pressures to provide education and training to a diverse student population, to serve community economic interests, and to support institutional operations with adequate fiscal resources will no doubt increase. To finance these activities, institutions will be caught between the need to turn more to the private sector for funds, especially fee payers, and meeting community needs for traditional education, such as literacy and cognitive development. Simultaneously, institutions will continue to face identity pressures, whether those be to preserve traditional community college missions and values or to expand into a higher status postsecondary institution. The pattern established in the 1990s toward a more corporate and businesslike approach to education along with the use of new technologies for both instruction and work is likely to be of central concern to both educators and governments. The purposes and outcomes of postsecondary education as embodied in the community college are undergoing significant change. So too are community college organization and work within these organizations.

Qualitative change, unlike quantitative change, is difficult to objectify or measure. Beyond their statistical characteristics—such as number of students enrolled, financial revenues and expenditures, and the like—community colleges can claim conceptual characteristics, features that give an identity, distinctiveness, and, some might say, life to these institutions. These characteristics are the objects of change, for to alter these is to alter the identity of the institution. And if forces of change, or globalization, or managerial responses to forces of change are to be designated significant and fundamentally altering, then change—that is, change to institutional identity, to the institution's purposes, actions, and to participants' understandings of these actions—will be qualitative. Levy and Merry, in developing a conceptual framework for organizational change, premise organizational change upon the concept of second-order, fundamental, and enduring change. Four categories of change are used in their framework: paradigmatic change, mission and purpose change, cultural change, and change in functional processes, including structures, management, technology, decision-making, and communication patterns.[18] These are the qualities that alter when change is lasting, becoming part of the patterns of organizational behavior.

There are numerous features shared by community colleges in North America, and to some extent these colleges can claim a common history in the 1970s, 1980s, and 1990s. Both community college literature and institutional mission and goals' statements combine to validate and proclaim similar attributes and intentions. The concept of "open access" is one of the fundamental attributes of the institution; access carries numerous connotations including geographical distance, finances, availability of programs, bureaucratic hurdles, as well as past academic achievement. The particular emphasis on one or more of these aspects of access is institutionally specific. Some community colleges permit students who have reached the age of 19 to enroll in any open enrollment course—that is, a course that is not part of a competitive entry program, regardless of that student's past academic record. Other colleges will place some qualifications upon this action—for example, requiring a student to take a placement test before enrollment.

Institutional emphasis upon students and on their interests, goals, and learning is another of the shared features of community colleges. As an educational institution, the community college has defined itself as student-centered, with a focus upon teaching as distinct from research or service. In the past decade, this teaching focus has shifted semantically to a learning focus. Other attributes of these institutions, either claimed or validated or both, include the provision of a comprehensive curriculum, community orientation, and a flexible and responsive institution.

Community colleges share three essential historical roles. These roles include education, training, and community resource. These are not independent, and emphasis upon any one of the three differs from one institution to another. Historically, these roles expanded in some areas and contracted in others. In the 1990s, the training role became more pronounced in colleges in which it once occupied a lesser status and institutional priority. As a community resource in the 1980s and 1990s, colleges lost much of their social function and gained a much more significant economic function. These alterations parallel the process of globalization identified for the late 1980s and 1990s.

This book addresses the period of the 1990s and is based upon a comparative study of influences of globalization and globalizing trends on community colleges in the United States and Canada, in order to identify and explain outcomes of responses to globalization in these institutions. The study was an examination of external forces acting upon seven institutions during the decade of the 1990s and the responses of institutions, including their organizational adaptation and institutional changes to mission and structures. In the most general terms, the study addressed change within community colleges during the decade of the 1990s. The specific focus, however, was upon external forces that influenced or precipitated internal change.[19]

The study used a qualitative, multiple case study design involving field methods—including document analysis, interviews, informal conversations, observations, and the use of informants. Furthermore, investigation included multiple sites or cases, and this approach was particularly appropriate for the understanding of institutional contexts.

In refining the design of the study, I narrowed the focus to a geographical area—the Pacific/Western region—to capture the concept of international and global economics and trade within what is referred to as the Pacific Rim and to identify and follow the development of international, cultural connections consistent with this region. Globalizing forces are likely more evident in or near large population centers, especially those with relatively large immigrant populations or those that depend upon international trade.[20] I concluded that I would need to understand not only the colleges but also their communities, however defined. The importance of the research methods to my analysis deserves some mention, although the details of these methods are contained in Appendix A.

Research on the colleges of two nations—the United States and Canada—was undertaken through methods that permitted both macro- and microanalysis. The use of federal documents for policy analysis, the use of both state and provincial government policy documents for analysis of government policy, and the use of institutional documents for institutional level analysis made up only part of the rich data collected and analyzed. Interviews at seven sites over a two-and-a-half-year period, involving over 400 people, and observations of institutional behaviors, as well as institutional questionnaires and demographic data for regions, states, provinces, and countries, all combined to provide large data sets. This in-depth examination of seven colleges and their complex contexts—local, regional, state and provincial, and national—informs this book and helps convey the story of these institutions and the emerging globalization of higher education.

Two theoretical domains guide the analysis: one is globalization theory and the other is organization theory. Globalization theory is used as an analytical tool for categorizing those institutional behaviors that have contributed to or defined organizational change. Organization theory provides several analytical frameworks for examining the ways in which organizations change, specifically changes in formal structure, organizational culture, goals, programs, or missions in institutions. Also useful as an analytical framework are theories of organizational adaptation. Two other theoretical fields—institutional theory and policy theory—are used, both to refine understandings of institutional behaviors and to clarify government actions related to community colleges.

Globalization is a multidimensional term. It suggests a condition: the world as a single place. It is viewed as a process: a linking of localities, separated by great distances and intensifying relations between these localities. Globalization is also implicitly connected to international economies, as in the concept of a world economy; to international relations or politics, as in the concept of global politics; and to culture, as in the concept of global culture. Furthermore, the term *global* is used as an adjective for both singular and plural nouns, suggesting that there are multiple economies, political systems, and cultures globally as well as a single integrative economy, political system, and culture.[21] As a practical term, *globalization* reflects a perception "that the world is rapidly being moulded into a shared social space by economic and technological forces and that developments in one region of the world can have profound consequences for the life chances of individuals or communities on the other side of the globe."[22]

While there is a wide array of definitions and conceptions of globalization, there is near consensus upon its impact on organizations. First, global forces drive production processes. This is a reflexive condition: transformations in production affect national economies and politics, as well as cultures. Global competition adds pressures to organizations in increasing profit margins or in decreasing expenditures, or both; or alternately in nonprofit organizations in increasing efficiencies. Second, global competition spurs technological innovation, particularly increasing computerization in the workplace. Technological innovation leads to the subordination and displacement of workers—that is, cuts in labor costs. These innovations and reductions lead not only to redesign and reorganization of the workplace but also to changes in the nature of work. Work changes, as well as production alteration, are oriented toward speed, to keeping up with market changes, responding to communications, and satisfying customers. The rate of production increases, the workload of employees increases, and the control of management over production increases.[23] The prime determinant of these alterations according to many scholars is technological advances.

And third, technological innovations and applications lead to more innovations and applications. "Globalization is both chicken and egg. It is driven by and driving the new technology that enables global action."[24] Technology is both   mulator and a product of globalization. Although the drive for profits and efficiencies makes the use of new technologies imperative, it is the new technologies themselves that transform the workplace and the organization.[25]

Organizational structures change in order to accommodate labor-saving technologies; labor is replaced by machines. New ways to manage production are inevitable: for example, network structures replace pyramids as ways to coordinate work, and both the speed of production and managerial control are increased as workers become more compliant with managerial imperatives.[26] In addition to its economic role, globalization also connects cultures and groups, integrating people and their differences, sometimes resulting in harmony, sometimes in a "complex, overlapping, disjunctive order."[27] The integration argument suggests that cultural differences are subsumed in a homogenous, overarching structure,[28] in which Western, particularly American, values are the dominant ones. This phenomenon is also referred to as "McDonaldization,"[29] a condition that, applied to higher education, views education as a commodity, readily available to all consumers, local and global. The Westernization or Americanization theme, however, may be a temporal phase of globalization, and the processes of contracting geography and connecting people socially, culturally, and economically may be the more enduring characteristic of globalization.[30] The point may pertain more to the homogenization of cultural attributes, such as ideas, language, and values and other related behaviors found in such areas as fashion and the media.

It may be that consciousness of a global society, culture, and economy and global interdependence are the cornerstones of globalization,[31] and these—consciousness and interdependency—have saliency in knowledge-based enterprises. Institutional theory suggests that there are organizational "fields," or institutional types, such as higher education institutions or hospitals, for example, in which patterns of institutional behaviors become similar across institutions.[32] Thus, there is a certain inevitability that higher education institutions, because of their cultural, social, and economic roles, are caught up in and affected by globalization.

The process of globalization has been connected to numerous alterations in higher education. For example, with emphasis upon international competitiveness, economic globalization is viewed as moving postsecondary institutions into a businesslike orientation, with its attendant behaviors of efficiency and productivity. At the level of universities in both the United States and Canada, globalization can be equated with corporatism, with the marketplace playing a more pronounced role than in the past. Furthermore, education is vocationalized, and training is driven by the demands of business and industry. Conceptually, training and education are synonymous, much like the interchangeability of "knowledge" and "skills."[33] The placement of higher education institutions in closer proximity to the marketplace, especially in fields connected to technoscience, through corporate partnerships and associations, is an obvious manifestation of economic globalization.

While no one theory of organizations is likely to explain organizational behaviors completely or satisfactorily, several theories have saliency for institutional change. These include organizational change theory,[34] theories of organizational power,[35] and theories of organizational adaptation.[36] For example, Cameron[37] employs a continuum to describe and explain organizational adaptation. This continuum is based upon the level of control over change to an organization: the level of control is framed as predominantly external control and predominantly internal control. This framework helps us to understand the role of internal organizational members on organizational action—that is, the extent to which organizational members are responsible for organizational change or adaptation. Sandelands and Drazin[38] refer to these two conceptions of change as exogenesis and endogenesis, with the former signaling change attributed to forces outside the organization and the latter signaling change attributed to the actions and choices of managers.

Related to organizational theory, institutional theory offers another perspective for examining organizational behaviors, advancing the view that institutional dynamics are best understood through an institution's relationship to other like institutions. That is, organizational behaviors and structures are part of a larger institutional context, a "field" of other organizations that includes constraints and influences.[39] In this sense, specific contexts, such as government policy initiatives, help to explain organizational change because change will occur not just at one site but at multiple sites that are part of the same organizational field.

But more importantly for this investigation, the emphasis on context in institutional theory—historical, political, social—and the behaviors of organizational members in response to that context suggest that the externally perceived and internally enacted identity of an organization figures prominently in what actions organizations take.[40] Thus, in this examination of community colleges in two nations and in several states and provinces, the institution, the community college, the country, and the state or province are contexts for organizational behaviors. Knowledge of these contexts aids in the understanding of organizational behaviors, specifically directing us to the changes occurring in institutions and the influences that give rise to these changes. The state is not just a jurisdictional context for community colleges but an actor through policy in organizational behaviors.

There are three streams of thought on the state that frame my analysis of government policy for community colleges. The first views the state as the nexus of the struggle of classes: that is, the state functions to preserve and expand modes of production.[41] State policy drives or influences production. The state "is an expression, or condensation, of social-class relations, and these relations imply domination of one group by another. Hence the State is both a product of relations of domination and their shaper."[42]

The second view of the state is that it is independent of capital and labor.[43] The state is an actor and, in the case of higher education, is intertwined and perhaps inseparable from postsecondary education.[44] It is composed of relatively autonomous government officials who serve their own interests as well as those of business and students.[45]

The third view of the state is that it is a multifaceted resource, within which policy formation is played out. Various branches or levels of the state respond to different and even competing constituencies.[46] That is, the state is not monolithic, and its behaviors are not necessarily consistent or uniform.

In addition to theory, some higher education literature, especially that literature with emphasis upon theoretical constructs to elucidate organizational behaviors, provides useful perspectives for the understanding of organizational change. In particular, the work of Slaughter and Leslie[47] is applicable because of their use of globalization theory, as well as their implications concerning the alignment of higher education institutions with resource providers, in line with the theoretical position of Pfeffer and Salancik.[48] Furthermore, community college literature in both the United States and Canada pertaining to the conceptualization of community college mission provides historical perspectives of institutional development. This includes the work of U.S. scholars, such as Brint and Karabel, Clowes and Levin, Dougherty, Richardson, Fisk, and Okun, and Roueche and Baker, and the work of Dennison, Dennison and Gallagher, and Dennison and Levin in Canada. The literature serves as a guide in the exploration and explanation of change to missions and structures of community colleges.[49]

In this book, I pursue the impact and influences of the globalization process and responses to globalization on community colleges, examining effects of organizational change upon organizational members and students. I uncover the implications of these changes for two nations and their respective societies. These implications address the purposes of higher education, whether those include the transmission of culture and knowledge,[50] the challenge to fundamental categories of knowledge and the modern tradition,[51] or training for the needs of capital.[52] I consider what we have gained and what we have lost as a consequence of globalization, and I suggest how community colleges might be conceived in the future.

This book not only tells the larger story of seven institutions but also conveys the ways in which community colleges have become globalized institutions. Globalization is reflected in institutional behaviors, in the changing and changed missions and structures of these institutions, and in the alterations to both education and work.

The Globalization Debate

Inconsistencies and contradictions follow descriptions, explanations, and judgments of globalization. Indeed, whether globalization is a process or a product is in dispute. Scholars suggest that globalization is a historical process, initiated in the fourteenth century,[53] with even its continental origin—Europe or Asia—in doubt. Analysis of present behaviors suggests "disjunctures,"[54] dichotomies, and contrasting alterations in resultant conditions and behaviors produced by globalization. Work has altered.[55] Economies have transformed.[56] Social dynamics have changed dramatically.[57] Such tensions, contrasts, and disruptions are defining characteristics of globalization.

Judgments about the consequences of globalization are also contrasting and to some extent polarized. A prominent camp opposed to globalization views its results as nearly catastrophic, alienating, and morally repugnant.[58] A second camp is more favorable to the effects of globalization and profiles a changed global environment.[59] A third takes a less judgmental view of globalization and its effects, preferring to explain the condition, its origins, and its implications.[60]

In the field of education, globalization and its effects are viewed largely by scholars from a negative point of view, giving globalization a derogatory connotation.[61] Privatization of services, institutional competitiveness, marketplace orientation, "vocationalization" of curricula, commodification of education and knowledge are among the numerous outcomes of globalization that are cast in this negative light. In the postsecondary sector, educational managers and government policy voice an acceptance of globalization, its effects, and its implications. This position is counterpointed with that of numerous higher education scholars, thus providing a polarized structure of judgment on globalization and higher education.

In order to understand the reputed effects of globalization upon higher education institutions and the import of institutional responses to globalization, there is a need for a more comprehensive perspective. Globalization is not simply an act done to an organization. Responses by organizational members to globalization have as much or more impact upon institutions as globalization itself. That is, organizational members play out or enact their understandings and judgments of globalization and global forces: they make changes to organizational structures and processes in response to their understandings of external pressures and forces. Critics of higher education who condemn institutional alteration as a consequence of globalization view organizational members as passive recipients of globalizing changes.[62] In contrast, organizational members can be seen as conscious, responsible actors, capable of forming intelligent and educationally beneficial responses to global conditions and processes. These responses are commonly reactions to other organizations, groups, and bodies, including institutional stakeholders such as business, industry, government, postsecondary institutions, and students. Global patterns of production, space and time compression of human communications, and ideological and even style uniformity are acknowledged characteristics of globalization, but there is no predictable certainty about their effects universally. Indeed, because globalization includes "contradictory trends towards... integration and differentiation,"[63] exemplified in the concepts of global and local, and "disjunctures"[64] between the spheres or dimensions of globalization, agency is a key variable or determinant of the effects of globalization. It is, therefore, important to acknowledge organizational and institutional theories, including scholarly understandings, in the examination of globalization and its influences upon organizational behaviors. These include organizational power, organizational response to an external environment, institutional context, and organizational change.[65]

Globalization and the Community College

This book addresses globalization as a process and examines its effects upon work and education in institutions of higher education. Effects upon work and education are noted particularly through the responses of organizational members to the process of globalization. Community colleges in two countries—the United States and Canada—are examined. These colleges and their legal jurisdictions serve as primary data sources. These data demonstrate that these institutions reflect globalization trends such as increasing the pace of work through the use of electronic technologies and reproduce globalization patterns as can be noted, for example, in how these institutions treat education as an economic commodity. The global context for the community college is not that of an institution that provides international education or one that interacts with institutions or agencies in other countries. Rather, the global context has become internalized, both reflected in and reproduced by the ideology of economic efficiency, productivity, and the commodification of education and training.

Behaviors and actions at community colleges underline the significant role of economic factors in globalization. But there is more to globalization than economic behaviors, labor and capital, and market forces. Specifically, electronic technologies not only drive globalization; they have also become part of the culture or behavioral patterns of globalization. Immigration, in both its patterns and its sheer numbers, also contributes to globalization, as do ideological shifts and international associations.[66]

For community colleges, economics, electronic technology, and immigration patterns serve as dominant globalizing influences upon the institutions. These constitute domains, or spheres of influence, of globalization. Economics include the wide area of global production, government and private sector behaviors in response to a global economy, and fiscal resources. Electronic technology includes computer-based information and production processing technologies, communication technologies such as electronic mail (e-mail), voice mail, and video broadcasting, and software programs from financial accounting packages to content-rich data sources that might be encyclopedic in nature. This technology grouping incorporates production, communication, and knowledge technologies. And finally, immigration patterns include the rationales for immigration, such as political upheaval, the geographical locations of immigration origination, essentially non-European and non-English speaking regions, and the demographic characteristics of immigrants, such as skill and income levels. In addition to these three domains of influence, the roles and actions of governments are significant catalysts and sustainers of organizational change. This fourth domain of globalization is one of politics, and government, specifically state and provincial government, is conceived as a principal agent of globalization.

Globalization is not a new phenomenon.[67] However, globalization in the 1990s was far different from and more influential than previously. The factors noted above were also not new phenomena: global economic behaviors, new technologies, and immigration pre-date not only the 1990s but also the twentieth century. Yet the nature of these factors, such as the reformation of management of production, the speed and capabilities of new technology, and the movement of large numbers of Asian and non-Western European immigrants to both the United States and Canada, were markedly different from previous decades.

In the 1980s and 1990s, these globalizing factors—production, communications, and immigration—were influential in altering organizational behaviors. Globally, there were shifts in production from material to information processing accompanied by changes in the management of production, in markets, and in labor requirements.[68] The pronounced shifts, while developed in earlier decades, were popularly identified with the fall of the Berlin Wall and the collapse of the Soviet system.[69] Globalization during the past decade and a half, from the 1980s into the 1990s, was generally acknowledged as a technological and managerial transformation of production and labor relationships in which economic values predominated and in which societies were equated with or reduced to economies.[70]

Although varying in their responses to external pressures, the colleges examined reflected the globalizing process and reinforced globalization in their internal relationships, demonstrating that organizations provide at least one means through which globalization occurs. This reflection and reinforcement were evident in the changing managerial ideology at colleges, with emphasis upon education and training as commodities, the actions to align the institution with the marketplace, and the drive in operations for economic efficiency. Reflective of globalization, college managers relied upon new technologies to propel change in both work and education. And with alteration to jobs in the labor market, both in number and kind, college programming changed to meet perceived marketplace employment and work-force requirements. Largely as a consequence of government funding constraints, colleges sought new revenue sources, particularly from private citizens through increased fees from international students, and from business and industry, as well as higher tuition fees from non-international students. Colleges worked at increasing efficiencies in production and did not diminish production; rather, colleges endeavored to expand production with fewer or the same revenues relative to institutional size.[71]

Electronic technologies accompanied production alterations and enabled higher levels of productivity. This use of electronic technologies mirrored globalizing trends: electronic technologies to drive production, to change labor and management relationships and relationships among the labor force, and to improve efficiencies. Colleges adopted various computer-based systems for enrollment and financial management in the 1990s. These systems altered production and relationships and increased operational efficiencies.[72]

Along similar lines of technological change, communications patterns and levels of communications changed over the decade with the addition of such tools as e-mail and voice mail. New "network structures" evolved through the use of e-mail, groups of "users" became established, and new relationships among these users developed. Voice mail as well as e-mail use led to the accomplishment of work outside of offices—for example, in automobiles and at home. Workers were thus available 24 hours a day. Work that formerly went through an outer office or assistant moved directly to managers and from managers directly to faculty and staff, as well as to other managers. These practices changed work patterns and work relationships.

Established patterns of communication altered in these institutions, driven by both the availability of electronic technologies and by external requirements or standards. As more and more information was available—and sometimes only available—online and more and more person-to-person communication was carried on through electronic mail, standard practices of previous decades became either obsolete or severely curtailed. In information dissemination, libraries and administrative offices lost their role as information centers and warehouses. For example, institutional data were more likely to be found at an institution's Web site than in an administrative office. In communications, collegewide meetings and memoranda as communication vehicles were rare, and messages by electronic mail were either posted on an electronic bulletin board or distributed to e-mail users.

Traditional organizational behaviors altered as well, as a consequence of changing student demographics. Large numbers of Asian and other non-Western European immigrants settled in the communities served by colleges. Public views toward these immigrants were ambivalent: on the one hand, social attitudes and government policy characterized and valued a multicultural society; on the other hand, public articulations and public polls reflected widespread negative reactions to immigrants.[73]

With large numbers of designated immigrants requiring English language training and many in need of skills development as well as socialization to their new country, local and relatively inexpensive public colleges served as principal sources of education and training of adult immigrants. The influence of global cultures, especially Asian, upon both U.S. and Canadian society was reflected in both curriculum and extracurricular activities at these institutions. Enrollments in English as a Second Language grew in the 1990s, international student numbers increased significantly, and college events and activities promoted multiculturalism.

In response to global forces, particularly production, communications, and immigration, colleges not only reinforced and reproduced globalization but also altered as institutions. Globalizing outcomes included the surrender to a market ideology, with privatization of goods and services and the commodification of products.[74] Ritzer and Ralston Saul see institutions becoming consumer oriented, aligned with the needs of the market. Ritzer sees educational institutions as following a pattern set by McDonald's, exhibiting production characteristics of predictability, efficiency, and managerial control. Ralston Saul views public education as responsive primarily to the job market. Dudley sees education and training as an instrument of economic policy, with emphasis upon markets for economic conservative policy and upon high skills and high wages for neoliberal policy. Marginson notes that the state has transformed its citizens into economic entities with education as a vehicle for economic objectives.[75]

In the 1990s, colleges became more market oriented in their goals and more businesslike in their behaviors. Colleges expanded their traditional mission by enlarging work-force training and by emphasizing skills development. This resulted in a more overt concentration upon private sector interests and reflected changing priorities for student learning.

The shift of community colleges to an entrepreneurial focus and to a more overt economic role is linked to both government funding and government policy. Thus, colleges were more decidedly instruments of government, particularly economic interests, than in the past and yet less dependent for their total revenues upon government.

At the extreme, colleges became several institutions structured within one institution. They were multi-institutions, combining an entrepreneurial college with a work-force training center, and yet they preserved much of the traditional institution, comprised of a comprehensive curriculum and open admissions practices. In the 1990s, community colleges maintained democratic principles, most notably open access to educational opportunities, a characteristic of "democracy's college,"[76] and responded more emphatically to corporate and economic interests of the local community. The shift was from community service to private sector interests while preserving and expanding education and training opportunities for community members.

Student learning priorities shifted from an acclaimed focus upon individual development and career and educational preparation to skills development and work-force training. Marketplace interests and employment training and retraining motivated institutional programming patterns. While numerous traditional vocational programs deteriorated, both in enrollments and in resources, vocationalism insinuated itself in higher level programming, such as business and computer-oriented programs and especially in Canadian institutions in baccalaureate programs offered at community colleges. Less priority than previously was given to remediation and to developmental education.

The changing institutional priorities to student learning included instructional delivery as well as curriculum. Moving in a direction similar to the ubiquitous claim of a paradigm shift in postsecondary education from teaching to learning, institutions justified institutional practices from distance education to computer based instruction as "learner-centered."[77] Institutional rationales paralleled the view of education and training as a commodity, students as customers, and business and industry as clients—all reinforcing market ideology.

Institutional change in this direction followed student, employer, and government preferences. Institutional revenues increased significantly in the 1990s, even with claims of government funding constraints. Tuition fees, contract service revenues, and temporary, non-base budget, and often competitive government grants comprised a greater share of institutional revenues, suggesting that resource providers including the private sector were favorably impressed with institutional responsiveness to economic interests. To what extent this shift to more job market responsiveness at higher costs to students affected both students and community members, who were not students, is uncertain.

There is ample demonstration of the expansion of mission, the growth in services, the elaboration of structures, the accommodation of more students, and increasing attention to new methods of instructional delivery and instructional strategies during the 1990s. The pattern of the 1990s indicates rising expenditures to support these behaviors. In order to meet the associated expenses and to acquire fiscal resources, community colleges turned increasingly to the private sector. With increasing reliance upon fee payers and business and industry, college programs and services inevitably reflected the needs and requirements of resource providers. This suggests that there was a decrease in the social community role of community colleges and an increase in the economic role. It also suggests that instruction developed in line with the needs of educational users. This included more work-based training, more non-classroom instruction that relied upon computer-related technologies, and greater emphasis upon what many college personnel called "employability skills."

Globalization and responses to globalization stimulated and sustained these institutional alterations. Community colleges were not passive recipients of globalization. They served as sites where globalization could be advanced, and indeed they modified and reinterpreted the globalization process. Each domain—economic, cultural, informational, and political—characterized a particular influence and effect of globalization. Organizational behaviors at community colleges were simultaneously mirror images of globalization and reproductions of globalization, advancing the process in an educational setting.

CHAPTER 2

THE CASES: SEVEN COLLEGES IN TWO NATIONS

The approach offered in this book to the impact and influences, as well as outcomes, of globalization on community colleges takes the form of an intimate portrayal of seven colleges in the 1990s as well as an examination of the domains of globalization as these pertain not only to the seven colleges but also to community colleges generally in North America. While community college doors are open wide to students, they are generally closed to field researchers. The rare glimpses into community colleges, views provided by a handful of scholars and graduate students who have gained access to sites, come from those who have actually walked and talked on campuses, interacting with college students, staff, faculty, and administrators and observing people in action. When the door is open, it carries a number of provisos: these might include limited responses to sensitive questioning, and they certainly include anonymity of respondents. These views of college behaviors are infrequent during each decade, because few attempt to carry out field methods research. Those who conduct field research on community colleges usually limit their focus to either one site or one topic, or both.[1] Howard London's *The Culture of a Community College* and Lois Weis's *Between Two Worlds* are cultural examinations of a single college, the former in the 1970s, the latter in the 1980s. Richard Richardson, Elizabeth Fisk, and Morris Okun's *Literacy in the Open Access College* is a field study of curriculum and instruction in one institution in the 1980s. In the 1990s, Dennis McGrath and Martin Spear, in *The Academic Crisis of the Community College*, use their own institution as a proxy for all U.S. community colleges in their exploration of academic drift. Robert Rhoads and James Valadez, in *Democracy, Multiculturalism, and the Community College*, investigated five community colleges on the topic of multiculturalism and democratic practices as these pertain to students. None of this handful of innovative examinations, however, looked at organizational behaviors beyond behaviors directed at or carried out by students. None addressed administrative behaviors, political behaviors, economic behaviors, or union and management behaviors. One of the most recent endeavors to study community colleges from a qualitative perspective, *Community Colleges as Cultural Texts,* is encumbered by an ideological overlay referred to as "critical qualitative research." This edited work obfuscates knowledge of community college behaviors, favoring instead to illustrate some key assumptions about community colleges, largely a cultural critique about institutional practices and outcomes. The volume sets out to show that community colleges need to "adopt a culture and set of educational practices that empower and transform students."[2] Overall, scholarly knowledge of community colleges is built upon data not generated from the field, with few exceptions. Because of the access issue, this is not surprising.

Community college practitioners do not want their work held up for analysis and they do not want their practices criticized. Operating under the shadow of higher status institutions and periodically ridiculed for not living up to someone's expectations, community college practitioners have little respect for scholars, especially those who have no practical knowledge of their institutions.[3] Insiders know best—at least that is part of the ideology of the "practitioner's culture."[4] Insiders, of course, know not only the answers but also the questions; and they know who has the answers if they do not. But insiders—that is, practitioners—have made little substantial contribution to the literature or to the understanding of organizational behaviors. A few articles in scholarly journals and a handful of book chapters that offer analysis of organizational dynamics—such as leadership, culture, and politics—constitute the depth of this contribution.[5]

To address how the globalization process and institutional responses to globalization affect community colleges takes both a scholarly approach and insiders' knowledge. It means gaining access not only to the institution and its members but also to intimate conversations involving organizational members and to confidential meetings of administrators and faculty. Furthermore, to understand the impact and influences of globalization on community colleges, the effects of organizational change upon organizational members and students, and the role of community colleges in advancing globalization requires knowledge of institutional contexts—such as governance structures and processes and institutional members' interpretations of institutional behaviors.

This book relies upon both historical analyses and sources and research data.[6] It looks at colleges from a scholarly perspective, incorporating the views of insiders at seven institutions. The seven colleges are actual institutions provided with fictitious names in order to give the institutions a sense of privacy. The necessity of anonymity of colleges is based upon the assumption that valid data would not be forthcoming without a guarantee of institutional anonymity and protection against making the names of interview subjects public.

The seven colleges are located in three states, two provinces, and two countries. Suburban Valley Community College (SVCC) is situated in California. Pacific Suburban Community College (PSCC) is situated in Hawaii. City South Community College (CSCC) is in the state of Washington. City Center College (CCC), East Shoreline College (ESC), and Rural Valley College (RVC) are in British Columbia, Canada. North Mountain College (NMC) is in Alberta, Canada. Names have a partial connection to location. For example, City South Community College is located in the south end of a metropolitan city; East Shoreline College is located near the shore of a large body of water; and Rural Valley College is located outside of a metropolitan area in a large river valley. While distinctive institutions, these seven colleges have representative characteristics of the vast number of community colleges in both the United States and Canada. Although community colleges differ along several dimensions, such as urban and rural settings, unionization, and formal governance, they share a host of common bonds with respect to mission, purposes, and goals. They adhere to a similar set of principles, such as open access and community responsiveness.[7]

Common Bonds

At the seven colleges examined, behaviors in response to both external and global forces differ among institutions, yet the institutions are more alike than dissimilar in their characteristics. They are all unionized environments, with behaviors subject to collective agreements and potentially to labor law. They are board governed, with either a system (or district) chancellor or institutional president accountable to the governing board. They fall under state or provincial legislation as public postsecondary or higher education institutions accountable to the government in power. Their students, while diverse in academic and ethnic backgrounds, age, and education and training interests, share characteristics that differentiate them from university students but that connect them to the general student populations in U. S. and Canadian community colleges. In comparison to university undergraduate students, they are older, averaging between 27 and 29 years of age; and they are more ethnically diverse. These students are from lower socioeconomic families; and they are less accomplished academically. They are much more likely to be part-time students than full-time, and much more likely to work well beyond ten hours per week. A substantial proportion of community college students are employed fulltime. They are largely commuter students and permanent residents of the local community.

In the 1990s, at all seven colleges examined, students were more diverse in the categories of ethnicity, socioeconomic backgrounds, age, and family status than previously. They worked more than in the past, had less time to study, and had greater financial needs than students of the past. Their faculty were considerably more alike professionally than not, with the possible exception of the faculty at City Center College, an institution with few program offerings designated academic and no formal university transfer program. But City Center did have a professional music program, and there were many faculty with academic credentials at the Master's level. Administrators and faculty had long work histories within the community college, and faculty especially possessed a long, single-college work history. Administrators tended to be more mobile, although with the exception of most of the college presidents, administrators in general were long-time employees of the colleges studied.

At the seven colleges, as at many community colleges, organizational culture—those customary patterns of behavior as well as organizational members' values—was relatively fixed.[8] That does not mean that organizational culture was uniform within each institution. There were clear areas of differentiation among organizational members' beliefs and values, common to other organizations.[9] But the patterns over time, such as friction between union and management over management rights and attention to students' needs, and value structures, such as personal development of students or cognitive development and teacher-directed learning or student-directed learning, were constant within the institution. These patterns and values underlie the literature on community colleges written by practitioners or former practitioners,[10] differentiating this literature from what Frye calls the "professional literature."[11] The behavioral patterns within community colleges are rarely about issues such as university transfer rates or social and economic mobility of students as the scholarly literature would have us believe.[12] Rather, organizational behaviors have to do with the preservation of institutional identity, accommodating growth, balancing education and training, among others, and of course power and authority, especially in relationships between the legal institution (for example, the board and its managers) and its employees.

Suburban Valley Community College

Suburban Valley Community College (SVCC) was a large community college situated in an affluent and productive region in Northern California, close to the San Francisco Bay area. Over 24,000 students were enrolled in credit courses at any one time. SVCC was part of a two-college district and had a national reputation as an innovative institution.

Organizational members possessed three distinct understandings or concepts of Suburban Valley Community College in the 1990s. One was envisioned but not realized by the district chancellor; the second was under development by the college president; and the third was a combination of traditional patterns of behavior and reputational myth adhered to by support staff, many faculty including the faculty union, and long-serving administrators. The college was both a complex and ambiguous site; it was also a contested terrain where struggles over curriculum, management and governance, organizational structure, technology, and fiscal resources and salaries were a backdrop for educating and preparing a diverse student body in a geographical region where the concepts of local and global coexisted.

As a California community college it experienced and was affected by broad policy changes, such as Proposition 13, which in 1978 altered funding for community colleges shifting authority from the local level to raise taxes to state control over revenue generation through taxation, and the state Assembly Bill 1725, enacted in 1988 and implemented throughout the early 1990s, which influenced governance behaviors. Furthermore, the California recession of the early 1990s gave rise to further restrictions on state funding.[13] Yet the 1990s also brought increasing numbers of immigrants to the area and growth in the local computer and electronics industry. While state government remained nonresponsive to articulated needs in education and increasingly restrictive in funding postsecondary education, demand continued from both the business community for well-trained workers and community members for education, from basic skills and language training to academic studies. In the mid-1990s, an enrollment fee for credit courses in community colleges was mandated statewide, and coupled with a resuscitated economy and employment opportunities both in the state and nationally, enrollments declined, notably in both college preparatory and university transfer areas. SVCC experienced financial difficulties in the early 1990s, and expenditures outpaced revenues. Employee downsizing or layoffs were the result, with support staff taking the brunt of the employment loss.

Against this fiscal context, SVCC endeavored to maintain its reputation as an innovative institution. Additionally, in the mid-1990s the college management, particularly propelled by the arrival of a new president, formalized a new organizational structure, one based loosely on an educational ideology that embraced interdisciplinarity, diversity, and teamwork. Moreover, adding complexity to this condition, a new district chancellor was appointed, and while embracing reform concepts of learning in postsecondary education that included the rejection of disciplinarity and the embrace of new electronic technologies, this chancellor brought a more strident managerial approach to both the district and the college. This approach favored pragmatism over tradition, rationality over sentiment, and supervision over autonomy. The district chancellor attempted to alter the past practices of the college in an effort to adapt the institution to a changing environment. For the chancellor, that environment was market-driven, high-technology, and global.

Organizational behaviors were influenced by the college's employee profile, including its aging faculty and its large percentage of part-time faculty that constituted approximately 80 percent of total faculty. Behaviors were also influenced by organizational members' memory of an "innovative" institutional past, including its former president and former chancellor. As a pattern of behaviors and as motivation for behaviors, the past had a significant effect upon present actions.

There was personal friction between the district's officers, especially the chancellor, and college employees, notably union leadership. There was also friction between the board, especially the board chair, and union leadership. There was a long-term pattern of declining state funding for higher education, and this condition in turn affected employer-employee relations at SVCC. Finally, a recent policy at state universities toward remedial education in effect dropped remedial education from four-year schools. This in turn suggested that the state's community colleges were becoming remedial education centers, a condition resisted by many SVCC members yet embraced by some, thereby creating institutional tensions.

Some college members and other observers believed that Proposition 13 in 1978 initiated the decline of public education in the state. Others were less historically minded but acknowledged severe decline and considerable college actions to "keep up," to maintain quality, and to attract both students and revenues from the state. At SVCC, there was a strong culture, one that fostered a belief in the college's qualities, including its members' work ethic; its student outcomes, whether those were manifest in transfer rates or job placement; and its historical legacy. It was clear from the images of the past that college members held up as ideals of the present that SVCC had not met its own expectations; yet, college members extolled the virtues of the school's past greatness and continued to work toward making their ideals concrete. They faced a nearly insurmountable condition: increases in workload; amplification of student and public expectations; changing student demographics with larger numbers of underprepared students; greater accountab... initiatives; aging employees, facilities, and equipment; greater workplace expectations for graduates; and finally, decreasing fiscal resources.

East Shoreline College

East Shoreline College (ESC) was situated in the Canadian province of British Columbia, where there was both a dynamic political environment and a vibrant although resource-dependent economy. ESC was an expansive institution, with a ten-year pattern of growth in programs, student numbers, employees, and facilities. In the 1990s, and especially the late 1990s, neither government funding nor institutionally generated revenues could keep up with growth. While the college "produced" more full-time equivalency student numbers, government funding to support this growth decreased.

The college possessed a historic reputation as an entrepreneurial institution. In the 1990s, it continued not only to maintain this reputation but also to further the practice of attracting new revenue streams. It competed for provincial and federal government contracts, for government agency contracts; it arranged contracts with foreign governments and institutions for training; and it secured contracts with private business and industry, locally and provincially. These behaviors and the marketplace positioning of the college evolved and co-existed with the development of a strong academic culture, in which the institution in the 1990s began, in several ways, to resemble a university. All of these conditions, including university status for a college with a mission of a community college, bicameral governance, rapid growth and funding constraints, and the several organizational schisms including vocational and academic, global and local, and capitalism and community of scholars, and others such as unionism and corporatism, suggested a dynamic environment in which mission was altering, structures changed frequently, and strategies were abundant but implementation was an act of considerable caution.

East Shoreline College expanded considerably in the 1990s, in student numbers, programs, and revenues and expenditures; at the same time, government funding did not keep pace with growth. Thus, in order to support and maintain growth, the college enlarged its resource-generating behaviors, focusing upon international markets as well as local markets. Although there was less government funding relative to institutional expenditures over a ten-year period, there was increased government influence and control over college behaviors and actions. Government funding behaviors had considerable influence over college actions, structures, and processes. These behaviors included productivity incentives and targeted funding for specific programs; government intervention in the collective bargaining relationship between faculty and the college, most evident in the establishment of a provincial-wide bargaining structure; and government legislative action, particularly in the change to governing board composition and in the establishment of a formal senate-type body to share governance with the governing board and administration. Moreover, government legislation that permitted the establishment of baccalaureate degree programs affected not only growth but also academic culture and institutional purpose at East Shoreline College.

Within the institution, there were rising expectations by specific program areas for growth and rising union demands for salary increases; externally there were government demands for productivity, efficiency, accountability, and marketplace responsiveness, placing pressures upon both curriculum and delivery. When in the late 1980s and early 1990s the provincial government authorized specific community colleges to undertake the development and offering of a limited range of baccalaureate degree programs, ESC was chosen and began to build programs, attract students, and hire faculty, staff, and administrators. Enrollments grew by approximately 75 percent in a decade. Much of this growth came in the baccalaureate degree programs, with over 1,000 full-time equivalency students added to the college in science, liberal arts, nursing, education, and business programs among others. Both academically oriented and occupationally oriented or applied degree programs constituted major areas of growth. At the same time, enrollments in traditional vocational programs faltered, and instructional expenditures increased up to 30 percent a year over a ten-year period in degree programs but climbed only 13 percent a year in vocational. The tensions between the degree programs and the vocational programs were accentuated because of the accompanying expansion and diminution of student enrollments, offerings, and resources. Friction in this area affected college actions.

Decision-making and deliberation, as well as day-to-day management of ESC, altered in the past decade, attributable in large part to government legislation that codified shared institutional governance, a bicameral arrangement in which a senate-type body of organizational employees and students deliberated over educational and educationally related issues, advising a college board of governors on some matters and conveying their decisions to the board on other matters. Alterations to governance structures and processes at ESC granted faculty greater decision-making authority and reduced the power of both administrators and the governing board in directing the college. While this legislation resulted in greater professional authority at East Shoreline, the intentions of government were to improve institutional productivity and to maintain labor peace.

In addition to legislation on governance, the provincial government and its department responsible for colleges were parties to two other major developments in the latter half of the 1990s: provincial-wide collective bargaining and a system-wide strategic plan for the colleges. These actions—the establishment of a framework for collective bargaining and the formalization of a strategic plan—not only coordinated college actions and decision-making in a number of areas, such as the use of electronic technology in instruction and faculty compensation, but also lessened institutional autonomy, making single institutions dependent upon all institutions as a whole as well as upon government. These actions increased the role of government in the management of colleges, including ESC.

There were several tensions within ESC over college direction, the allocation of resources, and institutional identity, which included how organizational members understood their institution and their work within the institution. There was the historical tension between academic and vocational program areas, accentuated with the arrival of baccalaureate degree programs. Since that arrival, a tension arose between those in the occupationally related baccalaureate degree programs and those in the more academically oriented programs. These were tensions about both the allocation of resources and the purpose of the institution—between training for the marketplace and educating thinkers.

City South Community College

City South Community College (CSCC) was a middle- to small-size institution (approximately 5,600 students) located in a major population center in Washington state. City South was part of a three-college district and is the smallest and most recently established of the three colleges. In the 1990s, City South Community College was buffeted by numerous external environmental forces, encumbered by its organizational history, and continually proposing and working on strategies to respond to externally influenced change. Its geographical location, the demographic characteristics of its local population, and the combination of unskilled employment opportunities and the college's historical emphasis upon vocational programming shaped college actions and outcomes over the past decade. To some extent, the college was a prisoner of its basic environment, its large immigrant and working-class population and its industrial base, as well as its history and continuing behaviors as a vocationally oriented institution.

The college possessed a historical reputation as a vocational college, with curricular emphasis upon vocational programs and ties to the industrial base of the region. But changes in workplace needs as well as available jobs for blue-collar workers translated into faltering enrollments in vocational programs during the 1990s. Furthermore, state financing of postsecondary education neither kept pace with growth nor supported the maintenance of existing quality. For City South, state appropriations fell over 7 percent in 1995 from 1994 levels, and a further 11 percent in 1996. In 1995, the president informed the college community that the institution would be restructured to deal with declining resources as well as to position the college for coping with expected external demands and changes to student needs, adapting the institution to a "highly competitive global economy." The restructuring proved to be a dramatic action both in the changes brought about organizationally and in its effects upon college members, many of whom appeared not to understand fully what was occurring or why. The restructuring altered the college's order, establishing administrative teams instead of divisions or departments, deleted positions especially support staff positions, and reduced expenditures. In 1996, expenditures dropped by over 5.5 percent from the previous year.

The 1990s was a period of considerable external flux for the college. The local population shifted in both socioeconomic status and in ethnic makeup as increasing numbers of new immigrants, as well as immigrants from countries not traditionally present in the region, came to reside in the community. The college was situated within a community that had a large and expanding immigrant population from Asia and Eastern Europe. Additionally, as the urban center population moved outward, the local community of CSCC was replaced by a slightly more affluent population, and local blue-collar families moved further away from CSCC, a condition arising from rising housing prices in the metropolitan area. The state economy went through a bust-to-boom cycle, including developments in the aircraft industry, increasingly rapid growth in the computer software industry, and declines in the resource extraction industries—mainly fishing and forestry. At the dawn of the decade, there was new senior management leadership for the district office and the entire system; before the close of the decade there was another change in leadership at the district office.

In other areas, particularly the workplace, influencers in business and industry promoted change, in order to keep up with global competition. Thus automation increased and electronic technologies were more fully integrated into both production and administrative work. Additional skill requirements placed stress on educational institutions to maintain pace with business and industry demands, and higher skill levels—such as those in engineering technologies, in professions such as health sciences, and in business itself—were needed and sought through university degree programs.

As a college with a traditional vocational emphasis, with little student population and minimal academic program offerings, CSCC found itself out of step with business and industry needs and public demands for higher learning and advanced university credentials. Demand continued for basic education, and the arrival of new immigrant populations generated new enrollments for English as a Second Language programs—these grew over 60 percent from 1990 to 1996, a 10 percent a year compared to a decline of vocational program enrollments of 5 percent a year, a 30 percent overall decline in 6 years.

This situation was not helped by legislative attitudes toward education and alterations to funding behaviors at the state level. Not only did funding emphasize productivity, specifically in increasing student numbers, but tuition revenues were added to the funding formula with colleges permitted to retain tuition revenues. The problem for several state colleges, including CSCC, however, was that some categories such as English as a Second Language did not generate as much revenue in tuition as did academic programs.

Increased government oversight and accompanying actual decreases in state appropriations placed other stresses upon the institution as its enrollments in traditional vocational programs declined and enrollments in academic and other occupational programs did not rise enough to offset declines. Thus, emphasis upon increasing productivity, on competition with other institutions, and on bureaucratic procedures to conform to state demands (for example, performance indicators, such as student enrollments and space utilization) along with decreasing revenues pushed the college to the category of marginality in the winners and losers dichotomy of the global economy.

College context, then, was significant to institutional behaviors. The college's connections to its external environment, to its local community, to the district office, to the state (its legislators and its economy), and to the business and industrial community weighed heavily upon college operations, from programming to recruitment of students to sources of revenue and governance and management. The college's positioning within its context was one of high dependency.

Pacific Suburban Community College

Pacific Suburban Community College (PSCC) was a midsize (7,300 student population) community college situated in the state of Hawaii, surrounded by a relatively affluent community. The college was part of the University of Hawaii system, the only public higher education institution in the state, and the state's community colleges and the university's several campuses operated out of the same structure, including a system chief executive officer and a governing board. Faculty at both community colleges and the university campuses were members of the same collective bargaining unit, a situation that was rare if not unique in higher education in the United States or Canada. PSCC's connection to the state, through the state government, and to the university system figured prominently in the historical development of the institution and in organizational behaviors in the 1990s. Furthermore, the geographical, social, and economic context for Pacific Suburban Community College, specifically its location in the Hawaiian Islands, helped shape college life—including college behaviors and members' perspectives and attitudes—and influence college growth and development.

In the mid and late 1990s, the state witnessed a sharp alteration in its economy, one largely determined by the decline of tourism. The California recession of the early 1990s and the Japanese economic slide of the mid and late 1990s translated into fewer Californian and Japanese tourists for the state. The historical dependency of Hawaii on offshore trade and travel and on its strategic location, whether historically for trade, or military conquest and defense, altered not in nature but in kind: the economy was singly focused upon tourists. Other natural resources such as sugar and pineapples have diminished in their economic worth; the military importance of the islands and thus the resources committed to the preservation of the military have declined substantially. It was culture and climate, along with vacation amenities, that provided the islands with commodities that brought others to the islands and sustained the islands' population economically. By the mid-1990s, the Hawaiian economy, used to ups and downs, moved into a period of decline. And because the state supported the public higher education sector with the majority of its revenues, supplemented in the mid-1990s by tuition fees, the weakening economy resulted in diminishing state revenues and thus reduced fiscal resources for institutions. Indeed, the vice-chancellor of the University of Hawaii, and the chief operating officer for the community colleges, noted to the state's legislative committee on Ways and Means in March 1997 that the colleges experienced a 32 percent decrease in funding allocations from the state between 1992 and 1996.Yet in spite of this decrease in state funding, the colleges served more students in 1996 than in 1992.

Thus, the higher education sector, including Pacific Suburban Community College, while influenced by the state, which in turn was dependent upon the tourist industry, was captive to a condition of fiscal decline. Against this economic condition of constrained resources, Pacific Suburban Community College maintained its programs, with one exception, and altered its structures, including curriculum, delivery, and administrative organization, in order to preserve not only its mission but also its distinguishing qualities. These actions—whether increasing distance education offerings, customizing training for hotels, or deferring facilities maintenance—were responses to declining resources and the need for PSCC to maintain or increase revenues. Increased revenues were generated almost solely by increasing enrollments, both through tuition revenue and government allocations.

Ironically, it was culture—the arts, languages, knowledge, and even ethics—that characterized and distinguished PSCC.Yet, the college was propelled by and responsive to a material world: driven by the need for more fiscal resources and reactive to the economic needs of the marketplace.

The island as both place and condition for organizational development was also influential. The island and the college were closed environments on the one hand and open environments on the other. They were closed environments because the population was stable, and organizational members aged and developed together over time. They were open environments because they borrowed from others: they imported both knowledge and goods, adapting these to their society. The college assimilated concepts and practices of distance education, service learning, and multiculturalism from the mainland. Pacific Suburban developed a culinary arts program amalgamating Asian and European cooking. Politically American, the island was South Pacific and Asian in its cultural orientation. The college's population, like the state itself, was multiethnic, with a predominantly Asian ethnic population. In 1995, 22 percent of the college student population identified itself as Japanese by heritage, with 16.5 percent Filipino and 10 percent Hawaiian.

But the college, like the island, was a closed environment as it served its island population; if it provided services offshore, then it did so to maintain its community role. Its faculty were long-serving, with little turnover in personnel. Its administrative group was largely former faculty or longserving administrators. Support staff, too, were longstanding employees, either of the college or another state institution, such as the university, government, or another community college.

The ocean surrounding the college's environment, it seems, brought the outside world in yet kept that world out. The college reflected its island environment and was subject to its many conditions, including its government and its economy.

City Center College

City Center College (CCC), with two campuses, was located in the province of British Columbia in an urban environment that had a large immigrant population. Campus locations were in working- and lower middle-class neighborhoods, and in a city core, although there were areas of affluence within close proximity. The college served the entire city, including both a large middle-class population and an affluent community. The college's history included considerable internal turmoil, including fiscal difficulties, with a major structural change involving the college's development from a three-campus operation to a two-campus one in the mid 1990s. The third campus became a separate college. The action of establishing two separate colleges from one was driven by both politics and economics: the faculty union at the departing campus had put the separation issue on the bargaining table during labor action over collective bargaining, and the fiscal crises of the institution were attributed to the management approach used in operating three campuses. Thus, the college altered from its position as a large institution to a smaller one. It altered its education services with a comprehensive curriculum to a more narrow and specialized curriculum focused upon adult upgrading and training in specific vocations. It changed from serving a cross-section of the urban environment to serving the greater part of the community that was less affluent and less socially mobile.

The political climate of the province in which the college was situated was a significant component of the college's development and functioning. Since the early 1990s, the New Democratic Party, a political party with a social democratic history and a left-of-center reputation,[14] was the government in power, and during this period the government and its agencies engendered considerable change to public institutions. City Center College was particularly subject to government initiatives, including the government decision to form a new college from one of City Center College's campuses. The government also acted to alter college governance, labor relations, and not only management of the institution but also—inadvertently—morale of employees through its funding behaviors. While the political party had a historical association with social causes, organized labor, and the disenfranchised, it did not have a good economic management reputation, and its record of staying in power was weak.[15] The government of the mid-1990s wedded its social programs to neoliberal fiscal policies and increased its expectations for public institutions to become both more accountable and more responsive to the public, especially to business and industry. Thus, the provincial government through its agencies exercised considerable control over fiscal behaviors of public institutions through its approach to funding and over programming and services of institutions through both its funding incentives and its government appointments to governing boards. Additionally, in the mid-1990s the government was a lead party in the multiparty agreement between colleges and their faculty unions to centralize collective bargaining. Finally, the government's postsecondary department headed a strategic planning exercise for colleges in the 1990s, and through multiparty agreement, including faculty unions, colleges, and community representatives as well as those from business and industry, committed the colleges to a plan that emphasized institutional productivity and provincial economic prosperity through training at the college level.

By the mid-1990s when City Center College had established itself as a two campus institution, it replaced the majority of its managers, leaving only a handful of long-serving administrators and the president, who was relatively new to the college, in place. Especially prominent in the new managerial group were the three vice-presidents, two of whom were formerly faculty members at the institution and the third who was recruited from the business community. Several daunting tasks faced this group. First, the college had to cope with an accumulated debt and a historical pattern of budget shortfalls and deficits. Second, the college had to "remake" itself from a three-campus to a two-campus college, losing in the process an extremely large program area, approximately 6,000 students, and hundreds of employees and services (for example, the library) that were formerly part of the same institution. Third, both governance and collective bargaining with faculty were undergoing substantial change as noted above. And, finally, the employees at the two remaining campuses—the faculty and staff—were not new; indeed, they were longtime, aging employees conditioned to and familiar with longstanding structures and practices.

City Center College was the product of historical forces—social, political, economic—as well as an instrument of government, a source of employment for staff, a place of professional practice for faculty, and a constant object of concern for administrators. It was a large, slow-changing bureaucracy. Its internal environment, including its fiscal and physical conditions, which were inadequate in areas of equipment, appropriate learning space, and in condition, as well as its union-management politics, was contentious and complicated enough to occupy organizational members full-time. Organizational members took their institution and their purpose seriously, convinced that in spite of their institution's shortcomings the college was the lifeline for its community.

Rural Valley College

Rural Valley College (RVC), a medium-size, multicampus institution, with one large campus, a second smaller campus, and additional sites, was located in a prosperous river valley, within commuting distance of a major metropolitan center, in the province of British Columbia. The college experienced considerable grov   the last decade, nearly doubling its fulltime equivalency (FTE) student numbers to approximately 3,800 FTE by 1996–1997. Institutional growth was precipitated by two major factors—local population growth and the establishment of a limited number of baccalaureate degree programs at the institution. This growth and the factor of baccalaureate degree status led to significant alterations in such areas as resources and facilities, personnel, curriculum, and governance. The college's budget, for example, expanded 200 percent over the period of 1990–1991 to 1995–1996, a 40 percent annual growth. In the 1990s, the college added approximately 100 additional full-time faculty. In addition, major facility expansion on the largest campus and dramatic curricular change, the development and offering of four-year degree programs in the arts and social sciences, in career-oriented areas such as nursing, and in selected science areas, altered not only the institution but also how longterm employees perceived institutional mission and internal relationships. For some, the increase in size meant that long-time colleagues were no longer "physically crossing paths" according to a department chair in the social sciences. For others, the historically close connection to the local community gave way to preoccupation with internal processes such as governance, coordination of work, labor relations, and, not least of all, academic professionalism, which included program and professional development. Finally, the development of baccalaureate programs, both at this institution and at others in the same provincial jurisdiction, led to reform in institutional governance. At Rural Valley College, with its history as a collegial environment, including a single bargaining unit for both faculty and support staff and a small cohort of excluded personnel or managers, the shift to a university style of governance brought on by provincial legislation was a gradual process but not one without conflict. While maintaining many of their former processes and behaviors of decision-making, college personnel continued to adjust to the new governance structures and processes.

Individual units or disciplines became more independent than in the past, likely the consequence of new faculty with doctoral degrees and experience largely in university environments. The institution was clearly "moving out of an older model," whether that model was a labor-management model, a collegial model of a small institution, or a traditional community college model that valued a "practitioner's culture"[16] rather than professional expertise and focused upon student development rather than cognitive and intellectual development.

In its first two decades of its history, the college was characterized by observers and institutional members as the quintessential community college, directing its services outward to its communities. Its reputation for community education and for harmonious labor relations was matched by its performance as noted in several reports and studies. But the alteration of the college from a two-year to a four-year institution at the beginning of the decade continued to affect RVC and its entire personnel, faculty, staff, and administrators. Adding to this concern over college purposes and internal relationships brought on by university-type status, college faculty and administrators reflected upon new labor-management relationships evolving as a consequence of the move in the latter part of the 1990s of the college union to join a province-wide bargaining structure of provincial colleges.

Furthermore, while government grants in the early 1990s not only kept pace with but also exceeded growth, the late 1990s can be characterized as a period of government restraint in funding, with an overlay of government direction on the uses of fiscal resources. For RVC, this meant that growth outstripped resources and that college operations were more directed to government priorities. The evolution of baccalaureate programs blossomed most in the liberal arts; yet the government's priorities were jobs and work-force training, with education seen as a means to decrease unemployment and improve the economy to stimulate government revenues. While government policy in the late 1980s and early 1990s, under two separate governing parities, was favorable to baccalaureate programming at community colleges, government policy in the mid and late 1990s emphasized institutional productivity and workplace skills in education, as well as closer institutional-private sector relationships and ventures. In responding to a faltering economy, the provincial government applied neoliberal approaches to funding the public sector. Some college programs as a result faced elimination and reductions, there was a provincial moratorium on facility construction, and base funding was reduced, with additional funds available on a competitive basis and criteria set by government. Moreover, in order to prevent colleges from seeking additional revenues from students to fund expansion, the government placed a freeze on tuition fees. Thus, government played a significant role in institutional actions.

North Mountain College

North Mountain College was a complex institution in the 1990s, influenced by its relatively lengthy history and by its growth. The institution had a long background as a two-year, denominational, liberal arts college, prior to its establishment as a publicly governed and funded institution. It was composed of a long-serving cadre of employees—faculty, staff, and administrators, with a substantial number of faculty moving to the administrative ranks. Through the 1970s and 1980s, the college possessed the image of an innovative institution, ascribed to it by its employees, given the widespread belief in individualized learning among college members in these decades. In the 1980s and 1990s, college planning and college actions furthered the image of innovation, or what some referred to as "the flavor of the month," with the elaboration of a 1980s plan to increase international activities, the development of four-year baccalaureate degree programs in the 1990s, and the infusion of electronic technology into both the workplace and into the learning environment in the 1990s. In the latter 1990s, "innovation" included the embrace by institutional leaders of outcomes based learning and assessment. Additionally, the 1980s was a time of facilities growth, and by the mid-1990s college enrollments approached 10,000 credit students, with large numbers in language institutes, a music conservatory, and continuing education programs. The college operating budget in 1997 exceeded $60 million. The college occupied one main site, where one exceedingly large building reflected not only college growth but also ample resources.

Resources, however, were an issue in the 1990s, as the provincial government of Alberta began serious public-sector restraint in the mid-1990s. Touted as fiscally responsible, public sector funding restraint was also ideological, as government endeavored to decrease institutional reliance upon the public purse and increase institutional productivity and efficiency. Furthermore, government policy clearly aligned public postsecondary education institutions with economic development of the province, particularly work-force training for the private sector.[17] Thus, government funding for NMC declined from 1994 to 1997, and targeted funding, the use of accountability measures, named "key performance indicators," and regulations about tuition fee rises all served notice that government policy was both directive and substantial. During the same period, the government authorized selective two-year colleges in the province to offer a limited number of four-year baccalaureate degree programs and the degree credential was referred to as "applied," so as not to transgress the rights of universities. North Mountain College lobbied to be one of these selective institutions and in the latter part of the mid-1990s began two baccalaureate degree programs, with three other programs developed and awaiting government funding.

It was during this period of government funding restraint that significant institutional change grew out of past initiatives and escalated, such as the infusion of electronic technology, and new institutional goals and strategies developed and were enacted. During government restraint, the college and its unions negotiated wage rollbacks, the institution began a minor restructuring effort, and NMC began a determined strategy to reduce its reliance upon government funding. By 1997, less than 50 percent of the college's revenues were from government grants. Thus, not just in plan but in execution, the college had generated alternate sources of revenue, and this was accomplished by altering structures and changing working conditions at the institution. In part, this led the college to model what many employees call a "business" organization or corporation, suggesting that college behaviors were directed, through incentives and coercion, to conform to managerial preferences and goals. In this way, the college imitated the business and industrial environment of its geographical location. Yet, there was also a large educational bureaucracy, a variation of a professional bureaucracy,[18] in which managers—president, vice-president, deans, directors, and even program chairpersons—were the institution's professionals, or at least dominant professionals, and the bureaucratic system was coordinated not by rules and regulations but by committee structures in which communication of strategies and actions and information dissemination ensured that institutional behaviors conformed to managerial preferences and goals.

With an immediate goal of resource acquisition, the college was not only resource dependent[19] but also resource driven. Thus, those areas of the college that performed the role of resource acquisitors, such as the continuing education area and the college foundation, as well as those areas that garnered resources from student tuition fees and government grants, were not just safe havens but influential determinants in college decision-making. Their opposites—those areas that were either not productive or a drain on college resources—were marginalized, downsized, or restructured. Such a condition correlated with a highly productive institution, a highly stressful workplace, but a flexible and adaptive institution. Furthermore, the behaviors of college leaders in resource acquisition led to tensions between groups in the institution over college purpose and practices. For example, there were differing views among organizational members about the purposes of the institution: the college as an instrument of business and industry, the college as a "second chance" institution for underprepared students, and the college as a liberal arts institution. Thus, there were numerous contested areas for organizational members, including the use of electronic technologies, especially in instruction, and the development and offering of four-year degree programs.

From Local to Global

There are numerous tensions evident at these seven institutions. While there are differing characteristics among the institutions, such as idiosyncratic histories, distinctive geographical locations and local community, and five separate legal jurisdictions—in two nations—organizational responses were directed to similar forces. These external forces included declining government allocations relative to institutional growth or expenditures or both, expanding demands from business and industry as well as from government, shifting local populations that were in part a result of new patterns of immigration, and altering workplace conditions that were in large part a consequence of technological change. These developments externally and institutional actions in reaction to these can be seen as contributors to organizational change in the areas of education and work. For example, expansion of curricula to encompass applied baccalaureate degrees at North Mountain College and the provision of distance education to South Pacific island countries at Pacific Suburban Community College were educational responses to altering economies and human resource needs within these economies. The emphasis upon efficiency measures through restructuring City South Community College and through the use of information technologies at all the colleges in such areas as registration, advising, and instruction was a managerial response to marketplace competition and restrained fiscal allocations from government.

Unlike earlier decades, these external forces are no longer local or regional. Their locus is not even at the national level. They include international economies, global communications networks, and the migration of people from Eastern Europe to Western Europe and North America, from Mexico to the United States, and Asia to the United States and Canada. The community college is an institution responding not simply to the local but to the global.

CHAPTER 3

THE DOMAINS OF GLOBALIZATION: THE ECONOMIC DOMAIN

Globalization exerts a number of influences upon both education and work in higher education institutions. Globalization of the workplace in business and industry also applies to higher education organizations as producers of symbols—knowledge and information—and service providers—education, training, and research.[1] The globalized workplace is geared toward speed, rapid product development, and faster service, all driven by technology.[2] The net effect is both higher productivity and reduction of labor. In education, institutional efforts both involve colleges as actors in a global environment and alter education to fit the global marketplace.[3] As a consequence of globalization, higher education may have accumulated more vocational objectives than those traditionally associated with a liberal education—that is, economic ends as opposed to democratic ones.[4] Even the new learning paradigm promoted at colleges can be viewed as a reflection of the imperatives of postindustrial globalization, in which capital and technology usurp the role of labor.[5] Changes to both work and education, then, can be linked to globalization as these are both fostered and sustained by globalization. There are changes in the nature of goods delivered (knowledge), the way goods are organized and presented (curriculum), the place where knowledge is conveyed (classroom), and the way knowledge is conveyed (pedagogy).[6]

Both positive and negative connotations are attached to these alterations and to the role of globalization. The changes wrought by globalization are on the one hand lauded and on the other condemned. But institutional behaviors in the face of globalization—in confronting global forces and the reactions of intermediaries who respond to global forces—are neither fully heinous nor altogether beneficent acts. Fundamental, second-order organizational changes are not accomplished quickly or easily.[7] Indeed, lasting changed means "changing the underlying assumptions and the abstract rules that shape and limit members' perceptions, beliefs, and behaviors."[8] We are thus too contemporary to judge the nature or the near permanency of organizational changes. Instead, we must observe the behaviors, identify temporal outcomes, and suspend evaluative judgement.

A number of behaviors of higher education institutions are not only consistent with globalization but also reflect the impact of global forces upon the institution and reproduce the globalization process.[9] Ten sets of behaviors are connected to globalization (see figure 3.1). One set of behaviors includes both internationalizing the curriculum and the campus and extending the campus in other nations. Specific behaviors are the recruitment of students from other countries, the delivery of college curriculum in other nations, and the inculcation of others' cultural values, including the promotion and display of international images, symbols, and practices. I refer to this set of behaviors as *internationalization*. Related to some extent to internationalization, institutions and their members adopt an ideology that on the one hand promotes equality among groups along the lines of ethnic origins, class, and gender orientation, and on the other hand favors strategies that give special status to underrepresented or historically less privileged groups. This set of behaviors is labeled *multiculturalism*. Higher education institutions create products and establish services that they take to the marketplace to sell, or private individuals or companies approach the college to purchase goods and services. This entails the development of programs to fit the requirements of a specific business. It also includes the delivery of instruction or training to the specifications, such as duration or place, of private business and industry. This set of behaviors represents *commodification*. Along these same lines, institutions make their products and services similar; they routinize work; they standardize practices, such as educational delivery; and most importantly, they attempt to objectify curriculum so that it approaches quantification or reduction to its basic elements. I refer to this set of behaviors as *homogenization*. Institutions also align themselves closer to the private sector, and they compete with other institutions and organizations for revenues. They form associations with private business and industry. They solicit private donations of money, goods, and services, which they acknowledge through publicity and tax benefits. I refer to this set of behaviors as *marketization*. Organizations make structural alterations to change work patterns and to change how and what they produce and the services they provide. This usually entails elaborate modifications that lead to job change, job loss, and the reallocation of resources. Indeed, resources and their scarcity generally motivate these behaviors. I refer to this set of behaviors as *restructuring*. Related are those institutional behaviors that change work patterns, including the nature and duration of work. These behaviors may entail additional students in classrooms or the implementation of online management systems—technological change—that modify workloads and work practices. I refer to these behaviors as *labor alterations*. To address and satisfy revenue needs, often the consequence of constrained government funding, higher education institutions exhibit two behaviors: they turn to the private sector, including fee-payers, a marketization behavior, and they pursue greater efficiency in work, including raising productivity of existing workers or lowering costs by reducing the work force. I refer to this latter set of behaviors as *productivity and efficiency*. Institutions adopt technologies that are perceived as both labor saving and normative. Higher education institutions use electronic technologies both for work processes, such as communications and information processing, and for education, such as online instruction. I refer to this set of behaviors as *electronic communication and information*. With the role of the state increasing in the affairs and operations of public higher education institutions, the state has become a more noticeable institutional actor, intervening or interfering in colleges actions. I refer to this set of behaviors as *state intervention*. Some of these sets of behaviors are not present in all organizations, not present simultaneously in an organization, and not enacted in all areas of an organization. Behaviors connected to globalization can be domain-specific.

Globalizing forces and the globalization process have impacted community colleges in several domains. One prevalent domain is **economics**, in which a global economy affects state revenues that in turn affects colleges through government funding alterations and policy initiatives. A second domain is **culture**, in which social attitudes and values are imported from the external environment and in which local populations reflect international cultures and are a consequence of international events, such as wars and political realignments. Electronic technology signals a third domain—**information**—including the acquisition, dissemination, and the structuring and management of both acquisition and dissemination.

In addition to these three domains is a fourth—**politics**—that signals the role and dynamics of the state in the organizational behaviors of colleges. The role of government in the behaviors and actions of colleges, however, is conditional, related to both the nature and severity of influence of global forces upon colleges. Under some conditions, government policy and actions detach colleges from direct impact of globalization; in others,

> internationalization
> multiculturalism
> commodification
> homogenization
> marketization
> restructuring
> labor alterations
> productivity and efficiency
> electronic communication and information
> state intervention

Figure 3.1 Globalization Behaviors

government behaviors place colleges in the vortex of global forces. Figure 3.2 illustrates these four domains.

The domains of globalization are not necessarily discrete. The economic domain contains behaviors such as internationalization that are also found in the cultural domain. Behaviors labeled electronic communication and information are found not only in the information domain but also in the domains of economics, culture, and politics. This suggests that these domains, in some organizational behaviors and actions, overlap.

The Economic Domain

In the 1990s, colleges were connected to global economies largely through state and provincial governments, through business and industry, through local employment conditions and patterns, and through workplace needs. Institutional behaviors included internationalization, marketization, productivity and efficiency, restructuring, commodification, and state intervention.

Internationalization

Internationalization was represented by a growing set of behaviors as college enrollments increasingly reflected more international students and college administrators and faculty participated in a wide array of international projects and meetings and engaged more frequently in international activities. Administrators, especially college presidents and those managers responsible for international programs, were aware of the revenue-generating potential of international students and contracts. Student enrollments in

THE DOMAINS OF GLOBALIZATION

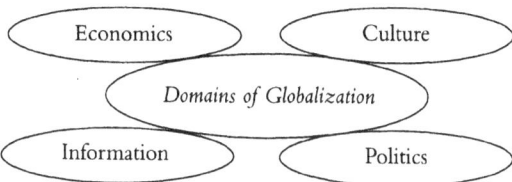

Figure 3.2 Domains of Globalization

community colleges grew significantly. International student enrollments at Suburban Valley Community College climbed from 659 in 1989 to over 1,800 in 1996, a rise of 173 percent; at City South Community College from 148 in 1989 to 224 in 1996, a 76 percent rise; at Pacific Suburban Community College from 42 in 1989 to 207 in 1996, a 393 percent rise; at East Shoreline College, from 92 to 337 students, a 266 percent rise; at Rural Valley College, from 11 to 175 students, a whopping 1,490 percent rise; and at North Mountain College from 69 in 1989 to 160 in 1996, a 132 percent rise. At City Center Community College where records covered only the period from 1994 to 1996, there was a 111 percent rise. By 1996, there were 3,275 international students enrolled in credit programs at the seven colleges. These enrollments generated considerable revenues for the colleges—for example, over $750,000 net at East Shoreline College, over $1 million gross at North Mountain, and $2 million gross at Rural Valley.[10] But, internationalization was not just represented by student enrollments. It also included contracted services with other nations for profits. East Shoreline generated considerable revenues from its projects in Asia, Central America, and South America. As well, East Shoreline established an international high school for private citizens of other nations, adding to the college's revenues, reportedly $1 million annually. Pacific Suburban developed distance education programs to serve Southeast Asian and South Pacific countries. North Mountain entered into training partnerships with Mexican institutions, generating revenue for the institution.

International revenue generation grew but there were both hurdles and hazards, such as problems with costs relative to revenues and especially with fluctuations in international economies. A case in point was the 1997 and 1998 academic year, when the Asian economy stumbled and went into a severe decline. South Korean students were forced by their government to abandon their studies at North American institutions, and Japanese students withdrew from colleges as well. Revenues at community colleges dropped, and program areas were affected, particularly English as a second language. Colleges reported losses of over 100 students at individual institutions between the fall and spring semesters, with corresponding revenue losses close to $500,000 for the year.

Marketization

In order to secure more resources, in part motivated by the strategy of growth and in part a consequence of government funding constraints, colleges focused more heavily upon the needs of the marketplace. Historically, funding for these colleges relied upon two principal sources—government and local students, with Suburban Valley Community College relying additionally upon local taxes. In the 1990s, colleges altered their dependency upon government to some extent, first, by generating revenues through training contracts with business and industry, as well as with government and institutions in other countries; second, by increasing tuition and fees for local students and recruiting international students; and third, through associations with the private sector whereby colleges traded donations of money or goods or both for either publicity or tax benefits. College efforts in generating revenues locally were more successful with government or government agency contracts than with the private sector. Basic operating grants from both state and provincial governments constituted a decreasing percentage of overall college revenues as the decade progressed (see table 3.1). This lessening of state support is clearly evident on a national level; in the United States,

Table 3.1 Government Base Operating Grants as a Percentage of Total Revenues

College	Pre-1990	Mid-1990s	Difference
Suburban Valley*	9%	18%	9%
East Shoreline	68%	60%	−8%
City South	59%	42%	−17%
Pacific Suburban	74% [1991]	73%	−1%
City Center	71%	68%	−3%
Rural Valley	73%	70%	−3%
North Mountain	72%	47%	−25%
Average change (of total revenues of all colleges)	-		−7%

*State legislation altered funding responsibilities, shifting greater responsibility to the state and away from local taxation.

state and local appropriations went from 68.7 percent of total revenues in 1989 to 60.6 percent in 1995 and fell by 12 percentage points since 1980), and in Canada, provincial allocations went from 76.7 percent of total operating revenues in 1991 to 67 percent of the total in 1997.[11]

Colleges pursued diverse avenues to capture additional revenues, but the outcomes intended were similar: generate revenues to support expenditures or to sustain growth, or both. North Mountain College saw its mission alter in "educating for the workplace," as one college official noted. The college established baccalaureate degree programs that were applied rather than academic in their curriculum, with emphasis upon "employability skills." Pacific Suburban Community College turned increasingly to contract training, providing workplace training for local hotels. City South Community College jettisoned vocational programs that were aimed at obsolete jobs, turned their energies towards contract training and generated as much as $6 million per year in revenues in the mid-1990s. Suburban Valley Community College established an occupational training institute, centralizing contract training, and emphasized cooperative education and community internships in occupationally related programs. The

Table 3.2 Contract Services as a Percentage of Total Revenues*

College	Pre-1990	Late 1990s	Difference
Suburban Valley	6.6%	3%	−3.6%
East Shoreline	12%	18.4%	6.4%
City South	1%	3.5%	2.5%
Pacific Suburban	1.7%	3.2%	1.5%
City Center	8%	7%	−1%
Rural Valley	7.7%	6%	−1.7%
North Mountain	2.4%	3.8%	1.4%
Total change (all)			5.5%

*It needs to be pointed out that in Table 3.2, contract services does not mean the same behavior for all colleges. There is considerable difference, for example, between U.S. and Canadian colleges in-as-much as in U.S. colleges, federal government–sponsored training programs are referred to as grants, and in Canadian colleges several federal programs are contracts. Thus, in the case of City Center College, a considerable portion of contract services is a service for the federal government. With a marked shift in federal policy toward less public sector funding, both Rural Valley and City Center show a decrease in the percentage of revenues generated by contract services. Furthermore, colleges over time change the reporting of revenues—for example, amalgamating sales and services. Finally, it should be noted that revenues are a gross figure and do not include the costs to the college for providing contract services.

college turned its curriculum more toward private sector interests, such as computer companies, the biotechnology industry, and the film animation industry, particularly Disney. For all colleges combined, an increasing percentage of college revenues was generated by contract services. Table 3.2 displays the percentage (%) of total college revenues generated from contract services at the beginning of the 1990s and at the latter part of the 1990s. The figures in this table do not show the considerable increases in institutional revenues during the 1990s. For example, Suburban Valley's revenues rose from $16,700,000 to $26,400,000, a 58 percent increase in an eight-year period. Even North Mountain College, faced with only a 6.5 percent rise in provincial government operating grants from 1988–1989 to 1995–1996, less than a 1 percent per year average, saw overall revenues rise from $37,420,524 in 1988–1989 to $61,113,445 in 1995–1996, a 63 percent increase. In Canada, revenues for community colleges nationally rose by 20 percent over the six-year period from 1991 to 1997. Evidently, decreasing provincial government support did not deter colleges from capturing additional revenues, because total operating grants from provincial governments over this period remained virtually unchanged.[12]

But college curricula altered as well in the 1990s in order to meet the needs of employers. Employment conditions and workplace needs were complex in their effects upon colleges. The truism that in times of unemployment enrollments rise and in times of high employment enrollments decline is not always correct. In some employment areas that saw heavy demand for workers, such as computer fields, health sciences, and business, enrollments rose and college actions were directed toward providing resources for these program areas. Suburban Valley gave increasing emphasis and devoted proportionately more resources to high-technology related fields. Some of City South's curricular offerings depended upon the local aircraft industry and its international performance. Too much economic activity from this sector, however, meant that there was an immediate need for employment and no need for preemployment training; too little economic activity, and the need for trained personnel diminished. The industry demanded specific training outcomes; the college fit the curricula to the industry, but program graduates were not hired in large numbers in the field. From 1990 to 1994 fewer than 25 percent of program graduates in aircraft maintenance were hired (out of a total of 181 program graduates) in their program field. Curricular change was thus both a risk and reward activity.

Workplace needs that require basic skills, including English language proficiency, placed pressure on colleges to provide instruction in these areas. Both employer needs and student demand were responsible for this pressure. City Center College, historically associated with English language training because of its programming response to a large population demand among adults in an urban area, shifted some of the focus of this activity from citizenship to vocational training, developing programs that combined English language training and occupational skills.

Workplace needs requiring specialized skills, such as computer or managerial skills, were influential in determining college curricula. This influence was exerted by program advisory groups, company or corporate officials, and faculty and those administrators who interacted with employers and observed the workplace. New skills for employment, such as computer and communication skills and a work ethic that included conformity to employers' standards were infused into the curricula of diverse programs in all colleges. At Rural Valley College, new skills in the health sciences followed the movement in that jurisdiction for "multi-skilled" health workers and more community-based nursing. Furthermore, at Rural Valley College, newly created baccalaureate degree programs in the social sciences and humanities were rationalized by their inclusion of "employability skills." A program in applied history, for example, served the needs of a mining company in course assignments. East Shoreline also turned toward a more economic focus in curricula, not so much in providing vocational programs to students, but in providing

Table 3.3 Tuition and Fees as a Percentage of Total Revenues*

College	Pre-1990	Late 1990s	Difference
Suburban Valley	12.6%	4%	−8.6%
East Shoreline	11.5	12.9%	1.5%
City South	12%	19.5%	7.5%
Pacific Suburban	14.5%	19%	4.5%
City Center	13%	17%	4%
Rural Valley	14.6%	21%	6.4%
North Mountain	23%	16%	−7%
Total change (all)			4%

*Over time, colleges in college districts or local systems—Suburban Valley, Pacific Suburban, and City South—do change the way they capture revenues from tuition. In some cases, district offices retain tuition revenues and then allocate part of these revenues to local colleges. This seems to have been the case at Suburban Valley College. At Suburban Valley, enrollments over the decade were largely unchanged; yet, costs and thus expenditure rose. Without massive tuition and fee increases, Suburban Valley was required to secure resources from other sources.

skills and job-specific training programs for employers and by emphasizing job skills in both two-year diploma programs and in four-year baccalaureate degree programs.

The marketplace also included fee-payers—students. Colleges relied upon increasing revenues from tuition and fees to meet expenditures and to sustain services. Tuition and fees reflected growing enrollments and a new clientele—international students. They also showed the increasing percentage of college revenues generated by tuition and fees. Table 3.3 displays the percentage (%) of total colleges revenues generated from tuition and fees at the beginning of the 1990s and at the latter part of the 1990s.

This increasing reliance on tuition and fees for community colleges is clearly evident on a national level where tuition and fees rose in the United States from 19.1 percent of general revenues in 1989 to 25.8 percent in 1995, a 6.7 percent rise, and in Canada from 9.5 percent of operating income in 1991 to 14.8 percent in 1997, a 5.3 percent rise.[13]

Productivity and Efficiency

Greater productivity and efficiency, as a consequence of lessening state support for education, were prominent influencers upon organizational behaviors at the institutions. "Doing more with less" was a slogan at more than one institution and a sentiment at all. Furthermore, as the decade came to a close, the state became more intrusive in promoting productivity. For example, performance indicators were one strategy the state used to tie funding to measurable productivity.

Suburban Valley Community College employees worked to increase productivity and efficiency, by featuring and expanding program offerings in high demand areas. As a consequence of less than adequate funding from the state, there were union-management tensions over salaries and over the demand for greater productivity. In the 1990s, there was a layoff of staff and elimination of positions, equipment in established instructional areas (for example, science) was obsolete, and there were incentives for early retirement to decrease salary commitments.

At City South Community College, productivity and efficiency behaviors applied to a variety of institutional areas. Three presidents during the decade attempted to improve cost effectiveness of college operations: the first by reducing employees and costs; the second by altering governance to induce more employee participation in decision-making, with the anticipated outcome of a rise in productivity. The third president pursued a combination of efficiency measures, including the "streamlining of operations," such as the elimination of redundancy or inefficiencies of personnel or both, the renewed efforts to capture greater numbers of students and provide services for local business and industry, and the rationalization of programs, including major program revisions or elimination. Furthermore, at City South, the use of distance education was viewed by managers as a cost-effective way to provide instruction and a key component of college strategy to improve productivity.

Other colleges exhibited similar behaviors. East Shoreline College emphasized productivity and efficiency, with larger class sizes, fewer administrators, and more reliance upon electronic technology for work: these actions were intended to cope with budget shortfalls. For Pacific Suburban Community College, declining state revenues and a declining economy at the latter part of the 1990s affected organizational behaviors, and managers placed greater emphasis upon cost cutting and revenue generation, including increased worker productivity and greater institutional attention to student outcomes.

The use of part-time faculty was one major answer in the United States to efficiency requirements. This class of faculty provided low paid labor to accommodate student demand. This pattern of efficiency was established in earlier decades, but by the mid 1990s, it was a condition where full-time

Table 3.4 Full-time and Part-time Faculty at U.S. Community Colleges[*]

Year (public or public and private)	Full-time Faculty (% of total)	Part-time Faculty (% of total)
1973, public and private	59%	41%
1976, public and private	44%	56%
1980, public and private	44%	56%
1987, public and private	42%	58%
1987, public	45.6%	54.4%
1991, public and private	35%	65%
1993, public	35.2%	64.8%
1995, public	35.1%	64.9%

[*]Kent Phillipe, *National Profile of Community Colleges: Trends and Statistics* (Washington, D.C.: American Association of Community Colleges, 1995), 73; U.S. Department of Education, *Digest of Educational Statistics*, Table 223 (Washington, D.C.: National Center for Educational Statistics, 1998), 252; U.S. Department of Education, *Digest of Educational Statistics*, Table 218 (Washington, D.C.: National Center for Educational Statistics, 1996), 229; and U.S. Department of Education, *Digest of Educational Statistics*, Table 210 (Washington, D.C.: National Center for Educational Statistics, 1991), 218.

faculty were a minority population at community colleges, constituting on 35.1 percent of all faculty (see table 3.4).

Restructuring

Although organizational restructuring was justified as improving operations, it was primarily fiscally motivated, at least on one level, and motivated by personnel on another. On the first level, colleges addressed revenue shortfalls. On the second level, personnel changes were the goals for presidents, district officers, and college boards. For some restructuring initiatives, both levels operated simultaneously. A third level of motivation—ideological—was not as common but was clearly evident at Suburban Valley, where an educational philosophy motivated structural change. (This topic is addressed in the section on the domain of culture.)

At City South, the restructuring effort of 1995 was a response to what the president viewed as "global forces of change" impacting the college. This effort led to outcomes not unlike those experienced within the larger corporate area of U.S. business and industry—downsizing and layoffs, greater loss of revenues, mission alteration—and greater dependency upon resource providers as well as an increased focus upon the private sector marketplace. The 1995 restructuring action was intended to help the college respond better to changing workplace needs. In 1997, however, college personnel were baffled by the rationale for the restructuring, with many viewing the outcomes as negative, such as altered work relations among workers and between workers and administrators and the de-professionalization of faculty by organizing them into "teams." At Pacific Suburban, remedial education programs shifted from credit to non-credit, enabling the college to use a different classification of instructors and to increase fees. North Mountain and Rural Valley altered managerial structures, primarily by eliminating positions. In addition, North Mountain shifted large program areas—English as a second language and college preparation—to the non-credit area to generate revenues for the institution and to cut the costs of the credit operations. And, at almost all institutions during the decade, distance education delivery was used for efficiency; administrative operations were streamlined; and positions were eliminated.

Commodification

All institutions moved increasingly toward the shaping of goods and services for either sale or imitation of business practices. International education, distance education, and high-demand programs were "packaged" and "marketed" as commodities. Services such as training for local employers evolved into key institutional operations whereby organizational members developed and delivered specialized training to private sector business and industry.

Economic benefits accrued to Suburban Valley by offering education as a service. The college developed and offered specific training for local business and industry; and the college relied upon distance education delivery, both to serve local needs and to position itself as a provider of education through distance education for a national and international market. Thus, education became a commodity. At East Shoreline, commodification of higher education was evident in the exportation and selling of both training and education in Asia, South America, and Europe: this exchange of goods and services for revenues was intended to support institutional growth.

As well as training as a service, curriculum was directed at the market and toward economic benefits. Curriculum featured marketable skills—computer skills, communications skills, and interpersonal skills. All of these became known as "employability skills" and "workplace skills" by the middle of the decade. Academic programs, including four-year baccalaureate programs in Alberta and British Columbia, were not immune from commodification. Indeed, outcomes-based learning and assessment—that is, focusing upon the end product, and a measurable product—were insinuated into liberal arts programs and courses.

State intervention

While colleges claimed that the state—particularly the states and provinces—had abandoned its traditional role as principal resource provider, the state was viewed as increasing its influence in college operations. In the 1990s, the state not only developed policy to direct colleges to a more economic role and to a role more closely identified with neoliberalism, but also began to act in accordance with is policies. Performance indicators were one blatant manifestation of state intervention. In the latter part of the decade, the state instituted performance indicators for monitoring and evaluating college outcomes, although these were largely in the form of quantitative measures such as increasing student numbers. These indicators were intended to be tied to funding, so that increased funding would depend upon increases in measures of productivity. Thus, the state influenced college behaviors because colleges were dependent upon the state for revenues. Only Pacific Suburban was spared this intrusion of performance indicators.

Pacific Suburban Community College was not immune, however, to state intervention. This just took a different form, and a more direct one. Lowering state revenues were simply passed on to Pacific Suburban—reduced fiscal allocations, a practice of government in the state. But the state intervened in another curious way as a party to contract negotiations for Pacific Suburban. With the governor's representatives present at contract bargaining talks between institutional officials and faculty, in 1997 a legally countenanced strike was averted not because the two sides—institution and faculty—found a compromise, but because the governor directed the institution and the union, to some changes in their position. Government "micromanagement" occurred not only for the state's economy but also for its institutions.

Behaviors and Outcomes in the Economic Domain

The most visible evidence might force a conclusion that economics contributed to organizational behaviors more than any other force in the 1990s. Integral to economics was economic globalization. Changing modes of production, higher productivity, increasing efficiencies, and expanding marketplaces, all driven by electronic technologies, characterize economic globalization. Within colleges, the economic domain was central not because colleges were profit-making enterprises, but rather because they were resource dependent and traditionally received their revenues from students, taxpayers, and primarily from government. Thus, global economic shifts and local behaviors that responded to global economies impacted community colleges in the main because of governments' susceptibility to globalization. Colleges were less and less protected from economic forces by governments; indeed, government manipulated colleges to conform to globally normed behaviors in the economic sphere—less reliance upon public sector revenues, increasing efficiencies, and competition for market position.

From the perspective of this domain, community colleges looked more like businesses and less and less like schools. They were more closely connected to business and industry, not just because they trained for the workplace as they had for decades. Their connections in the 1990s included a noticeable presence of the private sector on campus in advertising, in donations, in privatization of services, and implicitly in the classrooms. Ann, a department chair at Rural Valley College, noted that "the institution as a whole is much more focused upon the local business community. Programs as well as the institution are consulting more, developing partnerships and receiving funding or equivalents." For Ann, there is no turning back. But at her college, unlike some others, there were few visible signs of the private sector within the institution: no washroom advertising for commercial products as at City Center; no computer labs filled only with one company's product as well as advertising for that product as at Suburban Valley; no monopoly over food services by a private company such as at North Mountain; and no promotion for a bank that donated to the college as at East Shoreline.

These perceptions penetrated the consciousness of organizational members. The shift from an educational to an economic focus altered the thinking and subsequently the behaviors of organizational members. David, a department chair at Pacific Suburban Community College, reflected:

> We're going to increasingly be tasked to pay our own way. Raising tuition is inevitable. We have become more entrepreneurial and moved closer to the market. Rising costs will squeeze the college. The answer [to rising costs] is in changing operations to become more effective.

For David, the outcomes of economic globalization were "inevitable." Internalizing the ideology of business, he used the language of the commercial world to portray his college. Indeed, he did not object to these changes, or if he did, he failed to register his opposition. He also observed a present set of behaviors but identified them with the future.

Doris, a department coordinator at Suburban Valley Community College, saw the mission of the institution shifting from innovation to survival. "People are more desperate. In the past we could reflect. Now we think about survival. We cut here, we cut there, we reduce, taking the idea of permanency out. We have to make hard choices—eliminate the horse out of the pack, not just one leg of each horse." Not only did Doris not object to the changed environment, she promoted the speeding up of change so that the pain of transition would cease. But Doris was not talking about literal horses; she was referring to jobs and those who filled them.

Economic forces were among the most if not the most influential forces upon college behaviors and actions. These forces had a variety of effects upon colleges. Provincial and state economies and the political philosophies of the governments in power determined government fiscal allocations to colleges. Government policies increasingly reflected an economic role for community colleges and pushed for reform and productivity.

Federal policies were consistent with state and provincial policies. U.S. Federal policy documents were oriented in two directions: to improve the unfavorably perceived work-force productivity of the United States and to upgrade the work force and potential workers in order to remove a burden from employers and government. In California state policy, beginning in the early 1990s, and most apparent in the mid-1990s, there were descriptions of new and expanding roles for community colleges, including their role in economic development of California and in training a work force for global competitiveness of the state. For Hawaii, policy for the university and community colleges directed these institutions to be responsive to the state's economy and to economic reform. With acknowledgment in policy documents of declining state funds for higher education, the public higher education system was compelled to seek alternate funding sources and to achieve operating efficiencies. In the state of Washington, there was emphasis upon three themes: increased productivity (that is, efficiency); workforce training, with stress upon new workplace needs; and the state's economy, including a competitive environment.

In Canadian federal policy, emphasis was placed upon reducing unemployment, strengthening Canada's international competitiveness, and bolstering Canada's economy. There was little mention of improving the quality of education or training, but there was emphasis upon the need for training to become more marketplace-relevant, to meet the needs of employers. In Alberta, government policy documents were consumed with less public sector spending, greater efficiency and emphasis upon workforce training. Finally, in British Columbia, there were both implications and directions for postsecondary institutions to reform both curriculum and delivery, primarily to serve the private sector. Institutions in that province were directed to use more electronic technology and to increase collaboration with each other and with the private sector.

Because colleges depended upon these governments for their principal revenues, government funding behaviors were particularly critical. California's recession in the early 1990s, Hawaii's revenue shortfall in the mid and late 1990s, Alberta's debt in the early and mid-1990s, and Washington and British Columbia's declining resource economy all played influential roles in college behaviors. Furthermore, all jurisdictions were dependent upon international trade, and the U.S. jurisdictions of California and Washington were affected by military downsizing with the cessation of the Cold War, particularly evident in the missile and aircraft industry.[14] In adjusting to a global economy, state and provincial governments altered their practices of the past of expanding allocations to public institutions.

Colleges thus sought alternate revenue sources. In pursuing these new sources, colleges altered programming and services. For example, Suburban Valley Community College offered a biotechnology program through revenues from the local biotechnology industry, not through government allocations. The program was designed for and tailored to industrial needs; program students were largely those already employed in industry. East Shoreline College established a high school within the structure of the college, attracting Asian students who brought new revenues to the college. Pacific Suburban Community College pursued contract training for local businesses, developed curricula and delivered specialized programs to other countries through distance education technologies (online and Web-based), and expanded its culinary arts program to attract foreign students—all influenced by the need to compensate for shrinking government fiscal allocations.

Colleges expanded their traditional mission by enlarging work-force training and by emphasizing skills development. This resulted in a more overt concentration upon private sector interests and reflected changing priorities for student learning. Yet community colleges maintained much of their traditional curriculum and stuck fast to their traditional mission. Structural alterations occurred in the establishment of centers, institutes, and other new units or the enlargement of existing units aligned with revenue generation. There was increasing formalization of the entrepreneurial activities of the institution to the extent that colleges within colleges were developed. The non-credit divisions of the institution became de facto "shadow" colleges. These behaviors were not simply confined to the seven colleges but were evident in other community colleges as documented by Norton Grubb and his associates.[15]

Student learning priorities shifted from an acclaimed focus upon personal development and career and educational preparation to skills development and work-force training. College priorities shifted from the needs of individual students to those of employers. Work-force training was promoted by the state to serve the interests of employers not necessarily students. Employment skills were determined by the marketplace which propelled institutional programming patterns for training and retraining. While traditional vocational programs in several cases deteriorated, both in enrollments and in resources, vocationalism insinuated itself in higher level programming, such as business and computer-oriented programs and especially in Canadian institutions in baccalaureate programs. Decidedly less priority was given to remediation and to developmental education. At Pacific Suburban and North Mountain, these program areas were removed from the credentialing structure of the institutions and either became part of the revenue generating structure or were shunted off to other institutions. At East Shoreline and Rural Valley, as the curricular priorities focused upon higher level credentials, remediation and personal development slipped in institutional priority. City Center was the lone institution that did not abandon or retreat from remediation or personal development. In contrast to other colleges, City Center, as a result of losing substantial programming areas including academic programs when its third campus became an independent college, did not shift its curricular focus to more advanced programs. Nonetheless, undergirding its attention to remediation and personal development were the more strident articulations of City Center managers and the language of college planning documents stating that programming was directed at employment. City Center's increasing reliance upon English as a second language programming for revenues was a dependency upon federal government funding, allocated not so much for citizenship but for job preparation.

The changing institutional priorities to student learning included instructional delivery as well as curriculum. Moving in a direction similar to the ubiquitous claim of a paradigm shift in postsecondary education from teaching to learning,[16] institutions justified practices from distance education to computer-based instruction as "learner-centered."These practices were in fact prompted by both actual government fiscal restraint and government policy that directed institutions to become more efficient. Institutional rationales for a change to learner-centered education and training paralleled the view of education and training as a commodity, students as customers, and business and industry as clients—all reinforcing market ideology.

Institutional change in this direction followed student, employer, and government preferences. Enrollments in Canadian institutions rose substantially over the decade; in U.S. colleges, they rose modestly at Pacific Suburban, and they were relatively unchanged at Suburban Valley and City South. Institutional revenues increased significantly in the 1990s, even with claims of government funding constraints. Tuition fees, contract service revenues, and temporary, non-base budget, and often competitive government grants comprised a greater share of institutional revenues, suggesting that resource providers including the private sector were favorably impressed with institutional responsiveness to economic interests. To what extent this shift to more job market responsiveness at higher costs to students affected both students and community members, who were not students, is uncertain. Neither institutions nor governments possessed reliable data on student outcomes, such as job placements in program-related fields. No data existed that suggested the demands for education and training were not met—for example, community members who could not afford college or who had needs different from those satisfied by college programming.

Colleges drifted toward economic interests in the 1990s and shifted away from their collegiate role.The economic orientation of colleges was largely due to the reluctance of governments to fund these institutions relative to their anticipated expenditures. It is not that colleges in the 1990s became excessive in those expenditures; rather, growth as well as rising costs drove budgets to expand. As a consequence of government "underfunding," colleges turned to resource acquisition as a principal institutional activity. This consuming behavior led to the alteration of college structures and indeed to college missions. Institutions developed "shadow" or entrepreneurial colleges within a larger college. Organizational members and students were affected by the pervasive focus upon productivity and efficiency. Institutions used public money to serve private interests, particularly in offering education and training to meet the needs of specific employers and in using existing structures to provide services to private individuals for profit.

Some outcomes of organizational behavior, however, were more beneficial than others. Colleges lost some of their traditional, familiar, and even comfortable patterns of work, and educational priorities favored consumers, which included business and industry. Nonetheless, colleges gained new supporters, including business and industry, and certainly government, as well as new students.

Among the several gains that benefited the institutions, three of the more prominent are discussed. First, fiscal pressures sharpened the practice of college management. Second, colleges responded to the demands from external constituents for educational and training services to fit needs of time, place, and practical application. Third, the necessity of capturing both students and resources pushed colleges to become more sophisticated institutions, not just in marketing, which certainly mushroomed as an activity, but in operations and physical plant.

First, college managers became more strategic, not in planning but in thinking, working more collaboratively with each other and with faculty. They also became more astute by communicating with college employees regarding managerial actions. At North Mountain College, an elaborate committee structure within the institution served not only as an effective communication vehicle but also as a coordinating structure for ensuring that institutional levels and units were functioning with similar agendas and intentions. At Suburban Valley Community College, committees comprised of both managers and faculty served as work units for the management of the institution. Faculty were prominent members of these committees, and managers relied heavily upon their expertise. At several colleges, faculty served as managers while maintaining both their union status and faculty role. Because the institutions endeavored to curtail the managerial class at their institutions—certainly motivated by economic reasons, including employee productivity—potential administrative ranks, such as department chair, division chair, associate dean, and others, were staffed by faculty. In part, this behavior was consistent with that in the community colleges of the 1960s and 1970s, thus maintaining a tradition. But the institutions grew substantially since those decades, and in earlier periods, especially during unionization, there was considerable pressure to move faculty positions out of the union ranks into management. In the 1990s, this pattern and these pressures halted or were reversed. This approach of using faculty members as managers provided the institutions with considerable flexibility.

Second, flexibility was evident in the ways colleges responded and adapted to the demands of external constituents. In need of both resources and students, colleges altered their role from a social to an economic agency. They responded to the economic needs of community members, local business and industry, and to government policy, especially economic policy. New programs were established to meet the changing job market, and these included environmental management, computer software development, biotechnology, and small business entrepreneurship. Old programs were revised to include more job-relevant curricula. Even English language training at City Center College was given a face-lift, amalgamated with specific vocational programs, such as electronics and cooks' training, to join skills with employability. Most dramatic and unprecedented was the establishment of baccalaureate degree programs at community colleges—North Mountain, East Shoreline, and Rural Valley—fitting the needs of both students for higher-paying jobs and the economy for more highly credentialed workers. In a decade or less, community colleges were undergraduate institutions and sites of professional preparation. Community colleges in Canada offered baccalaureate degree programs in such areas as nursing, education, business, fashion design, and criminal justice, as well as in the traditional arts and sciences. Enrollments skyrocketed at two of the colleges at which a full range of programs was offered.

Third, in their quest for both more students, with a consequence of more state and provincial dollars and more tuition and fee revenues, as well as new revenues, colleges not only changed their programming but also altered their image externally. Colleges embarked upon extensive marketing campaigns and drives for donations, as well as the acquisition of private sector contracts. While not particularly a new behavior in kind, this approach to entrepreneurialism in the 1990s was larger and more sophisticated than in the past. In the 1990s, all levels of the institution, especially faculty, were involved in acquiring contracts with the private sector. In selling their services and products to the private sector, colleges had to market their institution as technologically fit, their programs as employment-relevant, and their personnel as appropriately qualified. One needs only to visit Pacific Suburban Community College to see state-of-the-art Web-based instruction, or Suburban Valley Community College to see computer animation equipment that is industry standard. Unlike the colleges of the 1970s, which conveyed the rhetoric of an advanced education institution, these colleges in the 1990s invested their resources in capital equipment, delivery methods, and qualified personnel, evolving the rhetoric into reality.

The considerable costs to personnel and to educational services need to be weighed against these material gains. While college marketing and promotional behaviors extolled the qualities of these institutions, such as "state of the art" equipment and "innovative," organizational members in solicited views were not as enthusiastic about institutional behaviors and outcomes in the economic domain.

At Suburban Valley Community College, "morale" became a major issue and problem in the latter part of the decade. Ventures in shared governance did not include shared decision-making, much to the consternation of faculty. Furthermore, the state-mandated pay for performance for administrators was "a thorn in everyone's side," lowering morale of administrative personnel and essentially pitting one against another:

> Folks are frustrated. People are starved for candor, faculty especially: they don't want the sham of shared governance. There are strained relations and conflicts between the Faculty Association and the administration. (Anna, senior administrator)

Additionally, new administrators at the district level altered the college's approach to labor relations:

> The new district people lack experience with collective bargaining. They hold a traditional view of industrial relations: bureaucratic, tied to the collective agreement. (Douglas, faculty union official)

According to Douglas, administrative decisions were motivated by finances: "money drives." But "there is no money for faculty and staff salaries." These behaviors demonstrated "how faculty are no longer necessary." This view is supported by another faculty leader. For Henry, labor relations dominated college life in the middle of the decade, and the college lost its "collegial" atmosphere. A district office administrator connected these behaviors to an economic context:

I think financial matters always influence. We had a short period . . . when there was more money to distribute for salaries and capital. . . . It is beginning to go dry. I've always said, "The table manners change when there are no longer enough muffins for everyone at the table." We will begin to see that this year. Next year, the situation will be worse and so will the table manners.

In the Canadian context, college finances were married to provincial governments and their management of the economy. As provincial institutions, community colleges in both Alberta and British Columbia were clear instruments of government policy and the benefactors and in part prisoners of the political economy.[17] A union leader at City Center College observed that the provincial government's emphasis upon deficits "stifles change" at the college:

We are simply maintaining the status quo; there is nothing innovative. The penalties are great and the rewards small.

For Janice, a college counselor, "economic survival is the real mission" of the college as a consequence of "government cutbacks":

We are trying to sell the place, almost exploitative behavior and the opposite of student centered. There is false advertising. There are no computers but we do have an internet address logo. We make students pay for placement tests and we make them take prerequisite courses. The commitment to our mission and goals' statement is not borne out by reality.

For Janice, the education of students as an institutional goal was superseded by financial behaviors.

At another Canadian college, North Mountain, the shift to an entrepreneurial approach was lamented by Mary, an English instructor:

There is a heavier focus upon entrepreneurship and money making. We have lost the focus on the soulful part of education. . . . Jobs drive students who want technical training and the college responds. . . . These influence the teaching of writing and [writing becomes] applied communications. . . . The social function is being lost.

A faculty union official at North Mountain noted that faculty were working hard but that their efforts were not recognized. Brian, an administrator in the human resources area, noted that there was "a massive increase in stress" as a result of "the volume of work, increased numbers of students and fewer support staff." An academic dean noted that the college's "mission has developed as the market needs and government expectations are identified":

> At one time, the college was content with student success and satisfaction, but now the college is more hard-nosed.

In reaction to these pressures at North Mountain, according to Jane, an arts faculty chair, "faculty are becoming a traditional bargaining unit, not a professional association—workers." A business instructor, Constance, referred to faculty as "volume oriented worker bees":

> Stress is placed upon instructors. They are not supported and have no time. There is no release time for curriculum development. Faculty are burned out with classroom size increased.

For Constance, the college became a business enterprise and as a consequence, "faculty [withdrew] emotionally."

At East Shoreline College, which even has a history of market-oriented behaviors going back to the 1980s, even the college president noted that personnel were "stretched" to their limits. Robert, a senate executive member, observed that East Shoreline was "a free-market organization: we offer what is marketable." In the 1990s, he noted, "economic expediency" and emphasis upon applied education within the provincial system had altered the "value placed upon education." East Shoreline nonetheless increased its emphasis upon a market orientation and the acquisition of resources became a central feature of institutional life:

> There is more pressure to be entrepreneurial. There is competition for offshore revenues.

Doreen, a nursing faculty member, noted, "in trying to deal with economic constraints, the college has taken on an entrepreneurial role, and competition adds to severe stress within the institution":

> There have been frequent government cutbacks. There is an incongruence between government articulations of support for students and funding resources required for education.

At Pacific Suburban Community College, the focus upon the "bleak budget situation" of the latter part of the 1990s resulted in what the president referred to as "a certain amount of chaos and uncertainty."

The decline in state revenues resulted in budget cuts. . . . There is too much work. Instructors have scaled back on assignments. (Moira, health sciences department head)

This condition of declining state revenues and subsequent budget cuts led to demoralization:

> I would say this is causing many of my colleagues to be discouraged from innovating because good quality requires training, resources, and infrastructure that allow innovative methodologies to be successful. (Janice, English faculty)

In the economic domain, organizational behaviors reflected increasing focus upon the acquisition of revenues or strategies to respond to actual or anticipated revenue decline. Stress upon organizational members to increase production, tension over job security, and frustration over the limits to the pursuit of qualitative approaches were among the outcomes. Labor relations suffered as a result of both financial constraint and managerial responses to revenue difficulties. Many faculty claimed that instruction suffered. Clearly, there were considerable effects upon employee morale at these institutions.

Outside the institutions, in the 1990s, state and provincial economies were clearly a major force in social and political life.[18] Inside the institutions, the external economy took on a more prominent role in the 1990s than previously. Revenues, their origins and their perceived scarcity, were more contingent upon global conditions and governments' responses to these conditions. Organizational actions affected not only institutional financing and finances but also work, including labor and management relations and employee morale, and education, including programs offered and methods of instruction.

CHAPTER 4

THE CULTURAL DOMAIN

The pervasive and invasive dynamics of what is in general referred to as a global economy have dominated thinking about globalization as an economic condition, with other global flows either downplayed or ignored. But economics are not the only global force. Indeed, it is argued by a few scholars that the transformation of labor and production relationships and the development of new global flows of communications, ideas, images, and people are the centerpiece of globalization.[1] Moreover, the role of economics and the behaviors of a world economy, especially since the 1970s, are associated with social and cultural change.[2] Another not dissimilar viewpoint is that globalization is a social process, with the current phase surfacing as neo-Fordism or neoliberalism.[3] A variation on this theme is provided by Ritzer and his MacDonaldization thesis—that the globalization process is consumption-oriented and has its origins in the United States,[4] suggesting that neither economics alone nor a global economy is the driving force of globalization.

Whatever the prevailing force of globalization, it is clear that globally there is a change in the conceptualization of the world as a single place[5] and an increase in the involvement of people with more than one culture.[6] Furthermore, there is an acknowledged presence of a dominant ideology (or ideologies) that accompanies globalization. For Ralston Saul, the ideology is "corporatism," the adoration of self-interest and the dismissal of the public good.[7] For Chomsky, the ideology is "neoliberal," the control of social life of the many for the maximization of profit for the few.[8] Teeple parallels neoliberalism to economic globalization. "The neo-liberal agenda is the social and political counterpoint to the globalization of production, distribution, and exchange."[9]

I focus upon three cultural aspects of globalization: (1) the dominant ideology associated with globalization, (2) the involvement and interactions of people in and with other cultures, and (3) the conceptualization of the world as a single place.[10] I turn to the first two of these cultural aspects and apply them to organizations, specifically to the community college. For the third aspect, I consider potential cultural change as an outcome of the use of electronic technology.

The Ideology of Globalization

In analyzing modern organizational management, Gephart equates the dominant global ideology with postmodernism, whereby management surrenders to market ideology. Followers of this ideology favor and pursue the reduction of goods, services, people, and organizational relationships to an economic value.[11] For higher education, this ideology underlies the fashioning of students as consumers and citizens as economic entities.[12] In this vein, if universities are knowledge systems, with academic entrepreneurs,[13] community colleges are handmaidens of technocracy,[14] institutions that incorporate academic knowledge and occupational skills training, relying increasingly upon new technologies and organizational network structures.[15]

Managers of community colleges have increasingly embraced a global ideology, either in the form of corporatism or neoliberalism in what I refer to as two organizational cultures—the managerial culture and the business culture. The managerial culture of community colleges can be identified by the emphasis in organizational behaviors upon systems' goals: survival, efficiency, control, and growth.[16] The business culture, in some distinction, can be identified by the emphasis in organizational behaviors upon performance, including productivity. Both managerial and business cultures share a number of features. The managerial culture can be equated with Ralston Saul's "corporatism," and with its central quality, rationality.[17] Mintzberg equates rationality with control. To rationalize, Mintzberg notes, is to cut, reduce, eliminate, and to avoid creative judgement or intuition.[18] This is in accord with Ralston Saul's view of corporatism as anti-individualistic, promoting individual passivity.

The business culture affects a more entrepreneurial, businesslike, and usually less hierarchical way of conducting organizational activities. Community college responsiveness to national requirements for competitiveness, work-force training, and dwindling public sector resources are complemented with practices that model those of business and industry.[19] The origins of the business culture in the community college can be traced to the early 1980s, to the rise in business of performance improvement, first publicized by Peters and Waterman and discovered in the earlier work of Deming.[20] In the United States, performance initiatives were linked to the underachievement of U.S. business, especially in comparison with Japan. Community college literature for practitioners reflected this bias for improved performance not only in the 1980s but well into the 1990s.[21]

Both the business culture and the managerial culture are sympathetic on the matter of employees: managers act to control the behaviors of personnel, whether for revenue generation (profits), as is the case of the business culture, or for systems goals, as is the case of the managerial culture. Arthur Cohen and Florence Brawer, the doyens of U.S. community college scholarship, isolate three concepts of import for contemporary management of community colleges, whether for the business or the managerial culture: total quality management, shared governance, and responsibility.[22] They do not reflect, however, upon the thread that ties the three concepts together and to the business and managerial cultures of the community college: managerial control. Measurable improvement of employee outputs, commitment of employees to institutional goals and cooperation with management, and accountability of employees are more apt descriptors of the three concepts. Paul Gallagher, a former Canadian community college president and one of Canada's more prominent educational practitioners, observes that the efforts to wed two value systems—the academic and the corporate—are bound to lead to an unhealthy relationship:

> Much conflict can be attributed to the fact that community colleges have attempted, on the one hand, to be collegial, participatory, and consultative, while, on the other hand maintaining quite traditional, hierarchical structures for administration and institutional governance. In a very real sense, many colleges and college systems have tried to marry the corporate sector's established methods of management with the university sector's sophisticated and subtle approaches to collegial operations.[23]

Gallagher attributes considerable labor and management disruptions to this arrangement. His point underscores the view that a managerial culture, modeled after the corporate world, is inimical to the more traditional values of the academy—such as peer evaluation and oversight—and to those values that community colleges adopted in their development—such as an emphasis upon teaching and learning and the "open door" concept that represents a commitment to a democratic society.[24]

A monolithic managerial ideology—the single belief system of college administrators—is neither a given nor likely, but there are recurrent images, themes, and observations both in how managers at colleges understand and assess their actions and in the assumptions that underlie the perceptions and behaviors of college managers. Alan, president at North Mountain College in Alberta, elucidated his rationale for altering his institution and modeling corporate behaviors:

> Enormous trend toward vocationalism. Jobs, jobs, jobs. Over 95 percent of students who come to us are looking for skills . . . in order to be able to get jobs and pursue successful economic careers. . . . The Pew Charitable Trusts in the United States concluded that the three major forces, external forces for change, were . . . vocationalism, information technology, and . . . privatization.
>
> In the college, there are higher levels of work; there are higher levels of stress. . . . We are confronted with a less supportive and more hostile government. We are being challenged . . . by government, by the private sector, by taxpayers generally. . . . People . . . at North Mountain are wondering whether their work is really valued or appreciated or understood. We are facing rising levels of expectation and demands.
>
> We are trying to inculcate at least some of these economy skills throughout our curriculum. That means fundamental revision to re-vamping the curriculum. . . . Education institutions: these are knowledge industries, companies. . . . They are also collegial. They are very radical in theory but very conservative in practice. . . . In this highly competitive environment, you feel enormous pressure to be adroit, nimble, flexible, and to respond to rapidly shifting corporate, government, student demands and needs. It takes years. We just had to operate . . . in a far more businesslike way: become a pattern now. The collegial culture suffers consequently. . ! . You have no choice.

For Alan, North Mountain College had little choice but to alter the institution to fit the expectations of "government," the "private sector," and "taxpayers." These expectations were primarily that college was a means for "jobs, jobs, jobs." And, the purpose of the curriculum was to provide students with "economy skills." As a consequence, the college became a different institution over the decade, operating less like an academic institutions and more like a business.

The business theme is evident in the description offered by Gary, president of City South Community College, on the college's rationalization of programs and services:

> Ray [the former president] and [I] worked together to reorganize, shrank administrative personnel, organize[d] a team concept . . . and reduced substantially the administrative personnel, put a lot more work on faculty and the use of technology. Enrollment was dropping. Ray saw the trend, just like in industry . . . to make it more lean and mean . . . to deal with issues, enrollment, community need. . . . And I agreed with him; so we worked to-

gether. . . . It's not always dandy; not many people like it: layoff faculty, eliminated position of associate dean, two or three of them.

Gary offered the view of a college that adopted a retrenchment posture: cut expenses by cutting jobs, because enrollments, and thus a source of revenues, were diminishing. Gary's explanation in 1997 took place approximately 20 months after the former president, Ray, sent a letter to the college community. Ray explained in his letter that a global economy precipitated change to the college's environment:

> All of us are aware, the tides of change are sweeping across our country, not only in a political sense but to the very core of our business, industrial, financial, governmental and educational enterprises. In this highly competitive global economy, change is no longer an intellectual activity to analyze and discuss, it has in every sense become a mechanism of survival—a way of life—regardless of where one looks. Re-structuring, re-engineering, reframing, downsizing, whatever you call it—it is with us and we *must* deal with it. . . .
>
> [W]e must accept the fact that change is constant and recognize that our structure, our processes, our procedures and many of our time-honored beliefs and past practices and methods will need to change. . . .
>
> To initiate the early phase of this philosophy I am proposing a rather dramatic change in our existing organizational framework.

At City South, enrollments had declined in the 1990s by nearly 15 percent in a six-year period, with the drop almost entirely in the vocational and occupational areas—those closest to business and industry. But following Ray's defensive action of "dramatic change," what Gary called the "lean and mean" approach, revenues also declined. Expenditures did not. The college lost state funding as well as student tuition fees. Surprisingly, in numerous areas, the college expended more, especially on personnel, after the rationalization than before. The greater change of the response to change—declining student numbers in program areas in which there were diminishing job opportunities—was on the one hand to employee morale and on the other hand to structures and process. Unilateral management action nullified even the slightest vestiges of collegiality or employee participation in decision-making, and the "team concept" modified the academic structure of the institution so that it reflected a business more than an academic organization.

Unilateral action, however, was not the only way to have employees comply with managerial preferences. A more subtle approach was described by Paul, the president at Rural Valley College:

> In our last contract... we negotiated quite consciously with our union.... Our thinking was if you wanted to make a flexible institution, you're not going to get flexibility where people are always worried about losing their job. People aren't going to take risk if their jobs are threatened.... No layoff clause. Give people an environment of security. I don't know if it's worked.... The theory was if you could provide people with that kind of basic security then you can more easily get them to take on things which they may not do if they are scared for their job. It's true of faculty and for staff.

For Paul, employee compliance with managerial preferences was the goal, and quelling employee fears was the avenue to realizing this goal. In order to accomplish this, the college's management agreed to contract language that guaranteed full-time employees their jobs for the duration of the collective agreement period.

Other college administrators both described and reflected upon the shift to a corporate or business ethos in their institutions. Carol, the vice-president at North Mountain, concluded that a competitive education environment required North Mountain to become "more flexible, changing [college] traditions and values." Brian, a dean at North Mountain, described the college's altered behaviors in noting that "the college has pulled back from the community, from non-corporate service." At City South Community College, a district office administrator noted twenty months after restructuring had been announced that morale at the campus was low and that "things [were] falling apart." City South's vice-president noted that "faculty [were] struggling with change" and that "the reorganization caused problems." At Rural Valley College, Denise, a dean, observed that "there's been a blurring of the public and the private sectors" whereby her college was compelled to be more entrepreneurial and to generate more revenue as a consequence of public resources going to the private sector. Denise's colleague, Robert, another college dean, saw the college shift in educational services to "linking training to education" to respond to "increased demands for the educated skilled worker."

Not unlike their administrative counterparts, faculty at these institutions acknowledged a corporatist orientation of their colleges and businesslike behaviors. At North Mountain College, where the president had noted that institutional members "just had to... operate in a far more businesslike way" that had "become a pattern," and consequently collegiality suffered, faculty reflected this trend. Doreen, a business instructor, observed in a less than flattering manner:

Power is centralized at the top. The president and vice-president are control freaks. . . . [The college is] bureaucratic, dictatorial, stultifying.

A faculty colleague suggested that organizational goals were shifting: "we are to a certain extent abandoning our community, looking for opportunity in a global marketplace." An English instructor, Randall, asserted that "the big change at the college is the orientation toward business and the business model of education." And another instructor at North Mountain, characterizing organizational change during the decade, responded, "I don't like seeing the college movement away from reaching the underprepared, remedial, and working-class students."

At Suburban Valley Community College, emphasis upon productivity, curriculum driven by private sector interests, and the loss of collegiality reflected an altered institutional ethos. One instructor noted that "productivity is the word—bigger classes, more students." Mark, a faculty union leader, asserted that "programs [are] set up for business interests." Ed, a faculty senate leader, reflected upon a changed institutional environment in which there was a "a labor-management mentality or atmosphere. [Both sides] bring out the contract: 'What does it say?' [The institution] is no longer collegial."

The pronounced shift in the community college both to corporatism and to a business orientation is evident in community college literature. First, the literature by and for practitioners both details and supports this shift. Second, the literature by and for scholars confirms the alteration both in institutional ethos and in the ideology of administrative leaders. Thor, Scarafiotti, and Helminski of Rio Salado College in Arizona note that the college president at Rio "believed that much as it had helped corporate institutions, a TQM (Total Quality Management) culture could help educational institutions survive in the coming new century."[25] They detail the implementation of TQM at their institution, where there was "emphasis on work teams," a "change in college values," and "a shared understanding of the meaning of customer service."[26] Gordon from Humber College in Ontario, Canada, outlines the collaborative actions between his college and business and industry, which he refers to as "partnerships." These partnerships are vehicles "for the development of the character and culture of Humber College."[27] Gianini and Sarantos of Valencia Community College in Florida discuss their institution's connection to business, noting that in the 1990s the college built "stronger bridges between education and the business world."[28] Institutional change at Valencia extended to instructional practices whereby "faculty members are being challenged to answer the question as to how they can integrate the economic development concept into the college curriculum."[29]

Academic scholarship on this topic is not as prevalent and not as effusive about the shift to the ideology of globalization; nonetheless, it does validate the claim of a shift. Johnson addresses the emerging and growing trend toward contract training, not just as an ancillary activity of colleges but as a central organizational function. He notes that numerous institutions whose practices he deems "high performing" operated in ways that were congruent with business and industry and different from the traditional college organization. Customized training, a subset of contract training and a new product of community colleges, served to gain community colleges "positive esteem within the business community and even earn profits to finance other operations."[30] Johnson's findings are supported by subsequent research carried out by Norton Grubb, Norena Badway, Denise Bell, Debra Bragg, and Maxine Russman, who found that new structures were established in community colleges in the 1990s related to business and industry, adding to the functions of the community college. This change included the creation of a new culture, with its own values, rules, and regulations, a culture separate from the traditional institution.[31] In a review of the scholarly literature in the United States, Meier suggests that these business-oriented behaviors favor or privilege markets over community and reflect the imperatives of postindustrial globalizing capitalism that embraces supply-side fiscal policy.[32] In observing Canadian community colleges, Schugurensky and Higgins conclude that these institutions are undergoing reforms, altering "from a developmental education paradigm" to "a global marketplace paradigm," which has resulted in an industry-driven model whereby colleges have adopted managerial systems typical of business and industry.[33]

People From Other Cultures

If the ideology of globalization in organizations sharply modifies organizational practices and the organizational ethos, then those behaviors that include the involvement of people with other cultures and the interaction of people from different cultural groups are less dramatic, less maligned, and less vaunted. Nonetheless, they were consequences of as well as contributors to globalization, and they did affect and help to alter community colleges. *Internationalism, multiculturalism,* and *diversity* are terms that both connote and promote increasing tolerance for other cultures, other people's physical and social characteristics, and other people's thinking and values.

The increasing emphasis in community colleges during the decade of the 1990s to "other"—that is, to other cultures and people—was a consequence of social and demographic conditions and resulted in curricular and policy change as well as behavioral change among organizational members and towards students. New patterns of immigration and the outcomes of previous decades of immigration for both the United States and Canada altered the demographics of college communities. Asian and Mexican immigrants and their offspring comprised a greater percentage of the total U.S. population in the 1980s and 1990s, and Asian immigrants and their offspring comprised a greater percentage in Canada during the same decades. Correspondingly, the percentage of Western Europeans of the total population in both countries declined. Immigration patterns for the decades of the 1960s, 1970s, 1980s and 1990s in the United States and the decades of the 1980s and 1990s in Canada illustrate the rising percentages of non-European immigrants (See table 4.1, table 4.2, and table 4.3).[34]

On campus, there was growing diversity among the student body, including the ethnic makeup of these students.[35] U.S. figures show that in 1980 those categorized as Asian made up 2.4 percent of total students at all institutions; in 1996, that figure rose to 5.7 percent of all students. Those categorized as Hispanic made up 3.5 percent of all students in 1980, whereas in 1996 they made up 8 percent. At public two-year colleges, 2 percent of students were categorized as Asian and 5.5 percent as Hispanic in 1980. By 1996, 6 percent of students were categorized as Asian and 11.9 percent as Hispanic. As well, for two-year colleges, those classified as

Table 4.1 Immigrants to the United States, by Place of Birth, 1961–1990; Total Persons and Percentage of Total Immigration

Country of Birth	1961–1970	1971–1980	1981–1990	1990–1996
All	3,321,700	4,493,300	7,338,100	7,682,800
Europe	1,238,600	801,300	707,600	988,000
	(37.3%)	(17.8%)	(9.6%)	(12.9%)
Asia	445,000	1,633,800	2,817,400	1,921,800
	(13.4%)	(36%)	(38.4%)	(25%)
Mexico	443,000	637,200	1,653,300	2,330,500
	(13.3%)	(14%)	(22.5%)	(30.3%)
Soviet Union (included in Europe figures)	15,700	43,200	84,000	365,400
	(.047%)	(.096%)	(.1%)	(4.8%)

"White" fell from 79 percent of the total student body in 1980 to 68 percent in 1996.[36]

At the same time that demographic change was underway, social change was reflected in government policy, such as affirmative action in the United States and access initiatives in Canada. Furthermore, within the academy, especially within the social sciences and humanities disciplines, the traditions of Western Europe were challenged and alternate epistemologies and metaphysical constructs were promoted and occasionally adopted. Backlash against these developments came from conservative and religious fronts but it was not enough to eradicate numerous changes. Even community colleges were affected by the multicultural debate.[37]

In higher education institutions generally, new attention to special student populations could be seen in recruitment and admissions policies and practices, support services, and programming. In the United States, this attention was directed toward minority students. In Canada, the focus was given to female, aboriginal, and disabled students. In community colleges, responses to these new populations led to organizational changes that made these institutions different in the 1990s than in previous

Table 4.2 Immigrants to Canada, by Origin, 1981, 1989, 1991, and 1993; Total Persons and Percentage of Total Immigration

Country of Origin	1981	1989	1991	1993
All	128,618	192,001	230,834	252,042
Europe	46,295	52,105	48,073	50,050
	(36%)	(27%)	(20.8%)	(19.8%)
Asia	48,830	93,261	120,019	134,532
	(38%)	(48.5%)	(52%)	(53.4%)

Table 4.3 Immigrants to Canada, by Origin, 1926–1991; as Percentage of Total Immigrants

Country of Origin	1926–1945	1976–1980	1991
British Isles: England, Ireland, Scotland, Wales	47.8%	14.1%	3.5%
Asia	.8%	31.7%	52%

THE CULTURAL DOMAIN 73

decades. Two specific sets of institutional behavior—internationalization and multiculturalism—were responsible for several of these changes.

Internationalization

In their pursuit of alternate revenue sources through international contracts and the recruitment of international students, community colleges in both the United States and Canada brought new students to their campuses and extended their institutions abroad. These students were characterized by their relative wealth, not only in their own country but in several cases in the United States and Canada at their community college, by their need for English language training, their cultural distinctiveness, and their personal and social needs as nonresidents, such as housing. Their effects upon English as a second language programming were considerable, and this area not only grew in student numbers in the 1990s but also achieved higher institutional status because of its wealth generation. For large numbers of international students, English language was their sole area of study.

The majority of international students at the colleges was from Asian countries (see table 4.4).[38] Thus colleges, their organizational members, their students, and their communities were affected not just by students from other countries generally, but specifically by students from Asian countries, with different backgrounds from students residing in Western countries. Institutions aligned their programming and cultural sensitivities to these students.

The large percentage of students from Asian countries on campus was not by chance. Colleges targeted Asian countries for both students and for service contracts, beginning in earnest in the 1980s. College officials traveled to these countries to establish links, personal relationships, and partnerships and to sell their institutions and their services. Suburban Valley Community College officials worked less diligently at this than the others because of the college's reputation and its location, which were significant attractors, according to college officials, for students from Asian countries. Nonetheless, at Suburban Valley in the 1990s, a program in intercultural and international studies was initiated and a campus center, multicultural and international, was established. East Shoreline College took a comprehensive approach to internationalization, not simply recruiting students but also undertaking projects in Asia (Indonesia, Japan, Thailand, Vietnam), Central America, South America (Guyana, Peru), and the subcontinent, India. Faculty and students used foreign sites for faculty development and student work placements, such as teacher training. These actions advanced the interactions of college members and their students with people from other cultures. The actions of providing services for a fee, placement of students abroad, faculty and student exchange, and the recruitment of students from other countries also connected the local institution with other countries and international regions. The community served by the colleges expanded beyond the local community and beyond the state or province. This suggests that colleges increased their global involvement in the 1990s, although perhaps more forcefully in the direction of more developed nations.[39] Together with the behaviors of multiculturalism, internationalization stimulated and advanced cultural change at community colleges enlarging and modifying the college mission as an agent of social change.

Multiculturalism

It was not only the rising international focus of community colleges that affected these institutions in the 1990s but also immigration patterns and local population demographics that molded college services and programming as well as college mission orientation. Both immigration patterns and local population demographics were contributors to the recognition and legitimacy of plural cultures, or what is generally known as multiculturalism. In the United States, the social movement of multiculturalism, including the growing liberalization of social behaviors and the public demonstrations of intolerance evident in the treatment of visible minorities, gays and lesbians, women, the disabled, and the poor, served to reinforce the elevation of multiculturalism on campuses.[40] In

Table 4.4 International Students, 1996

College	Total International Students	Students from Asian Countries (% of Total)
Suburban Valley	1,800	1,131 (63%)
East Shoreline	337	291 (86%)
City South	224	157 (70%)
Pacific Suburban	207	162 (78%)
City Center	372	355 (95%)
Rural Valley	175	129 (74%)
North Mountain	160	88 (55%)
Totals	3,275	2,313 (71%)

Canada, the pervasive emphasis in the late 1980s and 1990s upon a specific kind of access—the participation of targeted groups, such as the disabled, the poor, and aboriginal people—served as a proxy for multiculturalism.[41] In Canada, the goal for higher education was directed to greater inclusivity in educational participation and in social change as a consequence of participation.

The wave of immigration to the West of the United States in the past two decades—from Southeast Asia and from the former Soviet Union, in particular—altered the communities that the colleges occupied. In the community served by Suburban Valley Community College, the population growth rate was 7.6 percent from 1991 to 1996. During this period, the total population rose by 115,659, with 87,359 of that number comprised of immigrants. For the community served by City South College, the population rose by 103,914 from 1991 to 1997, with 36,587 of that number comprised of immigrants. And for the community served by Pacific Suburban Community College, the population rose by 33,626, with 30,622 immigrants contributing to that rise.[42]

Colleges altered their cultural emphases, becoming more attentive to students' cultural differences, more responsive in curriculum and instruction to multicultural needs, and more active in altering past practices of discrimination, with some colleges more pluralistic in their approach to both hiring and formal institutional governance. These changes served a number of purposes, from meeting student needs to benefiting the college through student recruitment and retention of students once in the institution. Additionally, cultural awareness and sensitivity were important qualities in international initiatives for colleges to secure work contracts and recruit students. The reasons for cultural change, with a shift to a multicultural focus, were both numerous and complex. The president at Suburban Valley Community College noted that "changing demographics" was a major force acting upon the college. Sara, a biology instructor at the same institution, observed that college energies were going to student retention: "we focus on student retention and success."

> We're hanging on to academic structures. Education is at the center in spite of technology and business push.

The term *multiculturalism* was used persistently at Suburban Valley Community College in a variety of ways to reflect not only student demographics but also institutional behaviors, including instruction and extracurricular activities. Locally, there were large numbers of immigrants, especially from non-Western countries. The college responded to its student population by altering programming, curricula, and college social life to fit student ethnic and cultural backgrounds. For example, non-Western writers became more prevalent on course syllabi, and extracurricular activities included international festivals and speakers. Furthermore, new organizational structures were established, such as a college reorganization of units in the mid-1990s to reflect multiculturalism and teamwork. Inter and multidisciplinarity in curricula gained prominence as the college adapted to college members' understanding of "new learning needs of students," especially part-time learners, non-native speakers, and students who were ethnic minorities. Suburban Valley Community College established an intercultural and international studies program and publicized its attention to ethnic diversity in both its college catalogue and its annual report. Additionally, college hirings, especially in the middle and late 1990s, accentuated minority status of candidates.

Similar behaviors were observed at the other colleges: City South Community College formalized a diversity task force that addressed institutional practices, including hiring of employees; City Center College established an aboriginal peoples' center; and North Mountain College dismantled its chapel, with its Christian referents, and set aside space for a meditation center with more universalistic connotations, to promote "self-development and spiritual and moral development."

The changing local population was reflected in college actions, as if the college mirrored its understandings of its community. At Pacific Suburban Community College, the college served the needs of its local students by its emphasis upon multiculturalism. Organizational members were fervent proponents of maintaining a cultural mosaic, both in college student demographics and in curriculum. Thus, cultural events on campus, such as International Week, and courses and programs that had cultural components and multicultural orientations (for example, culinary arts, humanities, languages, and business) were viewed as integral to college behaviors and actions. City South Community College was situated within a community possessed of not only a large immigrant population but also a changing immigrant population as the refugees—the 1970s "boat people"—gave way in the 1980s to the Chinese from Hong Kong, and these groups were added to by Eastern Europeans (for example, Russians). In the 1990s, the college placed increasing emphasis upon multiculturalism and diversity, serving a relatively large immigrant and refugee community population, many of whom were non-native-speaking students. The college added (in conjunction with the two other district colleges) a multicultural course requirement for the associate's degree in 1994 and added a cultural course requirement for the degree in 1996.

At City Center College, there was a large immigrant population both within the college and in the community. Included in this population were recent immigrants from war-torn countries (for example, Bosnia), from Asian countries in which the standard of living did not match Canada's, and from countries in which there were relatives of Canadian citizens (for example, Hong Kong, Korea). This population, in need of English language skills for employment as well as for citizenship and for coping with an Anglophone society, drove college enrollments and programming. This population was a large group within the overall urban community and in serving its community City Center College endeavored to meet the needs of a highly diverse population, one that had altered over time. Native speakers of English constituted 79 percent of the urban population in 1986, 72 percent in 1991, and 64 percent in 1996. Native Chinese language speakers rose from 5.75 percent of the population in 1986 to 13 percent in 1996, and native Punjabi language speakers rose from just slightly less than 2 percent in 1986 to 4 percent in 1996.[43] Thus, a large immigrant population was influential in the college's sensitivity to multiculturalism and diversity as well as its focus on job preparation and skills development.

But Suburban Valley's implementation of a "learning community" philosophy and organizational structure was the most dramatic and far-reaching of college initiatives in altering the institution. In part to deal with what the college president referred to as "changing pedagogy" to respond to a problem of "student engagement," the learning community concept evolved into "changing structures around the curriculum"—that is, organization of work units around curricular themes. In curriculum and in instruction, this philosophy was a "multicultural emphasis with a focus upon value"; it was publicized as "preparing students for a global society." Thus, the rhetoric of college members and college publications, such as the annual report, combined with institutional behaviors and actions tied multiculturalism to globalization.

Multiculturalism spread into formal governance of these institutions, and both ethnicity and "voice," the views of the traditionally excluded, became important factors. At City South Community College, the college president from 1995 to 1997 became the district chancellor, responsible for the management and governance of three community colleges, the first person of Asian origins to occupy such a role, not only in that college district but in the state. At Suburban Valley Community College, the college hired its first female president, and the district board elected an individual with Asian ancestry as its chair. In the three British Columbia colleges, government appointed board members reflected the considerable diversity of the local population, including Asian and Indo-Asian members, those who were individuals with disabilities, aboriginal people, and an equal or majority representation of women. Furthermore, legislation changed in the mid-1990s to include faculty, students, and support staff on the governing board. At City Center College, the board chair in the mid-1990s was a woman with a disability; by the end of the decade the board chair was another woman employed by the college in a support staff role. At Pacific Suburban Community College, a former female president of the college ascended to the role of chancellor of the entire state community college system in the mid-1990s. These alterations, unique in the history of these institutions, signaled greater tolerance for people from different cultures, for people with differing backgrounds, gender, sexual orientation, visible characteristics, and people with disparate communities of interest.

The World as a Single Place

To speak of a global culture or of the world as a single place is neither to promote those conditions nor to diminish culture to a homogenous phenomenon.[44] The experience of the world as singular or humanity as unitary is, however, conceptualized in numerous explanations of globalization. This is amply articulated in discussions of the local and the global and their interrelationships or interpenetrations.[45] Global culture is highly symbolic, idealizing individual behaviors, and is without memory or history, which characterizes national cultures. Global culture is an imaginary world experienced by people who live around the world.[46] It is a neoworld, riding on electronic communications systems and networks, sustained by various actors, media, financial and political institutions, and social movements' such as environmental and peace movements.[47] Human consciousness is its bedrock. For idealists and optimists, global culture is a communal unity of the human species, a global *gemeinschaft*.[48] For the antiglobalists, those who reject the contributions of globalization, global culture is hegemonic, a demonic Westernism or, worse still, Americanization.[49]

While the ideology of globalization is largely monolithic, a reduction of the world to economic entities and values, the experience of individuals and groups is less reductive and more integrative, connective, and animating. The focus on the globe as a single place does not negate "diversity, variety and richness of popular and local discourses, codes and practices."[50] These experiences of the world as a single place involve the intensification of worldwide social relations so that physical boundaries, such as time and space, are not impediments, and local and global are interdependent.[51] Social relations are initiated and sustained by the movement or flows of physical artifacts, people, symbols, information, and ideas across space and time and by the patterned interactions of networks between individuals, nodes of activity, or sites of power.[52]

Much of higher education scholarly literature ignores the cultural domain of globalization, preferring instead to conflate culture with economics, and in so doing connecting globalization processes almost solely to marketization.[53] Neglected in this literature is an acknowledgment, let alone comprehension, of generational change across communities and nations that reflects informative experiences of individuals worldwide. These informational experiences, especially in advanced societies, are propelled by economic, technological, and sociopolitical changes, not just locally but globally.[54] Although cultural change is slow, "fundamental value change takes place as younger age groups replace older ones in the adult population of a society."[55]

In higher education institutions, however, instruction and social interactions, as well as curriculum, are beginning to function as imaginary "scapes"[56] in which the world is experienced as a single place. Much of this is made possible by the use of electronic communication and information technologies. The rapture over the use of educational and informational technologies is based more upon an imagined future than an empirically demonstrated present.[57] In community colleges to date, this cultural shift is more potential than actual, as institutions begin to embrace electronically mediated instruction. This includes the use of the Internet and the World Wide Web as well as distance education by electronic transmission, such as interactive video.

While much or most of instruction mediated by electronic communications at the community colleges was localized or regionalized, there were preparations for transnational or global instruction. Curricula in English writing and literature, among others, were delivered online—that is, through Internet or computer-networked communications. Science laboratory curriculum and a microbiology course were "posted" on the World Wide Web. These were accessed largely by students who were local residents. But instruction went beyond local or regional borders. At Pacific Suburban Community College, courses in health sciences were offered to students in other countries through the Internet. Suburban Valley Community College and North Mountain College, while involved in electronically delivering courses and programs regionally, were well advanced in preparation to initiate international instruction, and both possessed sophisticated broadcast facilities and capabilities for synchronous instruction—that is, instruction that occurs in more than one site at the same time and is used regionally. Thus barriers of space and time can be removed: Internet and

Web-based instruction eliminate both, and synchronous instruction via broadcast video oversteps the boundary of space. These actions of communication and the experience that accompanies them may constitute new forms of social interaction,[58] with connectivity to networks globally. The relationships between and among those who participate in those networks may signal a global culture in which people experience the world as a single place.[59]

The embrace of these technologies at community colleges is therefore ironic, at least historically, as these institutions were characterized by their local orientation and to some extent vilified by their critics as socially reproductive agents.[60] Potentially, these colleges can function as global institutions, participating in the global flows of culture as conveyors and recipients of these flows, assisting in "the compression of the world and the intensification of consciousness of the world as a whole."[61]

CHAPTER 5

THE INFORMATION DOMAIN

The "information revolution" of the later part of the twentieth century is undergirded by microelectronics and manifest in electronic technologies that are the driving force behind globalization.[1] These technologies make possible the movement of information without the limitations of space and time.[2] If late twentieth century globalization is in large part built upon the compression of time and space,[3] then the production, dissemination, and management of information are the essential behaviors that sustain the globalizing process. The emblem of the information domain of globalization is information technologies.[4] In organizations, these include the Internet and Intranet, exemplified in electronic mail and the World Wide Web, as well as institutional computer operating systems, and are referred to as computer mediation technologies (CMTs). Information technologies also include voice mail and facsimile and video transmission. The information domain of globalization incorporates what is referred to as software and hardware—such as equipment and operating programs, the material manifestations—but also the processing and management of information, the behavioral manifestations.

In higher education institutions, information technologies and their accompanying behaviors are evident in both work, especially administrative work, and instruction. There are two parts to the presence of information technologies in higher education: one part is the expected outcomes of the use of informational technologies, particularly in instruction; the second is the current behaviors and effects of their use, particularly in administrative work.

The Promise of Information Technologies in Instruction

The claims of information technology for present alterations to instruction and future transformations are nothing short of remarkable. Computer-mediated technologies are viewed as responsible for a "revolution in learning and teaching" altering "what we teach, the ways we will teach, and the ways our students will learn."[5] Indeed, the literature on higher education in the twenty-first century gives a central role to information technology, including the reported "paradigm shift"[6] from teaching to learning, as well as the replacement of colleges and universities as traditional education structures by learning networks.[7] To date, however, there is little empirical evidence of specific learning outcomes that have been affected by information technologies.[8] Yet, the pressure to adopt these technologies, in distance education and in classroom-based education, continues unabated.[9] If change is occurring, it happens at the margins, in particular courses, such as composition courses, and in particular circumstances—for example, with working adults who are highly motivated learners.

The reasons for the push to adopt informational technologies are several. First, there is an educational reform movement, particularly aimed at higher education, which ties economic performance to skill development transferred to students at colleges and universities. This movement is prodded by business and industry and reinforced by government at the federal and state and provincial levels. Furthermore, this effort to reform higher education—to have institutions focus upon "employability skills" or market-oriented curricula—is supported by college and university administrators.[10] This set of behaviors is consistent with marketization.

There are additional rationales for institutional managers to support the adoption of information technology, and these include economic considerations. Colleges can become more efficient, generate new sources of revenue through services, and maintain or increase enrollments by projecting the image of technologically current institutions. Internet and Intranet-based instruction, for example, may mean more students served by instructors, or by less expensive instructors—thus the need for fewer instructors or fewer highly paid ones. This set of behaviors is consistent with productivity and efficiency.

But managers and other college employees, in line with community college missions, endeavor to meet the needs of students, who as consumers of education and training have their own demands. With greater numbers of students working, and working longer hours, and with older working adults serving as a significant institutional cohort, students expect instruction that is if not personalized then at least convenient. This in practice becomes instruction that is asynchronous—the reception of curricula and the interaction between student and instructor do not occur simultaneously with the communication of curricula. These behaviors may take place at great distances or within the institutional site, allowing students to undertake education and training during their preferred times. As well, students follow employer expectations for employment skills, and thus student demand validates instruction. If there is no demand for the study of ethics, there is no likelihood of instruction; and if there is demand, first from employers and then from students, for computer skills, then there is either instruction in computer skills or there may be fewer students enrolled at the institution. Students, then, play a consumer role, purchasing and consuming educational products that are expected to fulfill needs, from specific skills such as writing and computing to the acquisition of credentials. This set of behaviors is consistent with commodification.

Consumer-oriented education and training may then be the substance of the perceived shift from an emphasis upon teaching to a focus on learning. That is, learner-centered instruction is based upon consumption behaviors, not upon pedagogy. The learner or consumer has usurped power from the teaching professionals, turning colleges into facsimiles of fast-food outlets.[11]

It should not be surprising that community colleges have embraced information technologies for teaching and learning. Community colleges have a historical reputation as adaptive, responsive, and flexible educational institutions.[12] Their use of these technologies and the acceptance of the promise of change that accompanies informational technologies are consistent with the history of community colleges. Not only is there a pattern of adaptation and responsiveness but also there is a historical need for recognition and for establishing a reputable niche in the higher education hierarchy.[13] The use of information technology, particularly in distance education, has satisfied this need. "Technology-supported distance learning programs are key applications in which community colleges are leading higher education. They exemplify the fundamental elements of the transformation of the teaching and learning process: movement out of the classroom and replacement of the teacher with the independent adult learner at the center of the teaching and learning process."[14]

In characterizing their college, faculty, students, and administrators at Suburban Valley Community College emphasized the innovative and reputational image of the institution. Amanda, a senior academic administrator, noted that the college provided "an innovative environment." Her colleague, Bob, called the college "innovative." A student leader remarked that the college was "technologically advanced." A faculty member observed that the college "selects good people who are creative and innovative." A mid-level administrator, John, stated that the college's "reputation is centered around transfers and technology." And a faculty senate leader, Ed, provided this extended description of the institution:

> [The college is] always moving, never reflecting on projects, always go, go, go. There is a lot of cutting edge. It's always like being the first with something: the best and the biggest.

North Mountain College in Alberta, Canada, similar to Suburban Valley in California, adopted information technologies in part because of reputation. But reputation had an instrumental value—to attract local students in the face of competition from other higher education institutions and as a result gain additional revenues through enrollments. In refining the image of the college, the governing board commissioned a community study in the mid-1990s to capture the perceptions of community members concerning the college's present performance and future course. Of special interest to college officials were responses to the use of technology in instruction. Out of this study, the college administration developed an institutional strategy, complemented by a marketing approach to promote the institution as a high-technology college but a traditional institution nonetheless. The study indicated that community members preferred classroom based instruction with technology as an enhancement to rather than a replacement of traditional instruction. The official college position was to see "technology as a tool to support the learning process . . . a tool for interactive learning." In the traditional science disciplines, this translated into a "push towards digital technology and away from other technology . . . more lab simulations." In the arts, this translated into larger class sizes, with a "75-seat composition course . . . driven," according to Paul, an English faculty member, "by technology." For students, according to a student government leader, college actions favored a high-technology image over service to students:

> [The college is] . . . crowded. We're packed to the rafters. They're holding classes in portable classrooms, so space is a big issue that we all agree on. And then the college turns around and opens up this big multi-communications center with satellite links to campuses all over the world, which is great, but you've got that and we don't have space for another classroom where students can plug in their own computers or a classroom where we can just put in computers for students to use rather than the president talking to people

all over the world. They even put a class on the Internet, but that doesn't help the students that are here taking the classes. (Jenny, student leader)

As a strategy, the institutional promotion of and support for information technologies in instruction realized mixed outcomes in community colleges. Indeed, the implementation of new learning approaches sustained by information technologies furthered the hierarchies and status structures already in place in the institution. Thus, traditional arts and sciences in community colleges were not transformed or even enhanced but rather left behind. At North Mountain College, traditional arts and sciences—humanities, literature, philosophy, mathematics, chemistry, and the like—were neither areas of growth nor areas in which information technologies were in much use. Yet, the areas of nursing and business, in which these technologies were more evident, experienced growth in both students and in faculty. Faculty and administrators in the arts and sciences claimed that institutional "energy [is] around applied arts and technology to enhance [the] institution's image." In mathematics, faculty were "resistant" to college strategy on information technology, largely because the faculty were unclear about the outcomes of this strategy. Sandy, a department chair in the arts, noted that "pedagogical issues" were "less important" to the institution's managers than the information technology strategy. She observed that "faculty talk about technology, although their concern is about students." A science instructor noted that "Science [was] losing ground, moving backward." A similar observation was made at both Suburban Valley Community College and at Rural Valley College.

At Suburban Valley Community College, there was little evidence in the physical and biological sciences that a technological revolution in teaching and learning was underway. Science laboratories were largely intact from the early 1970s; instruction was traditional, unsupported by state-of-the-art computer equipment; and laboratories were crowded, with students cluttered around modestly furnished lab benches. A science instructor and former department chair, Dan, asserted that "the college is trapped in its own rhetoric—we were once innovative." "Now," he claimed, emphasis is placed upon " buildings [and] equipment . . . and [the college] lacks the old spirit of making things better." In response to the projected image of the institution as a leader in innovation and technology, Dan replied "Bullshit." Frank, the dean of science, characterized the faculty as "highly principled in their approach to science. They won't compromise, won't change teaching approaches . . . and embrace new technologies or delivery systems." Other managers referred to these behaviors as recalcitrant. One vice-president politely noted that "Faculty are just coming around to technology."

Enrollments in traditional science offerings lagged behind other program areas at Rural Valley College as well as at Suburban Valley. This was also the case at the other community colleges over the decade. The dean of science at Rural Valley noted that "if something new comes along, we have to cancel another thing." The "distance learning movement" and particularly "online courses" were not compatible with laboratory science courses, noted Ron, a physics instructor, and thus the emphasis upon information technologies in sciences was limited.

The "distance learning movement" was rarely embraced by science departments in the community colleges; exceptions were courses without laboratories, such as microbiology, as offered at Pacific Suburban Community College. Some community colleges, such as Pacific Suburban, were more practiced and more ideologically suited to distance-delivery technologies. At Pacific Suburban, distance education was seen not so much as an enhancement of reputation as providing for the mandated mission of community colleges in the state to serve all communities. Distance delivery served as the vehicle to fulfill the mission. A staff of ten and a manager supported Pacific Suburban's distance education services. The majority of distance education at Pacific Suburban was traditional instruction delivered by interactive video. With the exception of some online courses, especially English composition, distance education reinforced traditional pedagogy. Online courses—using Internet and Intranet—turned more of the responsibility of learning over to students, because it was asynchronous and devoid of in-person contact.

The growth of online instruction was significant during the decade. In the 1995–1996 academic year, there was only one online course at Suburban Valley Community College, the school's first. In the following academic year, 1996–1997, there were 21 online courses. During the fall 1997 term, the number of online courses was 15, compared to 3 the previous fall. At Rural Valley College's Web site, the transition from traditional to online instruction was described on the one hand as liberating and on the other as isolating, detaching the student from social contact:

> In effect students no longer go to school, school goes to the student, wherever the student sets up their computer and modem. (Rural Valley College Website, May 1997)

Online courses at Rural Valley in 1997 included baccalaureate degree courses in adult education and computer information systems as well as first-year anatomy and business communications. Online instruction constituted such a small percentage of college offerings that it was considered peripheral to college operations. This was hardly the transformation of teaching and learning promised or promoted in the literature, but it was consistent with other globalizing forces that compress natural boundaries of time and space and globalizing outcomes that commodify human activity, such as learning.

Commodification, marketization, and productivity and efficiency behaviors are far more important and pervasive explanations for the use of information technology in instruction than the promises of the gurus of paradigm shifts in teaching and learning, such as "student empowerment" and "faculty empowerment"[15] and other "extravagant claims for instructional technology."[16] In addition to these behaviors of commodification, marketization, and productivity and efficiency was state intervention.

The role of the state in promoting and supporting the use of information technologies in teaching and learning was evident in both policy and in funding behaviors. The state—the provinces and the states—used a mix of rationales, from training for a globally competitive economy to learner-centered education based upon new learning needs of students, to justify expenditures in hardware, software, and personnel to support information technology in instruction. The rationales were consistent from jurisdiction to jurisdiction: there are new students with different learning styles and needs from the past; there are fewer or at least not increasing funds available for public institutions, and therefore higher productivity or greater efficiencies or both must be realized by institutions; and the world of work—business and industry—requires well-trained and technologically savvy workers. The assumed logic was that these pieces comprising the rationale for the use of information technology fit together.

In the province of Alberta, both the government in power and its agency responsible for postsecondary education—Alberta Advanced Education and Career Development—promoted information technology in education as an efficiency measure. With increasing numbers of adult learners accessing postsecondary education and with government's ideology of less government funding for the public sector in the mid-1990s, the government turned to information technologies to raise system productivity, supplemented with the rationale of the need to have a more "learner centered" approach to adult education and training and to meet the needs of business and industry by having a globally competitive work force. The government agency tied the policy to funding incentives for the development and implementation of distance education, virtual learning, and computer mediated instruction.[17]

In its neighboring province, British Columbia, government was no less zealous in the 1990s to propel information technology to the forefront of postsecondary education strategies. Again, the need for a globally competitive work force was motivation for the reformation of postsecondary education, and coupled with expected decreases in public funding for education, the increased use of information technologies was identified as part of "a new course" for education and training in the province.[18] Furthermore, information technologies, particularly employed in distance education, were intended to solve the critical access problem in the province.[19]

In the United States, governments were less specific about the learning benefits of information technology in instruction but saw its use as a panacea for funding difficulties in the 1990s. In California, information technologies were justified as vehicles of productivity and efficiency: the method of delivering education to more students. The goal was to use these technologies to develop approaches to replace lecture-based instruction.[20] There was little apology among the policy leaders in California for moving toward the replacement of traditional instruction and instructors with computer-mediated instruction and distance education. As stated in the state's education code in 1996, a primary purpose of education and training at the community college level was economic, and the more education and training, the greater the contribution to the economy.

> A primary mission of the California Community College is to advance California's economic growth and global competitiveness through education, training, and services that contribute to continuous work force improvement.[21]

In the state of Hawaii, the use of technology in instruction was connected to access: to serve the Hawaiian Islands under conditions of revenue diminution for the state and yet to serve increasing numbers of students. Distance education, including the use of Hawaii Interactive Television System, was cited as the single mechanism for efficiency. Other references to information technology were vaguely characterized as effectiveness measures. In policy and in government legislation, a major purpose of the system's community colleges was to train the work force as well as provide access for the state's citizens to higher education.[22] But it was access that was served by the use of information technology in the state of Hawaii, and access, not vocational training, was a higher priority.

In the state of Washington, government financing of higher education was the critical issue of the 1990s, with the state government directing the system to increase productivity, promoting the use of both more part-time faculty in community and technical colleges to reduce expenditures and expanding distance education to increase enrollments. Even more blatantly than in California, work-force training and vocational preparation were emphasized as the purposes of Washington's community colleges.[23]

There were great expectations for information technology in instruction, but the anticipated outcomes expressed in policy and by practitioners were not about student learning, not directed to how students learn or to the connection between information technologies to learning styles, unlike the claims in the literature. Rather, both the expected and desired consequences of the use of information technology in instruction were economic.

Effects of Information Technology upon Administrative and Faculty Work

Although information technologies per se may not be the cause of altering arrangements of work and production, they are key ingredients of these changes and through them the process of globalization affects organizations and organizations perpetuate globalization.[24] Certainly, an intervening variable in the actual effects of information technology in organizations is the role and actions of managers.[25] However, through collective bargaining as well as through responses to the implementation of information technologies in the workplace, labor also has the potential to affect organizational actions.[26]

Information technologies are powerful, indeed in some cases organizationally transforming, tools for managers. They are viewed as labor saving, and indeed job reduction is attributed to their implementation.[27] They permit flexibility and decentralization in production and management, and their automating capacities help to remove the need for considerable human labor.[28] And, they further reinforce managerial hierarchies and enlarge managerial control over production.[29]

But these same technologies and their implementation have a less salient effect upon the work force. While there is considerable debate about job loss as a consequence of the use of information technologies, there is little doubt that information technologies are used as labor saving and jobs are replaced in certain sectors.[30] Work has altered over the century from extractive (agriculture, forestry, and mining) and physically transformative (construction, manufacturing, and utilities) industries to services, including transportation, sales, health, education, government, welfare, and personal services such as entertainment (see table 5.1). This suggests that as the century progressed, knowledge work replaced manual work, especially primary industrial work.

Table 5.1 Employment Distribution, Percentages by Industry, Canada and the U.S., 1920s–1990s [31]

Industry	1920s*		1930s		1940s		1950s		1960s		1970s		1980s		1990s	
	Can	U.S.	Can	U.S.	Can	U.S.	Can	U.S.	Can	U.S.	Can	U.S.	Can	U.S.	Can	U.S.
Extractive (agriculture, forestry, and mining)	37	29	34	25	32	21	22	14	15	8	9	5	7	5	6	4
Physically Transformative (e.g., construction, manufacturing, utilities)	26	33	25	32	28	30	34	34	31	36	30	33	27	30	22	25
Services (e.g., transportation, sales, health, education, government, welfare)	37	38	41	43	40	50	45	52	54	56	61	63	66	66	71	72

*The dates refer to the beginning of the decade, for example, 1920 for the United States and 1921 for Canada, except the 1990s where the U.S. figures are for 1991 and the Canadian are for 1992. The percentages are rounded to the closest whole number.

Furthermore, there was an increasing percentage of overall employment in information handling nationally (see table 5.2). Both U.S. and Canadian figures show a significant and parallel rise in the percentage of the work force employed in jobs classified as information handling. This category contains the work force in communications, finance, insurance, real estate, services, and government.

It should not be surprising that a substantial portion of scholarship on the use of information technology is a dialectical debate involving the benefits to management on the one hand and the detriments to labor on the other. Rarely are both brought together for an integrated discussion. Manuel Castells may be one exception as he neither predicts a brave new world nor laments the passing of an old order. He sees a large cultural shift underway, a technological global revolution that is "reshaping, at accelerated pace, the material basis of society."[32]

In higher education, there is little attention to the outcomes of the use of information technology for labor—administrative and faculty work— and for institutional management. The literature indicates that practitioners borrowed management uses of technology from business and industry, actions that include adopting new management rules for competition in a global economy. In the higher education sector, this translates into changing the labor structure, such as using part-time employees, fewer employees in targeted areas, and less expensive employees. An example of this in community colleges was the alteration to labor in student advising. One approach was to employ lower credentialed personnel—that is, baccalaureate degree holders and not master's degree holders; a second approach was to automate the process. Automation was realized through the use of e-mail or online advising, in which students did not meet face to face with an advisor; and the activity of advising occurred in conditions of controlled time, asynchronously. One of the results of these new management rules that emphasize global competition for both the business/industry and

Table 5.2 Percentage (%) of Employment in Information Handling in U.S. and Canada [33]

	1920s*	1930s	1940s	1950s	1960s	1970s	1980s	1990s
U.S.	26.7%	31%	32.5%	30.6%	34%	38.9%	42.7%	48.3%
Canada	27.6%	30.4%	30.4%	28.1%	32.6%	41.4%	41.9%	45.7%

*The dates refer to the beginning of the decade, for example, 1920 for the U.S. and 1921 for Canada.

education sectors was a weakening of unions or employee groups, changing the relationship between management and labor.[34] Jobs became more temporal, with lessening job security. This condition suggests that employees became more isolated—that is, less a part of a community—and more competitive with each other. As professionals, they were more likely to become independent operators, certainly at the university level. Sheila Slaughter and Larry Leslie capture some of this alteration in research universities in the four countries they examined.[35] David Leslie and E. K. Fretwell, Jr. offer a general and rather subtle analysis of new management approaches to address fiscal crises in 13 higher education institutions, with one community college district system among these.[36] They note in general that "resilient institutions" cope in the same way that successful businesses do—they are economically competitive, "giving society value for its money."[37] They do acknowledge that community colleges may be a special case, because "they perform a distinctive educational and social mission by serving the community of which they are a part."[38] This mission does not, however, make them immune from managerialism or globally competitive business practices. The findings of Leslie and Fretwell do not take into account the potentially harmful consequences of the serious rise of managerialism in higher education institutions and the capitalistic behaviors that are identified by Slaughter and Leslie.

Higher education institutions are included among those organizations in which there was increasing managerial control over work.[39] While describing managerial actions, both Leslie and Fretwell and Slaughter and Leslie ignore the diminution of labor unions' clout; they also ignore both the traditions and importance of academic values in institutional decision-making. Gary Rhoades, in reviewing labor-management collective agreements in higher education institutions, observes that technology expands managerial flexibility and increases managerial control over production, especially in areas with a part-time workforce.[40] Cynthia Hardy, in underlining the importance of collegiality in universities, reminds us that managerialism is instrumental power, whereas collegiality is "defined as a situation characterized by agreement around organizational purpose."[41] Jack Schuster and Associates, in attempting to incorporate academic values into institutional decision-making, observe that while businesses move toward collegial-style management, higher education institutions adopted more hierarchical and corporate modes of decision-making.[42] While few would accept the alteration of businesses to collegial institutions, most would acknowledge that higher education institutions became more corporate during the past decade and a half when new technologies emerged as pervasive management tools.

Two sets of behaviors accompanied the use of information technology pertaining to labor and to institutional management in community colleges. These behaviors were productivity and efficiency and labor alterations. These sets of behaviors are consistent with globalization, reflecting the impact of global forces upon the institution and reproducing the globalization process. Both sets of behaviors are interrelated to the extent that labor alterations were either a strategy of productivity and efficiency measures or an outcome or consequence of efficiency behaviors.

There were four major labor changes in the seven community colleges as a consequence of productivity and efficiency behaviors: (1) change to the number of workers; (2) change to the amount or quantity of work; (3) change to the pace of work; and (4) change to the quality or outcomes of work. With more automated systems and more computer-assisted work, the need for certain kinds of workers diminished, although the need for more technically proficient workers increased. Support staff reductions, although not in large numbers, were reported at the U.S. institutions, likely because unlike the Canadian institutions, their budgets were shrinking. In most cases, there was greater need for staff to provide support for informational technologies. Staff reductions seemed to have occurred prior to technological change. For example, at City South Community College, the staff reductions occurred as a result of the 1995 reorganization, before information technology use was implemented. This was also the case at North Mountain College in Canada, where staff reductions occurred in the early 1990s during fiscal restraint; by the latter part of the 1990s, fiscal restraint had ended. Thus, what was claimed for the noneducational sector—massive labor reductions as a consequence of technological change[43]—did not occur for community colleges in the 1990s. Technological change did not decrease either labor or work, except in very narrow secretarial areas; instead, work—and to some extent labor—expanded.

Employees, including administrators, faculty, and staff, at all colleges noted the increased workload and the increased pace of work as a consequence of information technology use. Voice mail and electronic mail were cited frequently as additions to work processes for U.S. institutions. At City South Community College, where voice mail and e-mail were new technologies 1997, administrators indicated that responding to messages was a time-related problem. A key issue was the difficulty of returning calls and electronic mail requests in "a timely fashion." At Pacific Suburban Community College, the use of e-mail was acknowledged to be an intensifier of the work process. "E-mail makes things go much faster," noted Heather, a staff union official. Indeed, support staff had mixed feelings about informational technologies; they assisted the work process by adding speed but encumbered that process by delivering too much information to users. The dean of student services remarked, "I can't keep up; [there's] just too much."

In Canadian institutions, online systems such as Banner operating systems for student records and human resources and financial management and online educational delivery were the drivers of increased work. Indeed, a faculty member at East Shoreline College noted that information technology made "faculty rethink how they teach." An instructor at the same institution who taught an online course emphasized the increased workload with online instruction. At Rural Valley College, while some faculty thought that technology was "too much: intimidating and time consuming," and responsible for changing jobs, others thought that information technology was a "positive addition to the college." There was considerable "debate" at Rural Valley College among organizational members about the use of technology both in work processes and in instruction. The stressors at these institutions were communications-related and included the expectations that accompanied the use of information technologies. Eleanor, a community education coordinator at East Shoreline College, succinctly described the predicament:

> Technology has increased the busy-ness of the job: [you are] pushed to your limit to communicate effectively, often because of the expected short turnaround time.

The quality and outcomes of work that resulted from the use of informational technologies pertained principally to services (to students, organizational members, other agencies, and the public) and to external expectations concerning the image of the institution. Information technologies were noted as improving services to students at all institutions. These services for students included online registration, online advising, and online information about the institution, its processes and structures. Information technologies also made possible student access to programs through distance education at remote sites and through Web-based or online instruction. For organizational members, e-mail and voice mail served to improve communications and helped people access institutional influencers. At Pacific Suburban Community College, one faculty member noted that through e-mail and voice mail they were "able to contact people at higher levels more frequently, thus get a more direct response." Furthermore, through online technologies, government and government agencies were served more effectively through a centralized and coordinated system; and through voice mail, the public received at least a voice response and a strong possibility of a reply instead of either a busy signal or an unanswered ring. Service in general was viewed as improved with the use of information technologies.

External expectations for colleges from both public and private sectors as well as from potential students were that these institutions were "technologically fit," current with business and government practices and with development in educational technology. The image of Suburban Valley Community College as a high technology-oriented institution was imperative to institutional managers if the college was to be successful in attracting students. These students were needed both for their tuition fees and for enrollment numbers that justified government grants. For North Mountain College, the expectations of business and the local community influenced college decision-makers in their implementation of electronic technologies. College officials at North Mountain College attributed both enrollment gains and financial donations from the community to the projection of an institutional image as a high technology college. Finally, government expected these colleges to be technologically adept, and it provided incentives for the institutions to adopt new learning technologies. This was especially the case in the provinces of Alberta and British Columbia where government planning documents identified technology as efficiency and productivity measures which government funding behaviors reinforced. Because the colleges met these expectations, they were rewarded financially.

The use of information technology was predominantly a productivity and efficiency behavior. To this extent, its use furthered the goals of management. But did information technology increase managers' control over employees or limit the freedom or independence of employees? Furthermore, did the use of informational technologies change organizational culture, altering work patterns and social relationships? Certainly, the use of distance education, such as Web-based instruction, made the instructional process more public. The use of electronic mail and voice mail, because of their storage processes, gave greater potential for surveillance by management over employee use. For example, at City South Community College, a district policy indicated that monitoring of e-mail use was a managerial prerogative. Faculty at the institution, however, viewed information technologies as a threat from the district office, especially the use of electronic mail.

Collective bargaining provided a venue for employees to negotiate with managers about some of these issues surrounding the use of information technology. However, unions did not resort to this approach to restrain management rights. At Suburban Valley Community College, there were no provisions in collective agreements in the 1990s that constrained management rights in the implementation of information technologies. At City South Community College in Washington State, the first implication of the use of information technologies was not present until the mid-1990s, with an article in the collective agreement on distance education. In this article, the word *technology* is absent, and reference is made to the selection and payment of instructors who teach distance education courses. The provision essentially protects the status quo and is silent on curriculum. Among the other six community colleges, there are no provisions related to information technologies and instruction. With the exception of Rural Valley College, whose agreement addresses technological change and the option of retraining or layoffs, there are no other provisions in faculty agreements at any other college on technology or technological change. The absence suggests either that faculty do not feel threatened by management in the use of information technologies in the 1990s or that management has triumphed at the bargaining table on these issues. The former is more likely because there was little evidence of concern among faculty members at these seven institutions over managerial control through the use of information technologies.

Rhoades in examining collective agreements of community colleges argues that "technology increases faculty's burden."[44] Out of 144 community college collective agreements in the United States, Rhoades found that 51 contained provisions related to instructional technology. Only 9 of these collective agreements contained provisions that addressed instructional duties. Rhoades concluded that contract provisions suggested reduced faculty autonomy in the use of information technology. It would be more accurate to say that the use of information technology in community colleges may slightly aggravate the condition of limited formal autonomy of faculty.

In community colleges, management—and this includes the governing board—has *de jure* authority over instructional issues: this condition is defined by legislation in states and provinces. Collective agreements may permit faculty participation in the process of college decision-making and in college actions; but collective agreements cannot countenance faculty authority, since legislation supersedes collective agreements. There is only one jurisdictional exception, a jurisdiction not covered in Rhoades's study, to the denial of faculty authority and that is in the province of British Columbia, where in 1995 government legislation permitted an authority role for faculty in specific actions. Thus, to expect faculty control over instruction, specifically legal or formal autonomy in curricular decisions, such as the use of informational technology in instruction is to misunderstand the legal framework for labor relations in community colleges.

Faculty participation in curricular decisions is the best that can be attained. In the states of California, Hawaii, Illinois, Oregon, and Washington and in the provinces of Alberta, British Columbia, and Ontario in 104 separate collective agreements, 34 agreements (33 percent) contained provisions that permitted faculty to participate in curricular decisions. Of the remaining 70 agreements, the overwhelming majority was silent on a faculty role in curricular matters, thus indicating that management had the right to include or exclude faculty in discussion on curricular matters, such as the implementation of informational technology in instruction.[45] For faculty to influence the use of information technologies in any formal way, legislation would have to be altered, then collective agreements could be negotiated to permit authority for faculty on instructional matters. It may be that the introduction of information technologies reduces faculty autonomy, but formally, autonomy is already circumscribed. More certainly, the introduction of information technologies increases the workload of faculty.

Information technologies (for example, Internet, electronic mail, voice mail, and fax) affected both administrative and faculty work at community colleges. The emphasis by managers upon productivity and efficiency as well as the perceived requirement for organizational members to "keep up" drove institutional behaviors toward increased use of informational technologies. Thus, work altered at these colleges as a consequence of the use of informational technologies. The industrial model of work and indeed of teaching underwent change and stress, although the institutions still clung to that model. In order to compete for students, to compete globally for international contracts, and to satisfy external demands—those of business, industry, and other higher education institutions—college members supported the increasing use of these technologies as well as their application to faculty work. To this extent, organizational culture altered: the general support for information technologies and their increasing use was evidence of at least a tacit agreement between labor and management to accept management's goals of greater efficiency and rising productivity. But there was little evidence that social relationships altered or that existing structures changed as a consequence of the use of information technologies. The behaviors surrounding the use of these technologies more likely supported existing power structures and hierarchies.[46]

CHAPTER 6

THE DOMAIN OF POLITICS

The role of government in globalizing community colleges was both manifested in government policies and perpetuated by those policies. The state largely reinforced and advanced economic globalization and the role of international capital not only through the establishment of policy but also through policy implementation. In the 1990s, public policy applicable to community colleges in both Canada and the United States directed these institutions to global competitiveness and to a refashioning of institutional mission. Government policies clearly endeavored to direct community colleges toward economic goals, emphasizing work-force training and state economic competitiveness as outcomes, compelling colleges to improve efficiencies, increase productivity, and become accountable to government and responsive to business and industry. Pressures for efficiency and productivity accompanied claims of government restraint on public sector funding and directed colleges to behave like globally competitive businesses. Pressures to orient institutions to the marketplace, evident in the emphasis placed upon vocationalism and commercialism,[1] were consistent with the needs of global capital. Furthermore, government responsiveness to economic concerns at the state and provincial levels became economic development policies applicable to community colleges. Institutional responses, evident in behaviors such as marketization and productivity and efficiency, altered community college missions, resulting in the pursuit of economic ends.

The domain of politics was the arena in which government policy and policy behaviors on the one hand and institutional responses on the other hand interacted. Policy can be seen as government efforts to control decisions and actions of institutions in accord with the objectives of governments.[2] Policy regulates institutions, permitting, requiring, or forbidding actions, which include those of both institutional members and government officials.³ Simply, policy reflects government objectives. Institutional responses are formally connected to policy implementation. For community colleges, the economic objectives of the 1990s overshadowed and in some cases replaced earlier objectives of accessibility, personal and social development, and a liberal or general education.⁴ Institutional responses to policy were varied, although in general colleges altered structures, processes, and institutional mission to align these more with economic interests.

The State and Higher Education

There is considerable evidence in government policy that the state was largely preoccupied with economic issues, specifically with improving its economic competitiveness on a global scale and reducing its public sector costs. Work-force training was the major focus of government policy directed to community colleges. And governments, particularly state and provincial governments, directed community colleges to alter institutional practices and become more productive and efficient—for example, to increase the number of students served, graduate more workplace-ready students, and reduce per unit costs.

There are three streams of thought on the state that frame my analysis of government policy for community colleges. The first views the state as the nexus of the struggle of classes: that is, the state functions to preserve and expand modes of production.⁵ State policy drives or influences production. The state "is an expression, or condensation, of social-class relations, and these relations imply domination of one group by another. Hence, the state is both a product of relations of domination and their shaper."⁶

The second view of the state is that it is independent of capital and labor.⁷ It is composed of relatively autonomous government officials who serve their own interests and may indirectly meet the needs of interest groups such as business and students.⁸ Nonetheless, government officials are assumed to possess independence from societal groups when they form policy objectives. Yet, this pattern of autonomous decision-makers is connected more to societies without a state tradition, unlike Canada or the United States.⁹

The third view of the state is that it is a multifaceted resource, an arena in which policy formation is played out. Various branches or levels of the state respond to different and even competing constituencies.¹⁰ That is, the state is not monolithic, and its behaviors are not necessarily consistent or uniform.

Goedegebuure, Kaiser, Maassen, and De Weert conceptualize two types of state influence or state behaviors with respect to higher education: the interventionary state and the facilitatory state.[11] In the former, government is actively involved in institutional activities and actions, intervening directly to ensure such outcomes as "economic efficiency . . . [and] student access and accountability."[12] If the state is the maintainer and expander of existing modes of production, shaped by classes or class struggles[13] and inherently capitalistic, then state policy reproduces production.[14] Furthermore, the interventionary state can be viewed as an instrument of economic interests and particularly capitalism. Thus, promotion of workforce training and emphasis upon economic competitiveness are behaviors of government consistent with the state as an "expression . . . of social-class relations . . . [that] . . . imply domination of one group by another."[15] If the state is an actor independent of capital and labor, and state officials are relatively autonomous, then the interventionary state may be seen as an agent of policy influencers of higher education that include the interests of business and students as well as state and institutional officials.[16] Thus, in this latter case, government social policy as well as economic policy and other actions that "attempt to reinforce the authority, political longevity, and social control of the state"[17] find a vehicle in higher education institutions.

Goedegebuure, Kaiser, Maassen, and De Weert view the state as either an expression of class relations or independent from class struggles. Slaughter[18] advances a different and more integrative view: that the state is de facto inseparable from higher education institutions, and therefore not an autonomous entity; and that the state is not monolithic, not a simple source of money or authority but a multifaceted resource. That is to say that at some levels, the state does reflect class and social struggles while at other levels the state is independent of capital and labor. This view suggests that although work-force training and economic competitiveness may indeed reflect the state's imposition of capitalistic behaviors on institutions, student policies and funding behaviors that support access could be seen as expressions of social policy that may not be in accord with capitalism or the domination of one group over another.

In my analysis of government documents, which includes U.S. federal and state documents and Canadian federal and provincial documents, government policies clearly endeavored to direct community colleges toward economic goals. The state was clearly interventionary rather than facilitatory. Policy emphasized work-force training and state economic competitiveness as outcomes, compelling colleges to improve efficiencies and to become accountable to government and responsive to business and industry. These findings are more consistent with the view that the state preserves and expands modes of production. But, there were also areas of compatibility that support the view of a multifaceted resource. There was little or no support for the view that favors autonomous decision-makers as drivers of policy.

The Policy Jurisdictions

In order to understand the explicit intentions of government policy for community colleges and to determine if these were consistent with globalization, I reviewed and analyzed policy documents of the 1990s from seven jurisdictions. These included the United States, California, Hawaii, Washington, Canada, Alberta, and British Columbia. Documents ranged from government legislation to government reports and strategic plans. I identified themes and coded documents by using the categories of globalizing behaviors set out in chapter 3. These categories are displayed in Figure 6.1 below. Findings from each jurisdiction are displayed in Table 6.1.

Federal: The United States[19]

Policy documents were oriented to two directions: to improve the unfavorably perceived work-force productivity of the United States and to upgrade the work force and potential workers in order to remove a burden from employers and government. Increasing work-force productivity was assumed to place America in a more competitive position internationally. Upgrading carried out by community colleges was viewed as meeting the needs of business and industry and aiding governments in ensuring that their economic and work-force policies were functioning. Federal goals

Category	Abbreviation Code
A. internationalization	[I]
B. multiculturalism	[MC]
C. commodification	[COM]
D. homogenization	[HOM]
E. marketization	[MRK]
F. restructuring	[R]
G. labor alterations	[LA]
H. productivity and efficiency	[P/E]
I. electronic communication and information	[ET]
J. state intervention	[SI]

Figure 6.1 Globalization Behaviors

Table 6.1 Themes of Globalizing Behaviors in Policy Documents

Jurisdiction	Dominant Themes	Explicit Intent
Federal U.S.	MRK, P/E	Meet national economic needs for global competitiveness through work-force training
California	MRK, R, P/E	Achieve economic competitiveness for business and industry through work-force training and increased institutional productivity to assist state economy
Hawaii	MRK, R, P/E	Assist economic performance of state by increasing productivity and efficiency and train a globally competitive work force
Washington	I, MRK, P/E, SI	Improve economic condition of the state within a globally competitive environment by training and retraining the work force
Federal Canada	I, MRK, P/E, ET	Reduce unemployment nationally and train for marketplace
Alberta	MRK, P/E, ET	Offer less expensive education, provide greater responsiveness to business and industry, and achieve greater productivity of institutions, with less reliance upon public funds
British Columbia	MRK, P/E, ET	Provide work-force training to meet the needs of business and industry and assist province in global economic competitiveness

included increasing skills and ensuring greater individual self-sufficiency—that is, improving workers' skills and removing the unemployed from welfare. There was considerable emphasis upon high technology and advanced manufacturing skills as well as on basic skills and literacy. Policy was occasionally ambiguous with respect to identified problems, such as the effectiveness of vocational education, and in proposed solutions, probably because there were differing assumptions about national competitiveness. These differing assumptions could be seen in the contrast between what policy documents refer to as jobs with high skills and high wages and jobs with some skills and low wages.

Federal policy documents were almost singly focused upon work-force training. The community college was viewed as a principal deliverer of work-force training and employment upgrading. Policy documents emphasized U.S. competitiveness and suggested that productivity in the U.S. work force declined in the 1970s and 1980s. These documents asserted an important role for postsecondary education, especially the community college, in providing training that was largely conceived of as skills development but included literacy and basic education, along with high-technology training in specialized fields. There was reference in some documents to underrepresented groups (American Indians and Native Hawaiians), to migrant workers, and to those already in the work force who needed upgrading. There was also the suggestion that the organization and management of vocational education were inadequate, that program quality was substandard, and that outcomes, such as job placement, were poor. As a consequence, there was the targeting of federal dollars to the states for reform of vocational education to ensure appropriate workforce training.

The major emphasis of policy was upon meeting national economic needs, especially national competitiveness within a global economy. Furthermore, the implication was that welfare and unemployment were detracting from national productivity and were a burden on federal expenditures. The themes of marketization and productivity and efficiency were most pronounced. Postsecondary education, especially community college education, was directed to improve work-force training, to assist employers in filling jobs, to support the economic competitiveness of business and industry, and to help those in the lower socioeconomic strata either find jobs or improve productivity within their jobs. The promise was that federal dollars would be used to improve vocational education and work-force training, with the community college as a major beneficiary of federal largesse. The presence of a global economy served as a motivating force for U.S. federal policy initiatives.

State: California[20]

Beginning in the early 1990s, and most apparent in the mid-1990s, descriptions of new and expanding roles for community colleges emerged, including their role in economic development of California and in training a work force for global competitiveness of the state. There were references to limitations on funding from the state, and little suggestion that state funding was going to increase in any significant fashion. Also, there were references to changing demographics, with increasing minority populations soon to become majority (by 2002). There was some reference to governance, characterized by tension between central and local governance. Yet, overall there was little expression of accomplishment for California's community colleges, and little reference in government policy to social issues. The dominant role of the state was funding, including policy directives to institutions for increased productivity and a greater economic role.

Prevailing themes in policy document were marketization, restructuring, and productivity and efficiency. Work-force training was promoted to meet the needs and requirements of employers, to assist the state economy, and to cope with new employment demands in specific areas and decreasing demands in traditional manufacturing sectors. Less public sector funding was available in spite of increasing student numbers: documents acknowledged that government funding did not keep pace with demand and growth. To increase productivity and efficiency, policy promoted the reform or restructuring of institutions to improve instruction. The policy message was clear: do more with the same or fewer finances. There was simultaneously recognition of changing demographics: increased immigration, increased minority populations, and increased needs for English language training.

Policy emphasized the requirement to meet state and private sector economic needs in light of changing economic environments, which were assumed to be driven by global economies. Postsecondary education, especially community college education, was directed to shift toward workforce training, both to assist employers in filling jobs and to support the economic competitiveness of business and industry. Also, corresponding with this role of work-force training and development came the directive from state government that institutions must alter, become responsive to external needs, and use electronic technology for efficiency and instructional innovations, including distance education and improved methods to assess students to ensure increased productivity. Overall, emphasis was upon productivity, as opposed to finding new revenue sources, in order to maintain services and programs.

State: Hawaii[21]

The economy, highly influenced by international trade and tourism, was the dominant issue in state documents. As a branch of government, the University of Hawaii and its community colleges were at once recipients of the economic woes of the state and vehicles to assist the state in coping with and reforming the economy. The University of Hawaii system offered strategies and plans to maintain programs and to expand facilities and higher education access. There was some evident tension between the demands of the university system's governing board and the legislature, particularly over funding.

Prevailing themes in policy documents included marketization, restructuring, and productivity and efficiency. State policy documents indicated that the economic performance of the state necessitated decreasing allocations to higher education, with the university system acknowledging the condition of fewer state funds for higher education. There was considerable emphasis in the state on preparing students for the work force, especially in community colleges. References were made to a consideration in 1992 and 1993 for applied degrees of three to four years in duration. Numerous new programs suitable for a changing economy were initiated in the 1990s. The underlying emphasis of these proposed initiatives was to bolster the state's economy with a trained work force. Calls for restructuring included the state's economy and both training and higher education. These calls were intended to improve the economic outlook of the state and to aid the public higher education system in coping with declining state revenues. Other calls for productivity and efficiency were efforts to cope with declining resources. The marketplace was identified as significant in policy documents: its prominence justified efforts and proposals to gear higher education to the state's economy and toward the private sector, including Asia Pacific countries.

Policy generated by the University of Hawaii system for the university and community colleges directed these institutions to be responsive to the state's economy and to economic reform. With acknowledgment in policy documents of declining state funds for higher education, the university system was compelled to seek alternate funding sources and to realize operating efficiencies. But the university system promoted quality in opposition to efficiency, providing potential conflict between legislators who promoted efficiency and educators who championed effectiveness. To deal with declining revenue sources, tuition was raised in the mid-1990s within the system; programs and personnel were cut; attractive retirement incentives were offered; and credit programs were shifted to non-credit, both to save and to make money. Distance education was also used to preserve and widen access and to attract international students as additional revenues sources.

State: Washington[22]

In policy documents there was emphasis upon economic behaviors within a competitive environment. Little attention was paid to social issues, with employment as the only socially related issue. Here, there was a focus upon retraining and training for the long-term unemployed or dislocated workers, with some reference to minorities and women. There were increasing government efforts to direct the institutions, including the development of a higher education system, first by amalgamating the state's community colleges and technical colleges and second by establishing a higher education coordinating board.

Prevailing themes in policy documents included internationalization, marketization, productivity and efficiency, and state intervention. On the topic of work-force training, there was considerable talk in early 1990s and action in the mid-1990s, with efforts to match education and training with the workplace. There was also increasing discussion of a competitive environment and "high skills/high wages," with acknowledgment of changing vocations and workplace needs. There was recognition of the loss of traditional manual and mechanical vocations and thus emphasis upon training for dislocated workers, immigrants, the severely unemployed, and people of color. Productivity and efficiency were tied to less government funding for institutions, with a push especially in the mid-1990s for community colleges to increase efficiencies, including the use of electronic technology, better student program completion rates, and employment rates for students. Colleges were also directed to use more part-time and fewer full-time faculty, and to use staff to do professional work, such as advising. Programming and operations were financially motivated, and institutions were assumed to be highly state dependent. The state directed institutions to greater efficiencies and movement toward increased work-force training. The state intervened in policy and fiscal support for educational technologies and distance education. The state changed fee collection so that colleges could retain tuition fees, and it changed criteria within categories of fee payers so that adult basic education and English as a second language programs became tuition free. In other programs, some categories of students, such as those who were unemployed, were not required to pay tuition fees. The internationalization process for colleges was mainly a means to locate additional revenues, although there was some mention (for example, in master plans) about the need for an internationally savvy work force and the need for community colleges to include internationally oriented curriculum.

There was a considerable shift in policy in the 1990s so that colleges would become more economic instruments of the state, driven through funding and policy directives by state government. Legislation supported greater centralization both statewide (amalgamation in 1991 of state community colleges and technical colleges) and at district offices (collective bargaining). Also there was centralization with a statewide higher education

108   GLOBALIZING THE COMMUNITY COLLEGE

coordinating body (promoting and overseeing collaboration); and through the legislature (general funding and targeted funding). Somewhat in contrast to this centralization tendency, new legislation in 1993 permitted districts to establish senates but forbade strikes.

Federal: Canada[23]

Canadian federal policy documents viewed postsecondary education as work-force training—that is, the federal role in education was confined to a training function, whereas education per se was seen a provincial responsibility. The federal emphasis was upon employment and reducing unemployment, upon Canada's competitiveness, upon Canada's economy, and upon federal/provincial arrangements. There was little or no mention of improving the quality of education or training, but there was emphasis upon the need for training to become more marketplace-relevant and meet the needs of employers.

Prevailing themes in policy documents included internationalization, marketization, productivity and efficiency, and electronic technology. Work-force training was the overriding subject relevant to higher education within federal documents. There was emphasis upon reducing unemployment and the promotion of international education, especially through student mobility (and related policy) to internationalize Canadian education to improve the work force. There was evidence of shifting responsibility for work-force training from the federal government to the provinces, and federal programs, such as the purchase of training, were cut. There was promotion of closer ties of training institutions to business and industry. Federal government policies and programs encouraged international education and partnerships with Canada and the United States and Canada and the European Community—for economic benefit. International education was viewed as an unexploited source of revenues for Canadian educational institutions. Electronic technology was tied to training and upgrading of the work force and associated with global competitiveness.

In Canada, there was a policy shift in responsibility, between 1993 and 1999, and from federal to provincial government bodies, for work force training and employment. The federal government claimed it had to pour billions of dollars into higher education and training and wanted to extricate itself from this commitment. A significant area of change was unemployment insurance: federal policy limited the duration that the unemployed could be on unemployment insurance. This necessitated that employment opportunities be available. There were, therefore, incentives to employers to hire the unemployed. This also required that the unemployed be trained or retrained, and incentives were provided to provincial. government bodies for such programs. What remains unclear, however, is whether federal money was transferred to provinces for these programs or whether provinces were expected to provide programs (training) from already transferred federal funds. There is some debate over this issue and over the actual nature of Canada's debt, which was used as justification to reduce federal transfer payments to the provinces.[24]

Province: Alberta[25]

Government policy documents were largely consumed with less public sector spending, greater efficiencies, and work-force training. Policy endeavored to situate the province in a globally competitive environment. There was acknowledged government intervention through funding behaviors—"envelopes"—and reduction in public sector funding in 1994, 1995, and 1996, down 21 percent. Government policy also used new applied degrees to satisfy workplace requirements. There was heavy emphasis upon electronic technology: learning enhanced by technology was viewed as cost effective, and the provision of access was couched in the language of the "new learner" and new learning needs. Overall, there was a business model for education with little focus upon content knowledge. There was pronounced government involvement with shifts toward education as a business, beginning in 1994 and including a considerable decrease in provincial government fiscal support for postsecondary education and increasing importance upon fee-payers (students) to be responsible for education and training. There was a marked increase in emphasis upon productivity and efficiency. Finally, there were references to government support for international education.

Prevailing themes in policy documents included marketization, productivity and efficiency, and electronic technology. Work-force training was emphasized to meet the needs and requirements of employers, to assist the provincial economy, and to make Alberta competitive globally. Less public sector funding on the part of government included actions to reduce debt and end deficit financing. Productivity and efficiency were tied to the reform or restructuring of the adult learning system: to improve instruction and do more with the same or less finances. Finally, to meet the needs of business and industry and to improve productivity, government policy promoted the use of electronic technology.

In Alberta, government took an active role in directing the province's higher education system, particularly colleges and institutes. Government promoted education and training that supported government policy, expecting institutions to produce and provide education and training that was less expensive, served more Albertans, and was responsive to business and industry. Education and training were viewed as economic supports. Government also tied funding to institutions' willingness to conform. In the mid-1990s, government cutback their grants to public institutions so that provincial deficits and debt would end. Institutions were asked to be less reliant upon government. Finally, government moved to legislate four-year applied degrees, largely to meet the higher skills needs of business and industry.

Province: British Columbia[26]

There was a growing mantra over the period of the 1990s, beginning in 1991, on economic competitiveness of the province, on work-force training to meet the needs of business and industry to enable these to compete internationally, and on skills acquisition—"employability skills," applied skills, workplace skills. There were also both implications and directions for postsecondary institutions to reform both curriculum and delivery in order to meet the needs of the private sector. Institutions were directed to use more electronic technology and to increase collaboration with each other and with the private sector. The assumptions were that there was a changed workplace; that there was a high level of international competition for business and industry; and that there were new learners (that is, different from the past). Furthermore, there was the assumption that "job shift" was occurring, mainly toward more service sector jobs. Finally, government legislation regarding governance of colleges and baccalaureate degree granting status suggests an ambiguous message about the purpose and operations of colleges. While much of government policy was directed toward economic ends, legislation could be interpreted as emphasizing the more academic aspects of colleges, giving a more pronounced role for academic education and its traditions, such as collegiality.

Prevailing themes in policy documents included marketization, productivity and efficiency, and electronic technology. Work-force training was emphasized for colleges to meet the needs and requirements of employers and to assist the provincial economy. There was acknowledgment of a rapid increase in the use of electronic technology in the workplace and thus the need for institutions to increase use in both curriculum and instructional delivery. Productivity and efficiency were promoted to reform or restructure institutions to improve training (for example, modularized instruction, distributive learning, prior assessment); and to do more with the same or less money. Partnerships were encouraged, with the private sector to meet its needs, and with other institutions to improve efficiencies. Tied to productivity and efficiency were social programs including a focus upon underrepresented groups, greater equality for women and the disabled, aboriginal self-determination, and multiculturalism.

The major emphasis of policy in British Columbia was upon meeting provincial and private sector economic needs, although in the context of government social programs. That is, the needs of special groups such as women, aboriginal peoples, and the disabled were part and parcel of expected and promoted policy change. These two priorities were not necessarily compatible, especially as economic interests were those of private business and industry and social interests were those of marginalized or disadvantaged groups. Nonetheless, postsecondary education, especially community college education, was directed toward work-force training, both to assist students in obtaining jobs and to support the economic competitiveness of business and industry.

Government Policy for Community Colleges

There were remarkably similar emphases across jurisdictions, from province to province, from state to state, and from one country to another. The global economy occupied center stage in government initiatives and directions for community colleges. There was also considerable consistency in the perspective of policy, and the underlying assumptions, with Carnoy's view.[27] Within the economic domain, which includes work-force training, the dominant category, state policy reproduces production. Higher education institutions, specifically community colleges, were directed and coerced to serve the needs of capital through supplying business and industry with a trained work force. At the same time, these institutions were asked and pushed to increase efficiency—that is, to reduce per unit costs. Restrictions upon and even reductions of government spending were strategies to cope with both declining revenues and increasing demands for government services. In other words, public education served private interests in at least two ways: first in containing private taxation and second in supplying labor for the private sector.

However, in some cases, most specifically in U.S. federal policy, and in Washington, Hawaii, and British Columbia policy, there were modest signs of the relative autonomy of the state, free from the domination of capital over labor or of one class over another. Here, social programs had a noticeable place in policy. For example, within policies on work-force training, the U.S. federal government highlighted the importance of serving underrepresented groups—for example, American Indians and Native Hawaiians. In Washington State, work-force training policy featured dislocated workers, minorities, and women. In British Columbia, the social and economic needs of special groups—women, aboriginal peoples, and the disabled—were addressed along with the needs of the provincial economy. The presence of social issues in these jurisdictions may suggest that the state had influence and power distinct from the power of capital or of a dominant economic class.

Non-economic issues were not forgotten entirely in government policy. Independent of business and industry and capital, government promoted social issues, even though these were largely tied to economic matters such as employment and training for employment. Alberta was clearly the only jurisdiction in which social issues were not topics of government policy related to higher education. In contrast, British Columbia not only promoted issues of equity but also acted in its legislation to democratize institutional governance. In the United States, while there were fiscal pressures to close the doors of community colleges, access for all was maintained as a primary value. For all three U.S. states, expanding and even maintaining access, according to government policy, required "doing more with less."

Surprisingly, in the U.S. jurisdictions there was no specific reference to multiculturalism even though the three colleges in these jurisdictions featured multiculturalism in their curriculum, extracurricular activities, and institutional value statements. In Canada, consistent with federal policy, which expressed a devolution of responsibility for training to provinces, there was a pronounced emphasis upon provincial priorities in government policy related to higher education in general and community colleges in particular. In both Alberta and British Columbia, planning documents assumed that community colleges were part of a provincial system, serving the needs of provincial citizens and aiding the provincial economy.

Policies suggestive of a relatively autonomous state—autonomous from capital or class struggles—were few, leading to the conclusion that in the case of community colleges, government policy was primarily oriented to reproducing production. The relatively autonomous state may have been applicable to an earlier era, the historical period before the 1990s that concerns Dougherty[28] especially during earlier developments of the community college, but government policy in the 1990s clearly favored the interests of business, industry, and capital. The state's attention to issues of equity, access, and an informed citizenry—issues that could be held up as critical to the community college movement—was marginal.

The state—province, state, and federal government in the United States—used the community college as a vehicle of government economic policy and as a model of production, directing these institutions to greater efficiencies and less reliance upon the public purse. Furthermore, government policy fashioned the community college as an economically globalized institution, adhering to global competitiveness and its attendant behaviors.

Government Effects upon Community Colleges

The role of government in changing community colleges was significant, and organizational change was influenced by the responses of government to a global economy. Hartmark and Hines[29] identify five areas in which government policy can influence higher education institutions. These pertain to the goals and purposes of higher education, values and norms, programs, management, and resources. Government policy and policy implementation affected goals and purposes through legislation; values and norms through major social policies, such as access and affirmative action; programs through planning documents, the budgetary process, and targeted funding; management through collective bargaining; and resources through fiscal allocation. In all cases, government was interventionary, endeavoring to influence community colleges directly in programs, management, and resources and indirectly in goals and purposes. To conform to government policy, community college norms and values were expected to alter. The path to globalization for government policy was a path of economic growth.

The behaviors and influences of governments were also dualistic regarding the colleges. Governments persuaded and coerced colleges to increase their productivity, to respond to workplace and business needs, and at least to affect an accountability posture to the public. Colleges responded to workplace demands but also neglected aspects of their mission and thus their communities because their focus and their resources were directed to government priorities. Colleges endeavored to increase productivity but in so doing precipitated tensions in labor relations; for example, management asked for and expected faculty to teach greater numbers of students and to use technology to support their added responsibilities. In this sense, governments directed colleges to become more efficient and more oriented toward global competition. But governments also shielded or detached colleges from global forces not only by translating these forces for colleges but also by mediating between global conditions and local conditions. Governments used colleges as instruments of policy and they also protected colleges from market forces by subsidizing their operations. These actions were significant contributors to the conditions of colleges as buffered from or buffeted by global forces.

The British Columbia provincial government was the principal agent for City Center College to deal with global forces, as well as with social, cultural, and political issues. The government and its agencies interpreted global forces for the college, for example, declining revenues as a result of decreasing exports, such as lumber, to Asian countries. City Center College was the recipient of government initiatives that responded to global forces: policies on productivity and efficiency, proposals and incentives to engage in private sector partnerships, and no measurable increases in overall government grants to the college. At the same time that government constricted its fiscal support of City Center College, it increased its oversight and directing of the college. The government's interpretation of global forces was balanced with its ideology as a social democratic government. As one senior college administrator noted in an articulation that expressed the sentiments of others, "the government is schizoid, contradictory, combining politics and economics: they want productivity and efficiency but also want to protect union jobs; they also want more entrepreneurship." Government thus acted within the context of a global economy as a neoliberal, capitalistic force trying to respond by legislating productivity and economic growth. But government also acted within the province with a socialist ideology promoting its embrace of multiculturalism, equity, and the underprivileged. On the one hand, the provincial government directed colleges to freeze tuition so that students could have access without a greater financial burden. This freeze constrained productivity behaviors and limited colleges' funding sources. On the other hand, government required colleges to seek alternate sources of revenue to public sector funds, captured from taxation. The government supported the worker, for example, assisting in raising the salaries of faculty unions, and yet the government asked for greater institutional productivity, which may indeed have meant the displacement of workers either by technology or because of financial exigency.

At Pacific Suburban Community College in Hawaii, the state was accused of "micromanaging the university and college system," and college observers noted that the college was viewed as another department of state government. In short, the state government was not viewed in a favorable light by higher education system officials—"The only snakes on the island are in the government." The intrusive role and influence of government in higher education began with the governor's office: the governor not only appointed board members but also became involved in labor relations through collective bargaining. The state legislature influenced the college through policy, funding, and championing of specific programs:"Downsizing is politically popular," noted one college official showing the impact of political behaviors upon college funding reductions from the state. Indeed, the government in the 1990s was particularly involved in college operations and actions including the governor's office, which intervened and diverted a 1997 faculty strike, and a state-mandated tuition policy in 1995, in which the college retained revenues but government operating monies decreased in nearly equal amounts.

During the decade, the state of Hawaii had not moved toward greater accountability measures for Pacific Suburban Community College. This was likely because of the state's ability to control and influence higher education institutions through its fiscal behaviors and especially through its bureaucratic and funding relationships (for example, statewide contract negotiations for faculty, with government as a third party, and state appointment of governing board members). The speculation by organizational members that the future held greater institutional autonomy from government was at odds with the view of a governing board member who noted that neither the university nor the colleges were economic players or global competitors. Thus, according to this board member, they might have to reconsider their future role, including educating and serving the state's population in a changed economy, one in which subsistence might be a realistic condition. This is not a mission that is applicable to an entrepreneurial institution or one free from heavy reliance upon government fiscal support. Furthermore, the assumption that a lessening of government fiscal support for the college would lead to greater independence from government is not borne out by either research[30] or by the reported experiences of other colleges in this study.

According to organizational members at City South Community College in Washington, the state, especially through its funding behaviors, treated the college as a branch plant operation, much as large corporations behave toward foreign production sites. The state established funding policies and used targeted funding for an agenda not favorable to colleges or students, set tuition fees, used its agency to demand specific forms of accountability, and controlled collective bargaining in part by its state salary allocations. Educational policies that might benefit students, such as university transfer articulation policies that facilitate student mobility or support for excellence of student performance, were either nonexistent or below the level of institutional consciousness because neither organizational members nor institutional documents referred to state policy that had educational salience. Finally, the state's welfare-to-work program was, from the perspective of college faculty and administrators, a regressive action that moved students out of the classroom and onto the streets looking for work, even below poverty-level wage work. This policy was viewed as partially responsible for the loss of those programs that could help students attain careers and occupations rather than temporary or unstable jobs in a global economy. The program encouraged short-term training and thus detracted from the more educational and long-term employment orientation of a two-year associate's degree programs. At City South, in 1998, between 500 and 600 full-time equivalency students were categorized as welfare-to-work, close to 20 percent of the college's total student body.

Also at City South Community College, state influence was largely fiscal, directing programs through enrollment-based funding and operations through the use of performance indicators. Increased government oversight and accompanying decreases in state appropriations placed other stresses upon the institution as its enrollments in traditional vocational programs declined and enrollments in academic and other occupational programs did not rise enough to offset declines. Thus, emphasis upon increasing productivity, on competition with other institutions, and on bureaucratic procedures to conform to state demands (for example, performance indicators) along with decreasing revenues pushed the college to the category of marginality in the "winners and losers" dichotomy of the global economy.

At East Shoreline College in British Columbia, although there was less government funding relative to institutional expenditures over a ten-year period, there was evidence to suggest increased government influence and control over college behaviors and actions. Government funding behaviors had considerable influence over college actions and in the development of college structures and processes. These behaviors included productivity incentives and targeted funding for specific programs; government intervention in the collective bargaining relationship between faculty and the college, most evident in the establishment of a province-wide bargaining structure; and government legislative action, particularly in the change to governing board composition and in the establishment of a formal, senate-type body to share governance with the governing board and administration. Moreover, government permissive legislation for baccalaureate degree programs at East Shoreline affected not only growth but also academic culture and institutional purpose.

In California, the role of the state was evident at Suburban Valley Community College in at least two areas: college finances and accountability. The California system of education funding was based upon limits to property tax assessments. This led to a shortage of funds to support the demands of higher education. Furthermore, the state targeted funding to support specific areas of its interests, but faculty salaries were not among those interests, to the consternation of faculty. College enrollments either grew or remained stable and costs rose, but government funding did not keep pace with increased costs.

Also at Suburban Valley, the state intervened in college management and operations through its demands for greater productivity and its requirements for increasing accountability. Mandates in the 1990s included a "pay for performance" administrative plan, enrollment fees, performance indicators, and various laws that constrained both the offering of distance education and student registration. As a major action, the college endeavored to increase enrollments because state funding was enrollment driven.

Overall, community college responses to policy and to government actions differed not only along institutional lines, but also along national lines. A marked difference between Canadian and U.S. institutions was particularly evident in institutional association with government ideology. In Canada, the institutions in Alberta and British Columbia exhibited close ties to provincial government departments and the ideology of provincial governments. Funding behaviors of government influenced institutional behaviors, and government policy was evident in institutional behaviors. In Alberta, government policy to shift the financial burden of government to taxpayers[31] and reduce public sector funding[32] had a dramatic effect upon the actions of North Mountain College and upon the thinking of organizational members. The college made a deliberate shift away from reliance upon government funds and altered its programming to reduce dependency and to increase its opportunities to secure private sector revenues. Additionally, college tuition fees rose in the late 1990s so that students paid a greater percentage of the costs. Government behaviors actually led to a change in thinking (for example, on the public role of the institution) on the part of many organizational members, especially managers.

Particularly noteworthy were governance alterations in the province of British Columbia in the 1990s and the evidence from City Center College, Rural Valley College, and East Shoreline College where organizational members repeatedly acknowledged significant changes to decision processes and structures. Government legislation in the mid-1990s formally established a role for college faculty, support staff, and students in decision-making in British Columbia colleges. The legislative alteration clearly moved these groups from an advisory-only role to a decision-making role. The legislation provided for an educational body with powers that not only paralleled the administrative bureaucracy but also in some cases superseded administrative authority. While governance changes were not rationalized responses to global forces, they can be associated with globalizing behaviors promoted by government, including worker productivity and labor-management stability, both of which promoted investment, especially international investment.

In the United States, college members did not exhibit the same association with government ideology as in Canada. Colleges were affected by financial allocations, not by government policy, although some policies, such as affirmative action, did have impact. Other external organizations, primarily universities and specific businesses and industries, had more influence upon college behaviors in the United States than in Canada. For example, university positions with respect to remedial education affected two of the U.S. colleges: that is, university policy influenced college practice. University positions and policy on community college transfer of credits to the university were deterministic of college programming. And the status accorded to a local university was much greater than that of the local community college. This suggests an important difference between the two countries and the role of government policy in institutional behaviors. In Canada, community colleges are extensions of the state, provincial institutions conforming in large part to the ideology of the government in power. In the United States, community colleges are vehicles or recipients of government policy but are affected as well by business and industry and other higher education institutions, such as state universities, in a much more obvious way than in Canada.

Notwithstanding these national differences, in both the United States and Canada, government—especially state and provincial—served as what Wheeler calls efficient managers or facilitators for "a world governed by global markets."[33] Cultural and knowledge-related issues, those matters associated with a liberal education, were superfluous in government policy. College purposes and mission, values and norms, programs, management, and resources were affected by an interventionary state. In large part, this state directly or indirectly reproduced economic globalization, which was as responsible as any other force for the globalized institution.

Refashioning Institutional Mission

Community colleges, at least since the 1970s and perhaps in their entire history, have not been the institutions that McGrath and Spear[34] suggest they were: academically oriented and disciplined-based. Indeed, there has always been ambiguity over the purposes and identity of the community college and its predecessor, the junior college.³⁵ The impetus for the rise of the junior college at the beginning of the twentieth century in the United States, is somewhat in dispute as a consequence of social pressures, such as immigration and changing family structures, or as the extension of an American ideal of personal achievement through social mobility.³⁶ Arthur Cohen at the end of the 1960s captures the comprehensive and convoluted identity for the community and junior college in an articulation that looks both forward and backward:

> The community junior college . . . is viewed variously as democracy's college, as an inexpensive, close-to-home alternative to the lower division of a prestigious university; as a place to await marriage, a job, or the draft; and as a high school with ashtrays. For many of its enrollees, it is a stepping stone to the higher learning; for most, it is the last formal, graded, public education in which they will be involved. The community college is—or attempts to be—all things to all people, trying valiantly to serve simultaneously as a custodian, trainer, stimulant, behavior-shaper, counselor, adviser, and caretaker to both young and old.³⁷

In Canada, Dennison and Gallagher acknowledge that jurisdiction's reliance upon an earlier U.S. tradition in higher education, suggesting a similar pattern of institutional development. Yet, they emphasize that community colleges in Canada were decidedly unlike other postsecondary institutions and primarily established by provincial governments to serve the public and the needs of the public in all its ramifications, from recreational to advanced credential requirements.³⁸

The multiple purposes of community colleges in both countries run parallel to heterogeneity of their students who have both diverse abilities and diverse expectations.³⁹ The refashioning of mission at the community college, consistent with the responsive character of these institutions in addressing local community needs and the alteration in demographic and economic conditions,⁴⁰ is both a consequence of government pressures and institutional responses to these pressures as well as to global forces. These global forces include most prominently a global economy, but also global cultural flows⁴¹ and global forms of communication, epitomized by the concept of a "networked society."⁴² Economic ends dominated the mission of community colleges in the 1990s, refashioning traditional missions of access and responsiveness to community educational and training needs so that these became means not ends. Instead, improving economic conditions of regions and nations, through such activities as work-force training, both to compete in production globally and to attract investors with a competitive economic environment, became a preeminent, articulated concern. Furthermore, by "economizing"—that is, by operating institutions more efficiently—colleges imitated the behaviors of businesses or corporations and became participants in the global economy. This was precisely the intent of government policy for community colleges in the two nations.

CHAPTER 7

THE PROCESS OF GLOBALIZATION

The process of globalization in the community college did not eradicate behavioral patterns associated with the preservation of institutional identity, the accommodation of growth, the balance between education and training, and many other traditional patterns. The globalization process accompanied these behavioral patterns and in some cases initiated others, such as marketization. Institutional responses to both global forces and to the responses of intermediaries, such as government, to global forces resulted in considerable alteration to institutional mission and structures at the seven colleges.

All seven community colleges responded to and were affected by external and global forces in distinct ways. The amalgamation of these behaviors for each college furthered the movement of these institutions along a path of economic globalization. Each institution has its own story.

Suburban Valley Community College: The Image of the Past and the Embrace of Technology

Globalization affected Suburban Valley Community College in several interrelated ways. First and foremost was the college's location in a region nationally and internationally renowned and highly competitive internationally in high technology industries, especially computers and computer software. A global economic and cultural environment was adjacent to the college. The college served this environment through training the work force and by applying the products of these industries, such as computer software. The area attracted workers internationally. A social web of organizations in the region masked or ignored distinctions between private and public spheres, and both private and public educational institutions interacted with the computer industry in similar fashion. The increasing use and pervasive influence of electronic technology was a second force acting upon the college. Historically, the college established a reputation as an "innovator" and "educational leader," according to both insiders and observers of community colleges nationally. Thus, such a role, if to be maintained, had to match external expectations. That is, SVCC was compelled to adopt electronic technologies such as information technologies (for example, e-mail, voice mail, online registration) and educational technologies (for example, Web-based instruction) to achieve recognition nationally. Additionally, in order to attract students to increase enrollments and to gain needed revenue, the college offered what the public and business and industry expected: this included current electronic equipment and user-friendly instructional approaches. The expectation was for a computer-literate student. This suggests that a particular segment of the marketplace played a prominent role in organizational behaviors. Finally, the use of electronic technology was increasingly supporting distance education, the delivery system that not only satisfied the needs of the public, especially the adult working public, but also increased productivity through distance education enrollments. The potential of distance education for revenue generation was dependent upon electronic technology for delivery—including online instruction and satellite broadcast video.

A third globalizing trend, multiculturalism, was the result of large numbers of immigrants, especially from non-Western countries. Asian immigration was a consequence of numerous factors including political conflicts, rapid industrialization, and the promise of economic prosperity in California.[1] The importance of Asia globally was both as a market for products and as a source of labor. This suggested the need to cultivate closer ties to Asian cultures and the need to integrate Asians into other societies. The large Asian population as well as the other non-Anglo population at SVCC meant that diversity and multiculturalism were practical concepts. Overall, 56 percent of students were visible minorities, including Asians, in 1996, compared to 27 percent in 1989. Thirty-six percent of students were identified as Asian in 1996, compared to 21.5 percent in 1989. The college responded to its student population by altering programming, curricula, and college social life to fit student ethnic and cultural backgrounds. Furthermore, new organizational structures were established and inter and multidisciplinarity in curricula gained prominence as the college adapted to college members' understanding of "new learning needs of students," especially part-time learners and non-native English speakers, and concepts of "learning in a global context."

The role of the state in institutional behaviors constituted a fourth globalizing trend. The state's role in leading, or indeed in stalling, technological innovations and economic restructuring is a significant factor of globalization. The state "expresses and organizes the social and cultural forces that dominate in a given space and time."[2] Greater productivity and efficiency at Suburban Valley were a consequence of lessening state fiscal support for education, statewide. Actions of restructuring and increasing workloads for college employees were connected to the drive for increased productivity. Furthermore, even though there were limitations to state supported education, the state was viewed as increasing its influence in college operations. In the latter part of the 1990s, the state instituted performance indicators for monitoring and evaluating college outcomes, although largely in the form of quantitative measures such as increasing student numbers. These indicators were intended to be tied to funding, so that "increased funding" was dependent upon "increases in measures of productivity." Thus, the state directed the college because the college was largely dependent upon the state for revenues. Also, state policy initiatives such as increased emphasis upon training of students and greater infusion of technological equipment into the workplace affected both instruction and administrative and clerical work.

College members, especially managers, relied upon various strategies to adapt the college to its environment, to maintain its reputation, and to aid in the survival of the institution. The college was influenced by its local environment, including its students and their social and cultural backgrounds, the expectations and demands of business and industry, and the expectations of its affluent community members. The president was viewed as responsible for a restructuring decision, to alter both administrative operations and to adjust instruction to match learner needs. College employees acted upon managerial decisions to emphasize diversity—in hiring faculty, for example—and to commit fiscal and human resources to the acquisition of technology facilities and equipment. Additionally, the goal of increasing enrollments and improving productivity led to a strategy to increase distance education. Furthermore, the use of distance education complemented the maintenance of the college's image as an innovative institution. These strategies accompanied a trend in declining enrollments and declining state resources for students (that is, declining per unit revenues) and were largely motivated by the need to gain revenue from the state so that the college could survive.

Strategy at Suburban Valley Community College entailed responding to external forces yet maintaining historical patterns of behavior and institutional identity. The image of the college, both locally and nationally, as an innovative and sophisticated institution was maintained and indeed developed further, not just to provide employees with a valued self-image but also to increase enrollments by attracting new students. The college responded to its external environment by promoting diversity and multiculturalism, by emphasizing high technology education and its use of electronic technology in both administrative work and instruction. A restructuring of the organization was a specific action of major proportions, occurring in the mid-1990s to address both internal and external needs, responding to both new students and new understandings of students—both their learning needs and their sociocultural backgrounds—as well as the size and dynamics of the college's work force. The structure encouraged matrix management, teamwork, and fewer administrators, with faculty and staff involvement on committees and faculty interaction with each other and with different student populations through inter- and multidisciplinarity. The result was a form of learning community and its variations, including an organization structured around themes associated with education and training (for example, Multiculturalism-International Programs and Services, and Science and Technology). The college's emphasis upon electronic technology—for example, its use in distance education—was a strategy not only to attract and serve more students and to increase institutional productivity but also to maintain its national reputation. Thus strategies included the preservation of institutional image, social responsiveness, student focus, the use of technology for work and learning, changing organizational structures for both productivity and inculcating teamwork, and finally increasing enrollments to achieve productivity gains and thus acquire more fiscal resources.

In spite of strategies to emphasize high technology and higher status programs, the college actually became more remedial in its educational services and more of a skill provider for the work force in its training. While college enrollments in the university transfer area rose approximately 2.5 percent per year in the 1990s, English as a second language enrollments rose by 53 percent per year. The college endeavored to accommodate new learners, part-time, working adults or aspiring workers, with general skill and language and mathematics deficiencies, in order to serve these students and to gain enrollments. To serve these students, the college increased its use of electronic technologies to deliver curricula, through distance education practices, and to provide assistance to students. Changing student demographics (for example, in 1997–1998, 35 percent of students worked 40 hours a week or more), changing industry needs, new government welfare policy that required short-term training, and new immigrants with diverse backgrounds contributed to the changing student body.

There was considerable ambiguity over the primary articulated role of the institution—to educate and train students. This ambiguity involved, for example, the outcomes of instruction and the extent to which education and training were responses to learning needs or to the values of business and industry, and the expectations of government. For business, industry, and government, education and training were more of an inculcation of acceptable behaviors to serve employers rather than addressing the needs of individual learners. A palpable tension was present within the college between the drive to increase enrollments in order to capture greater state funds and the desire to maintain a high profile image as an innovative, prestigious institution. This tension could be seen in the conflicts over staffing the technology facility and in hiring full-time faculty for the arts and sciences. Some organizational members attempted to mollify the tensions by promoting technology as the vehicle of access, the means of improving student learning, and as a strategy to increase enrollments and thereby gain the needed fiscal resources to support education.

College mission and structures altered in the 1990s, and these alterations suggest that the institution was itself undergoing change. But alteration was impeded on the one hand by the college's reputation as an innovative and leading community college and on the other hand by resistance from faculty and some long-serving administrators who valued the practices and goals of the past, such as less formalization of operations and greater emphasis upon academic education. There was an informal interest group of faculty and some administrators within the college who did not want to see the college mission altered to become a tool of business and industry, and to lose its educational leadership position. While they compromised on some issues, such as accepting the president's restructuring of the college, they rebelled against increasing district control and increasing managerialism and formalism. They developed alternate agendas such as innovating through interdisciplinary studies and personal gain such as early retirement packages and teaching overloads so that faculty could earn more than administrators. Faculty turned to union militancy during conflict over productivity or over issues of unilateral decision-making by district managers or the governing board. Organizational behaviors played out tensions that parallel those intrinsic to globalization. These include conflicts between the global and the local and between homogeneity and heterogeneity, intensifying interactions and broadening connections between disparate spheres, such as the private and the public and nation-states.[3]

East Shoreline College: Entrepreneurialism, University Status, and a New Mission

Government policy, government funding behaviors, greater institutional alignment to both international and local markets, and growth itself aided in increasing globalization of East Shoreline College. Commodification of higher education was evident in the exportation and selling of both training and education in Asia, South America, and Europe: this exchange of goods and services for revenues was intended to support institutional growth. Internally, the college emphasized productivity and efficiency, with larger class sizes, fewer administrators, and more reliance upon electronic technology for work: actions intended to cope with budget shortfalls. The college also turned toward work-force training, not so much in providing vocational programs to students but in providing skills and job specific training to employers and by emphasizing job skills in baccalaureate degree programs. Additionally, privatization grew with, for example, the establishment of an international, private secondary school under the jurisdiction of the college, drawing resources from private citizens in Asia, particularly Japan. In this environment, the college created "winners" and "losers," imitating global economic behaviors. At ESC, degree programs were viewed as productive and were in high demand; traditional vocational programs—the trades—lost their once-prominent position and faltered both in acquiring resources and in demand. College structural change was continual, with restructuring as a consequence of the establishment of baccalaureate degree programs, and program growth in student numbers with accompanying human resource growth and governance changes that followed their establishment.

While the state, the provincial government, was particularly directive toward the college, both in curtailing public expenditures and in advancing social and economic policy, East Shoreline College responded neither by adhering literally or completely to government policy nor by challenging policy. Instead, college members responded to policies and government actions as stimulation to act according to college self-interest or college traditional patterns of behavior. With public sector funding constraints, the college increased its efforts to secure alternate funding sources through both public government contracts and through the private sector. With government incentives to develop programs that were workplace and marketplace relevant, the college responded by combining curriculum from a declining or static program area—vocational—with academic degree programs, resulting in applied degrees.

Although numerous external factors contributed to the actions of East Shoreline College, the college adapted to its environment largely through institutionally generated strategies. The provincial government especially, growing local populations, and international economies contributed to organizational actions. But these acted more as stimuli for the college leadership, in concert with other organizational members, to respond and react to external forces by pursuing new program areas for baccalaureate degrees (for example, liberal studies), expanding existing programs (for example, nursing), adding work-force training and retraining programs (for example, forestry technology), increasing an already active international program and contract services area, and marketing the college both locally and internationally. Government funding constraints confronted the college with choices about growth or reduction: the college chose growth. Government legislative actions pertaining to governance confronted the college with choices about employee participation in decision-making or faculty-dominated committee structures for governing and managing the institution: the college chose the faculty-dominated committee structure, suggesting a movement of the institution toward a professional bureaucracy,[4] in which managerial authority was limited and professional authority—the power of expertise—was emphasized. This emergent professional bureaucracy resulted from the rise of the baccalaureate degree programs as the dominant curricular area of the institution, where growth in students was considerable and where new institutional hirings were directed to the addition of faculty expertise to arts and sciences degree programs as well as career programs such as nursing, education, and social work.

Academic strategies invariably have a symbolic intent.[5] In the case of East Shoreline College, academic strategies of formalizing and strengthening committee structures, negotiating workload changes to recognize scholarship as a requisite for baccalaureate instruction, and the pursuit of Canadian university status altered the identity of the institution, changing its power structures, its work, and its purposes. The institution altered not only legally from a two-year to a four-year college but also in practice, with academic work taking precedence over other forms of work. Moreover, the institution extended its mission to include both the traditional mission of the community college and the mission of a four-year college. This mission extension was not without its internal costs.

There was friction between degree program faculty and vocational faculty, largely as a consequence of status and resource differentials. This friction, while acknowledged by college managers, was in part a result of increasing competition among faculty groups for both resources and institutional power. The college president, formerly a vocational instructor and dean, was a champion of vocational education, yet he was unable to stem the tide of vocational program contraction. The vocational area diminished in both resources relative to other program areas and lost its influence in institutional actions.

Strategy at East Shoreline College was a continual response to changing external conditions, including government policy, government funding behaviors, the local demands for education and training, and to a lesser extent changing global economies. But strategy also included responding to internal demands for change, most particularly and recently for alteration of college purposes and of identity as a university. Fiscal behaviors were predominant, especially in the latter half of the 1990s, as college members deliberated over actions dependent upon funding and resources. The college management actively pursued funding sources outside of the traditional government operating grants, and the president of the college devoted considerable time and energy to fundraising and to the acquisition of international contracts in concert with other college officials. Strategy was not solely about survival, however, but motivated by the desire to grow and to change, to adapt East Shoreline College to external requirements such as changing student and workplace needs.

The college pursued international connections, associations, and partnerships among private and public consumers for its products, largely for the acquisition of revenues and as well to provide faculty and students with international education, training, and professional development experiences. It attracted a substantial number of foreign, particularly Asian, students to its campus (for example, over 300 in postsecondary programs). While the college was influenced fiscally because of a downturn in the Asian economy as it was in the spring of 1998, it was not so severely affected that it altered its international focus and its pursuit of international sources of revenue.

A number of strategies were at work at East Shoreline College, some complementary, some potentially in conflict with each other. Furthermore, some strategies were overshadowed by others. Overall, there was a preponderance of actions directed toward specific strategies, and organizational members expressed both a condition of fatigue over their numerous activities and confusion about institutional direction. While academic faculty, and particularly those teaching in baccalaureate degree programs, worked toward the development of a more prominent academic institution, with increased professional authority and a university culture, vocational and collegiate or non-degree program faculty worked toward program and job survival. Educational services to students at the lower end of the educational hierarchy were jeopardized by the increasing emphasis on higher learning—that is, baccalaureate degree programs. Administrative leadership strategies involved actions directed to growth, productivity, and labor-management stability. These strategies translated into administrative work in securing resources, in managing budgets with both art as well as craft and in intense political lobbying, internally with organizational members and externally with government officials.

But in these strategies and their attendant actions, there was little evident behavior directed to student needs. While students may have benefited from the byproducts of these strategies, such as improved facilities or the preservation of courses and programs, they were not the object of these strategies. This omission may have been a consequence of the changing student body over the 1990s, both in growth and in student characteristics: for example, the addition of an international secondary school to the campus that brought teenage students from Asian countries whose native language was not English and whose socioeconomic background did not match that of local 18 to 24-year-old students, which was considerably lower.

The comprehensive nature of the college curriculum, from college preparation to trades training to baccalaureate degrees, meant that the student body was diverse in interests and abilities. Strategies directed toward student interests and needs were thus diffuse. This suggests that useful learning strategies for students would have to occur at the unit or program level, not at the institutional level. Thus, the forestry technology program altered curriculum and instruction to adapt to a changing workplace and therefore increased student opportunity for employability. The nursing program dramatically changed its curriculum so that graduates could adapt to the changing health care environment of the province. These unit or program strategies, however, were not always compatible or consistent with larger institutional strategies, but because the college operated as a collection of relatively autonomous work areas, the inconsistencies were not regarded by organizational members as problems. The overall institutional strategy of environmental responsiveness through growth likely bound organizational members and units to the institution, indicating that strategies were grounded in organizational beliefs and aspirations, at whatever level.

Organizational members had various perceptions of the state of the college's mission, yet consistent views on its essential content. Several indicated that the mission was not changing; others modified this perception, suggesting that the mission was "not consciously changing;" one faculty member noted that the mission was changing by default; and a few faculty and administrators observed that the mission was changing slowly in spite of the intentions of organizational members. The mission of the college was changing dramatically, yet organizational members wanted to preserve the best of the past and deny the extent of change that was occurring. In part, institutional growth drove mission change: the college was a larger institution in the late 1990s than it was in the 1980s, and the relatively moderate-sized organization had become a large organization with thousands of students, hundreds of employees, and four campuses spread out over a number of communities. Its expenditures exceeded $50 million (Canadian) annually, compared to just over $32 million at the close of the 1980s. But mission altered more because of curricular focus than because of growth. Changing structures both supported and followed from a changing mission.

The establishment of baccalaureate degree programs, coupled with alterations to governance whereby faculty involvement in institutional decision-making increased, marked the entry to institutional transformation from a two-year postsecondary training and education institution to a university. Mission expanded to include baccalaureate education, including professional education in the fields of social work, nursing, business, and education, among others. The transfer function, long a tradition of the U. S. and Canadian community college, was no longer a major function of East Shoreline College, because students no longer needed to transfer to attain further education and a baccalaureate degree. While ESC maintained its community college role, it added a university role.

Moreover, in an effort to sustain its various roles and its activities, including its growth, ESC expanded its mission in another direction—toward the secondary school mandate of preparing school children for college. ESC established an international secondary school, not only enlarging its institutional functions but also altering its educational role as a public institution to include a private institution as well. This action was consistent with the college's historical behaviors as an entrepreneurial institution, but in overtly privatizing education in an institutional setting and on-campus, the college demonstrated a more marked shift to a mission responsive to a more corporate agenda—educating economic elites. While providing revenues through their tuition fees to support public education, private school students from Asian countries were also supported by a public infrastructure and the benefits of a public system, including all of the organizational features of a public college such as a highly educated faculty, a legitimated curriculum, and the service, much of it voluntary, of internal and external community members on committees and on the governing board of the college.

A palpable manifestation of this mission change was the presence of dozens of Japanese students (private, fee payers), ages 15 to 18, on campus. Their presence was obvious, not because of their Asian appearance but because of their behaviors—adolescent—and their dress, which was expensive, trendy, and inconsistent with the dress of other students. They gave a secondary school atmosphere to the cafeteria and to the library, and instructors reported that these Japanese students were not dedicated to their studies. Thus, the price of privatization for the purposes of resource acquisition was a structure at odds with the new university structure, in which scholarship and higher learning took precedence over adolescent development and developmental education.

Another influence upon mission was the increasing influence of government not just on fiscal conditions and behaviors within the college but upon curriculum. Few condemned the government for adding baccalaureate degree programs, but most acknowledged the role of government in pushing the college through policy and through funding incentives and disincentives toward workplace training, and several organizational members decried this alteration. Government policy favored applied skills suitable and appropriate to the marketplace, particularly the private sector. College curriculum was thus developed and judged on workplace utility. This emphasis was at odds with traditional understandings of liberal education, and there were points of friction between academic faculty who promoted learning as knowledge acquisition and other faculty and administrators, as well as students and support staff and board members, who pressed for applied knowledge or practicability of learning. Even though mission altered as a consequence of the early development of baccalaureate degree programs, there was pressure from government upon these programs to provide more workplace skills for graduates.

Through the shift to baccalaureate degree granting status, East Shoreline College became a university—perhaps a hybrid type, but a university nonetheless. The college maintained its community college mission and expanded that to include not only baccalaureate degree curricula but university values and behaviors, such as professional authority and formalizing the role of scholarly research. ESC was responsive externally, locally, provincially, and internationally, with this latter response driven by revenue generation. Its global emphasis and involvement was predominantly an economic condition.

The provincial government and its responsible education government office—the ministry—was a major external influencer of college behaviors and actions. Government policies and legislation contributed to significant organizational change in the 1990s, including the addition of baccalaureate degree programs, the addition of organizational employees and students to the governing board membership, the reshaping of institutional governance so that organizational members shared responsibility for the institution with the governing board. These contributed to the college's alteration to a professional bureaucracy[6] where faculty professional authority prevailed and where baccalaureate degrees were seen to drive institutional decision-making. But the provincial government also influenced the college through its funding behaviors and its labor-relations policies in constraining government allocations so that they did not keep pace with institutional growth and in sponsoring a provincial structure for collective bargaining between faculty and colleges.

The college shifted its practices and its purposes in response to external forces including the provincial government. The changing workplace and the changing nature of work, both globally and locally constituted other forces influential in college behaviors. Because the province was historically a resource-based, extractive economy, the decline of both the forest and fishing industries meant severe dislocation for workers, declining profits for investors, and declining revenues for the government. The trades that either supported these industries or developed with them declined as well, and thus trades training in these areas faltered. Furthermore, the increasing emphasis in the workplace of the 1990s on computer skills, electronic communication, and the manipulation of data influenced postsecondary education generally.[7] New skills not old knowledge were preferred, and thus ESC responded to changing workplaces and work through curriculum and instruction and contract training.

East Shoreline College's responses to globalization redefined the concept of the institution as a community college. In the 1990s, ESC did not eliminate its mission of the 1980s, but it added to and expanded that mission. The two-year postsecondary institution that provided training and education for its community became a university, providing educational services, training, secondary and postsecondary credentials, as well as baccalaureate degrees, to its local and provincial communities as well as internationally. The actions of East Shoreline College demonstrated how a community college provided services formerly foreign to these institutions, adding structures and processes to accommodate an expanded mission.

City South Community College: Reorganization in the Face of a Globally Competitive Environment

Globalization for City South Community College was a complex phenomenon, colored by the global connectivity of two state and local industries—aircraft and computer software. The college's history as a vocational institution, "Paycheck College," in which students enrolled in programs, finished and obtained jobs with satisfying remuneration, was like a microcosm of the global economy's affects upon America. Blue-collar, trade-oriented jobs declined both through automation and outsourcing (that is, to other countries). The call for American competitiveness was not to address the decline in industrial manufacturing but to stimulate training in the high technology fields, the professions, and business.[8] CSCC was caught in a time warp in which old, successful programs lost enrollments because of structural changes in the political economy, yet the college's image and its community demographics limited its movement toward evolving as an advanced educational institution.

Ironically, while highly influenced by global forces, the college's connections to intermediary organizations and systems impeded—even directed—college responsiveness. Economic forces impinged upon college behaviors, which became mirror images of globalization. Institutional emphasis upon productivity and efficiency, especially in the face of declining revenues, increasing accountability from government, decreasing program demand, and changing workplace requirements had several effects of substance upon the college. The restructuring effort of 1995 was a response to what the president viewed as global forces of change impacting the college. This effort led to outcomes not unlike those experienced within the larger corporate area of U.S. business and industry—downsizing and layoffs, greater loss of revenues, mission alteration—and greater dependency upon resource providers as well as an increased focus upon the private sector marketplace. While the college president may have acted to save the college from collapse, he did not adapt the institution to a new global economy. There was essentially no strategy, no replacing of content to what was altered and jettisoned, and no new programs to take the place of the deteriorating vocational programs.

The district office, for example, acted as an intermediary buffer between the state and the college and between external global forces, which included rapid technological change. District office officials endeavored to increase efficiencies on campus and to develop a more salable image to the community for the three district colleges as a whole. Thus, the district office acted according to global patterns—centralizing control, information, and decision mechanisms and decentralizing production. The district claimed to "subsidize" City South Community College, but it also may have been responsible for influencing its management, by selecting and influencing its chief executive officers, and by moving the college away from its local community to serve district interests and needs. Again, this behavior of district personnel may indeed have saved CSCC from collapse and from further erosion in state funding.

The college was affected as well by its organizational development and the characteristics of its organizational members, many of whom were long term employees. While its faculty and administrators remained relatively stable over the decade, its senior leadership—both the college presidency and the district leadership—altered. The college in the 1990s experienced serious organizational decline and at the end of the 1990s attempted to adjust to mission alteration and programming changes with a new president.

Innumerable strategies emerged in order to cope with both external forces of change as well as with subsequent college generated strategies in response to these forces and to earlier strategies. The 1995 restructuring action stands out, not only for its radical approach to both external change and internal fiscal decline but also for its influence upon the future. While this strategy was a deliberate one, rationalized in several documents written by the president to college members, more recent understandings of the restructuring reflected denial of the president's justifications and an inability to repair dysfunctional outcomes or reverse the structural changes imposed by the act of restructuring. Efforts from subsequent presidents were directed by both presidents to reform the governance process of the college: to increase diversity in college hirings, to stop the decline in enrollments, and to solve fiscal problems that the restructuring action was intended to remedy. Late 1990s strategies of the college involved ways to deal with state imposed performance indicators and a planning process to focus upon college directions and put into action various intentions. Continued and significant emphasis was placed upon diversity and multiculturalism, largely as a response to the student body and the local community.

In spite of these strategies, the college was without a marketable image largely because of its past emphasis upon vocational programming, an area that no longer had salience. Its historical development did not include the maintenance of an academic culture or even the substitution of another strong culture aside from job training. Attempts in the latter part of the decade to strengthen the student services area placed greater emphasis upon students' needs but largely viewed students as customers.

Viewed and self-defined as a vocational institution, City South encountered serious budgetary and enrollment difficulties in the early and mid-1990s. The image of the college and its patterns of behavior perpetuated both its mission and its problems. The college president who proposed a major restructuring initiative in 1995, carried out some of this plan, and then moved to serve as a senior administrator at the district office before his retirement in 1997. The new president on leave from another district college while not overturning the restructuring initiative did alter past practices in governance and began to emphasize other organizational behaviors, including attention to multiculturalism. While the college mission did not change during this two-year period, both continuing patterns of enrollment decline and employee involvement in college decision-making, as well as recognition by organizational members of changing student demographics, the return to the former mission—as a vocational institution—was over. By 1998, mission alteration became institutionalized, with activities directed at planning for change.

But the 1995 restructuring had realigned units, altered working and personal relationships, and effectively de-professionalized faculty, although this condition was promoted long before the restructuring. This structural alteration was an impediment to mission change, as the college was organized along the lines of a business or company more than as an academic institution. College efforts in the latter part of the 1990s were directed to focus more on students and student needs. One manifestation of this was the attention to multiculturalism. Another manifestation of the focus upon students was in addressing the needs of adult part-time students through advising and admissions. But the structural changes of 1995, including the de-emphasis of a strong academic culture, meant that attention to students was also a businesslike process: that is, defining students as customers and not as learners.

New efforts to reverse enrollment declines meant an increased emphasis upon instructional delivery: developing courses to be delivered online, in flexible formats; changing course offerings from daytime to nighttime; and approaching business and industry to gain contracts for training. But these actions took place in a context that suggested an unstable mission and an uncertain faculty. Furthermore, the district office was viewed as a guiding force in new delivery systems, such as distance education, with faculty especially leery of central influence and control.

In the latter part of the 1990s, the college established a task force to address mission and planning, with support from all internal sectors. While committee generated change is slow, it does benefit from the advice and participation of a broad segment of the organizational membership. This task force structure was to some extent the mirror opposite of the 1995 restructuring act—a solo, top-down decision that disconnected work from purpose and left organizational members wondering about its intentions. Although some organizational members, especially new ones, doubted the significance of the 1995 actions, these actions represented the autocratic environment of the previous decade and the early 1990s that not only de-professionalized faculty but also denied self-efficacy to most organizational members.

Several prominent influencers loomed large in the organizational behaviors and actions of City South Community College in the 1990s: these included the former president, the local and state economy, the changing workplace, the district office leadership, and population demographics. While the college was not progressing well as a vocational institution, even in late 1996 and again in 1998 organizational members continued to view the institution as vocationally oriented. This self-defined image tended to impede the college from moving away from past patterns of behaviors and past memories, largely the consequence of the actions of the former president. Declining enrollments, decreases in state appropriations for the college, and changing student populations to some extent forced the college to change its mission; nonetheless, the mission as a social construction—that is, how organizational members conceived of their mission and how they enacted and played out their beliefs and conceptions—remained largely intact from at least the 1980s.

While there was widespread recognition about the need for change and there were numerous actions to promote change and responsiveness to external conditions, these recognitions and actions were not founded upon a pervasive or deeply believed set of assumptions about the college's purposes or about its role as a postsecondary educational institution. Even in the most recent iteration of the college's revised mission in March 1998, there was an articulation of intentions and a listing of commitments (for example, "commits to meeting the changing needs of students by providing . . . programs which prepare students to succeed in their careers or further their education") but no compelling and convincing identity of the institution, beyond the introductory assertion that the college "is a community of educators." There was little other institutional evidence to support this assertion.

Faced with a changing local population and with altering and sometimes contradictory demands from the workplace, City South Community College could not preserve its vocational image and reputation. Jobs which were once filled by CSCC graduates either disappeared or were filled with unskilled labor. The student population that the college drew upon in the mid and late-1990s, was predominantly minority, recently immigrated, and in need of language and other basic skills. Students who required or demanded occupations that were more than temporary jobs needed programs that were either sophisticated training that took two years' minimum to complete or were articulated with baccalaureate degree programs so that students could transfer to a university and eventually attain baccalaureate status. Without curricular change, CSCC could not sustain itself as an independent college.

The institution was a recipient of several deleterious effects of economic globalization as well as changing demographics, themselves a consequence of immigration largely from Asian and Eastern European countries. Like primary industries in the state and nation, and several related industries such as steel, City South Community College experienced a type of postindustrial stress. Its central mission was eroding and adaptation to a new economic environment was destabilizing organizational practices and culture.

Pacific Suburban Community College: Preserving Culture and Serving Industry

On the one hand, Pacific Suburban Community College continued its historical pattern of contracting geographical distance between South Pacific and Asian countries, as well as between in-state islands, by increasing its development and use of electronic technologies (that is, distance education) and unifying cultural differences among its various ethnic populations through greater emphasis upon multiculturalism. On the other hand, PSCC was an object—even a victim—of economic globalization as others' economies (for example, California in the early 1990s and Japan in the late 1990s) had a significant bearing upon college actions. The state economy, as several organizational members observed, had a pervasive influence over college behaviors and actions: "everything pales in comparison to the economy." This economy was dependent upon tourism and its related spinoffs, such as retail merchandising. State tourism declined as did the revenues associated with this industry. The past pattern of expansion ended, and public institutions, such as PSCC, were at a crossroads, either at the mercy of a declining state economy or preparing to alter sources of funding. The state did not seem prepared to raise taxes to support the public sector. Observers saw that the effects of the state's high salaries attributed to the large percentage of unionized workers—approximately 22 percent statewide as compared to the 12 percent national average—had to be modified by reduction in work force and by curtailing public sector expenditures. But the state's high costs of living, a product in part of Asian capital, without expanded revenues for the state and resultant increases in state expenditures, furthered the existing situation in the state of haves and have nots.

The intrusiveness of government, a fact since the inception of the college and reported as increasing, was expected to diminish both as a result of declining state fiscal support for the college and rising dependence of Pacific Suburban upon other resource providers. By the end of the 1990s, Pacific Suburban planned to move closer to the marketplace and further from reliance upon government in the belief that the private sector would respond and provide needed revenues for the college. State economic woes meant that some societally beneficial actions by the college—such as the provision of relatively inexpensive training and education—were coming to an end. The college set itself on a course to raise productivity, and with increases intended to come from international sources who could access college programs and pay the costs.

The college endeavored to maintain its cultural and social emphasis while addressing its economic situation. The economic situation of decline led the college to plan on a major restructuring process, altering organizational structures to reduce expenditures and to focus upon several strategies to raise revenues. In short, the college began to de-emphasize bureaucracy and emphasize "Adhocracy,"[9] becoming more entrepreneurial by loosening controls over units, diminishing both the role and numbers of managers, and expanding the role of faculty by flattening the hierarchy, encouraging and even requiring faculty to engage in capitalistic behaviors individually and in groups. That is, PSCC intended to connect more closely with the business and industry community as well as with South Pacific and Asian customers of education and training.

Pacific Suburban Community College's adaptation to its environment was both complex and rational, or close to predictable. A host of environmental forces were at work influencing the college: these included the very geography and geographical location of the state and the size, in geographical area and in population, of the state; historical connections to Asian countries; and, most prominent in the 1990s, the economy. The college undertook a considerable number of strategies, as if the primary actions in the late 1990s of the college were deliberate forms of adaptation. While a major strategy was the preservation of programmatic strengths and multiculturalism, other strategies might be seen to undermine these or ignore them. While university transfer was not just a programmatic strength but where close to 70 percent of students undertook coursework, college strategies put emphasis upon marketplace—private and international sector—needs, specifically training. Whereas nursing job placements were declining in the state, the college addressed the needs of a health-science work force in a South Pacific country. Locally, the college developed programs for the training of retail merchants and for hotel service employees.

Strategy at the close of the 1990s was for restructuring the institution, not just reduce expenditures but also adapt the institution organizationally and in its services to the marketplace in order to generate fiscal resources. A predictable response to resource decline, to reduce expenditures in areas that do not affect production (in this case instruction), restructuring in U.S. companies has led to expenditure reduction without accompanying increases in productivity.[10] Furthermore, the desire to reduce reliance upon the state means that the college will increase its private role and become dependent upon other resource providers, whose goals may not be in line with the educational mission of the institution. Additionally, the international trend of governments to reduce funding for institutions has not led to less state intervention in the management of higher education institutions: performance indicators are one of the many levers that governments have used to continue to hold institutions accountable to legislatures. Thus, PSCC was heading down a path that suggests that adaptation is a process of undoing its strategic intent. What was somewhat surprising was the extent to which faculty, normally a critic of managerial strategies, accepted the restructuring plan or what they knew of it. But perhaps this acceptance was a manifestation of the environment, both historical and current, in which faculty resided—for example, an island state and thus an institution dependent upon international economies for its tourist revenues.

The historical strategy in the late 1980s and early 1990s for Pacific Suburban Community College was largely directed to the elaboration of mission and the maintenance and indeed improvement of reputation. The emphasis was upon quality programs, especially academic and a few occupational programs (for example, health sciences and culinary arts), with innovative instructional approaches (for instance, writing across the curriculum) as important adjuncts to college behaviors. But by the mid-1990s, the economic situation of the state worsened with respect to public sector funding, and PSCC began to plan for structural change. Several years of deferred physical maintenance, the curtailment of offerings that were not productive, and even the movement of remedial education from credit to non-credit in order to change expenditures into revenues did assist in protecting core operations but did little to change the pattern of reduced revenues. Even the emphasis upon students and the ongoing preservation and growth of multiculturalism brought neither increased enrollments nor new revenues or revenue sources.

The major two strategies, both interconnected, entailed restructuring the institution and positioning the college closer to local business and industry and to international consumers of education and training. While moving closer to the marketplace was a progressively growing action, including greater development of distance education programming, restructuring was a plan intended to go into effect in July 1998 provided that the expected budget shortfall was not altered by some final act of government. The strategies in short were intended to reduce expenditures that were not central to core operations, increase expenditures in growing and promising areas, and develop and promote products (for example, training) that would generate revenues. The outcomes of the restructuring strategy depended upon the ability of the new structure to facilitate revenue generation and to cope with expenditure reductions. That is, the reduction of an associate dean's position would not only save the college a salary and benefit costs but that reduction would also be expected to be accommodated by more efficient management and gains in effectiveness—for example, departmental cooperation in pursuing and acquiring contracts for training. Faculty work expanding into the development and delivery of distance education would have to include the acquisition of either more students or more revenues or both.

While college members worked to protect and sustain the basic college mission and to preserve several qualitative aspects of the college, such as its multicultural heritage and its curricular strengths, they also worked toward moving the college closer to the marketplace to acquire resources so that the college could sustain itself. On the one hand, the mission expanded—college members were doing more, reaching international markets and students, increasing distance education offerings, adding service learning programs, integrating multiculturalism into the curriculum. But on the other hand, in moving closer to the marketplace the college set priorities, establishing a structure for areas of the mission that would increase or diminish. Those areas that brought financial benefits to the college, either through increased enrollments or increased revenues or both, gained a higher priority. Those activities that did not perform in this way and that were peripheral to the financial aspirations of the college achieved a low priority. In the case of remedial education, those who could afford to pay, the lower socioeconomic division of the community, had their education threatened, removed. But remedial education as a program remained at the institution in a non-credit, continuing education area, because its enrollments did not falter and the program paid its way. Thus, while the mission of providing remedial education did not change, the population served by this program altered. The new, targeted population was intended to be those not only locally but those in other countries, and thus the traditional community college mission of serving all of society began to alter as the college increasingly served a specific segment of its own society and the elite of other societies.

For Pacific Suburban Community College, both geography and history were destiny: that is, location of both the institution and the state as well as institutional history were highly influential for the actions of the college. These actions were strategies for adapting the institution to its environment. In the late 1990s, the college was consumed with its fiscal situation: dependent upon a state government that had declining revenues as a consequence of its reliance upon a single industry—tourism—to support the economy. Tourism in the case of the state of Hawaii was tied to the fortunes of the Asian economy, particularly that of Japan. The state was vulnerable to international economic shocks, and the college was in turn vulnerable to the state and its economic performance. The island economy, like many of its natural attributes, was fragile.[11]

The stable pattern of the 1980s and indeed the early 1990s began to give way to market forces—international forces—and Pacific Suburban Community College turned its assets into products to sell on the local and international market. With more dependency upon students as fee payers and non-governmental resource providers, the college moved down an unfamiliar path. Furthermore, the college planned to alter how it managed itself, turning to current business practices, particularly high technology business models of entrepreneurial and highly responsive operations, a model rare in the public higher education sector. This suggests that faculty work would alter too, with faculty required to become more entrepreneurial, more engaged in the development, marketing, and delivery of their products. But at the close of the 1990s, the college remained predominantly an academic environment serving largely university-bound students, through traditional methods of instruction, within a bureaucratic structure. In altering its operations, Pacific Suburban Community College would have to undo much of its history.

City Center College: Buffered by Government, Bound by History

Population demographics of the local community as well as institutional history and government actions were influential in organizational actions at City Center College. The college had a reputation as a basic education institution with major emphasis upon English language training. In this context, the college served its local community, which had a large immigrant population, particularly a large Asian population, and this service emphasized English language training, with close to 50 percent of the college's students enrolled in coursework. Although students from Asian countries had professional expertise in their country of origin, in Canada that expertise was questioned and employment in any field for these students required English language competency. Accompanying population demographics, federal government immigration policies, and federal funding for language training were heavily influential in college programming.

The college was connected to a global environment through its large immigrant population both within the college and in the community. From 1992 to 1997, over 30,000 immigrants a year settled in the college's community. Of the total population of this community for the early to the mid-1990s, immigrants comprised 10.8 percent of that population.[12]

Except for this large, local immigrant population, Asian and Eastern European dominated, the college faced little direct confrontation with global forces. The college was largely bounded by other systems, agencies, and structures—from the provincial government to the provincial collective bargaining framework to the federal government's immigration department—and hence buffered from global forces. Instead, City Center College responded to others' responses: for example, to the actions of government funding of public institutions to cope with declining taxation revenues from industry involved in Asian markets. In the past decade, City Center College reduced its interactions with an international and global environment, first by reducing its international education operatior second by narrowing its curricular and programming focus as a consequence of the loss of its third campus. While the international education activities reportedly did not generate expected revenues, they did focus the college outside of its community and led to international associations, training, and reputational image. In this way, the college was not as bounded by the provincial government and looked beyond its role as a social agency or community resource. Its narrower curricular and programming focus, while likely strengthening its local community responsiveness, limited the college's educational connection to larger-scope institutions such as the local universities and detached the college from high-level skills and advanced technologies that come with such programs as engineering, computer systems, and undergraduate science.

The role of the provincial government in organizational change for City Center College was significant. Not only was government the principal funder of the institution but also government was the only creditor of the college, as the institution found itself in an illegal debt situation in the early 1990s, and government concessions enabled the college to pay back the debt without penalty. This financial relationship no doubt increased institutional dependency upon government and furthered adherence to government policy. Additionally, government actions in the province to oversee the establishment and functioning of a province-wide collective bargaining process with college unions and the government moratorium on capital projects and on raises in student tuition increased City Center's dependency upon a government and its agency, the department responsible for postsecondary education. Government policy emphasized public sector responsiveness to the economic sector, greater institutional productivity, such as the training and education of more students with the same or fewer resources, and the preparation of a work force for global competition.

Although the college was heavily influenced by its context—its history, its local community, and its relationship to government—managers ironically relied upon symbolic behaviors to direct organizational actions. Managers were limited in the objective manipulation of the college and its environment; instead, managers functioned symbolically, managing and manipulating meanings and interpretations. For example, in the mid-1990s while the college budget was almost fully committed to specific expenditures, college managers engaged with other campus members in extensive planning about the direction of the college, both on a day-to-day basis and over an extended period of time. City Center College organizational members, including board members, devoted considerable time to internal organizational matters, such as review and revision of mission, integration of campuses, and meetings and internal communications. Nonetheless, adaptation did not rely upon symbolic action, largely because managerial and other institutional actions did not alter environments. Instead, symbolic behaviors constituted coping mechanisms for college members.

From one perspective, the college adapted to its environment in two traditional and foundational ways. First, organizational managers defined CCC's environment as its local community, and thus they conceived of the college's role as a responsive institution to its immediate external community. To some extent, college members acted to give the institution a specific identity and to meet goals consistent with that identity. Second, the college responded to student demand, and that demand was a local demand for language training, basic skills, employment preparation, and specific vocational training. Its programs reflected the demographics of a large segment of its immediate community, particularly its immigrant and lower socioeconomic status community. Not only were there large numbers of immigrants in the college's community but also a large number of those who were unemployed. During the decade, the unemployment rate was between 8.1 and 9.3 percent.[13] Thus, college actions conformed to environmental characteristics.

The prominent influence of the college's local and student population cannot be overestimated. The high percentage of immigrants and non-native English language speakers were the instructional focus of CCC. Thus, the college adapted to its local population, based upon their demographic characteristics. Furthermore, college members were internally focused. That is, their energies were directed to maintenance, especially the preservation of historical patterns in personnel practices and employment gains, such as worker benefits and job security, as well as formal bureaucratic positions.

Changes in the 1990s to the governing board of City Center College were also influential in organizational actions. Foremost among these changes was the appointment of board members whose personal backgrounds matched the prevailing policies of the government in power. Furthermore, this government's ideological orientation matched that of the college's local community, whose demographic characteristics corresponded to the targeted population of government policy, including visible minorities, displaced and unemployed workers, social assistance clients of the government, and new immigrants.

Strategy at City Center College was two-pronged: address expectations and learning requirements of the local community and attend to internal organizational structures and finances. The college's history of financial difficulties, especially prior to the mid-1990s, sensitized college members and especially administrators to budget deficits. A college debt and earlier deficits provided a considerable incentive to the college's leadership to ensure that finances were managed prudently. Thus, the senior financial officer of the college claimed a position of influence in college actions, the board of governors served as an important watchdog, and college managers were charged with controlling expenditures. While this emphasis on fiscal matters had justification, the fear of debt, deficits, and ultimate cutbacks led many college members to a condition of stasis. The strategy worked, but the consequences led to other problems, such as low employee morale and an entrenched mission.

The mission of the college was largely built upon a programmatic foundation: developmental education, remedial education, and language education and training. In this way, the college responded to and interacted with an external environment. Other actions of the college, such as securing fiscal resources through the private sector, were acts to preserve and support the mission of the college. The college lost its academic programs, through the establishment of its third campus as an independent college. But college administrators were not seriously concerned about either the loss of academic programs or the focus upon a narrow curriculum. A board member noted, "We are good at what we do. . . . We have the market on the group we serve. . . ." Other college members indicated that altering mission was neither of interest to them nor part of the college discussion.

What was of interest to college members was personal welfare for many and college survival for others. That is, issues of employment security, workload, and retirement, as well as concerns over the college's ability to maintain itself economically, were foremost in the thoughts of college members, administrators, faculty, and support staff.

There was therefore a conceptual tension here between the college mission of serving its local community, including serving community members with appropriate educational and training programs, and the condition of college insularity with regard to its external environment, especially the environment beyond its local community. There was an apparent stasis because of economic and personal fears. While the college viewed its actions as serving its community, it was also becoming more internally focused upon governance, upon facilities and their need for improvement, upon fiscal resources, and upon internal politics. It was as if a hostile environment—the emphasis provincially upon economic globalization, the sophisticated needs of a competitive work force, and the complexity of electronic communications—had pushed members underground.

City Center College was tightly bounded by its environment. This environment included not only its local community but also the provincial government, the provincial government's agent for postsecondary education, the provincial structure for collective bargaining, and the college's own collective agreements with its employees. The college was also clearly directed by its institutional history. That history included not only the existence of a third campus, now an independent college, but also fiscal debt and financial crises. The financial history shaped present behaviors, making college members both fearful of economic ruin and partially immobilized in acting to alter college behaviors. The loss of the third campus significantly altered the college's curriculum and thus its mission.

Nonetheless, City Center College adapted to its new environment and to its own history by identifying and attempting to secure a credible position in the educational system of its region—bounded by universities, public colleges, proprietary schools, and secondary adult education institutions. To some extent, the college became a specialized postsecondary educational institution, emphasizing programs and services required by community members. In this vein, the college returned to some of the foundational principles of the community college including responsiveness to community needs and facilitators of democratization.[14] Yet, the college's reclaiming of a foundational role of the community college could also be seen as a response of localism, a rejection of globalization but an acknowledgment of its influence.[15] In college identification with its particularly narrow definition of its local community—what Appadurai calls a local fetish[16]—college members may have expressed their sense of alienation from the larger society.

Rural Valley College: Mission in Transition

Four dominant behaviors signaled the impact of global forces upon Rural Valley College. These included education and training, governance, financing, and labor relations. All of these behaviors emanated from the provincial government and its departments or agencies. To improve the economy, buffeted by international markets and economies, government policy supported and indeed promoted work-force training, higher-level educational attainment, and higher-level participation rates, not least to reduce the high provincial unemployment figures, which ran close to the 10 percent rate. Government expended millions of additional dollars in the early 1990s to support the evolution of university-colleges—four-year degree-granting community colleges. Rural Valley College was a recipient of a share of these funds. The outcomes of the development of university-colleges in the province, and this was the case for RVC, included significant growth in student numbers, faculty, and facilities. An unintended outcome was major growth in fields not traditionally connected to employment or job training—the liberal arts. Accompanying this growth was increasing academic professionalism and provincial faculty union power. In the mid-1990s, the government enacted legislation to alter governance structures at colleges so that faculty had not only voice in decision-making but also a partially shared role with administrators in managing the institution, because faculty were given the dominant role on an educational council, a senate-type body and the preeminent academic decision-making body in the institution.

At Rural Valley College, alterations from a two-year to a four-year institution led to reduced attention to the local community and greater attention to internal academic concerns and governance and management matters, such as scholarship, program credibility, and university status. It also led to tensions among groups, as some areas prospered and others became impoverished and disillusioned, reproducing in microcosm the concept of "winners" and "losers" characteristic of economic globalization. Thus financing was a factor of institutional change. Following the early 1990s efforts to establish university-colleges, government funding altered both in its *largesse* and in its *laissez-faire* approach to oversight.

Beginning in the mid-1990s, government funding behaviors were more restrictive and controlling. There was less public sector funding from the provincial government relative to institutional growth. As a share of revenue, provincial grants fell from 73 percent of total revenues to 70 percent, whereas tuition fees rose from 14.6 percent to 21 percent of total revenues. This suggests that public sector spending reductions meant private consumer spending increases, a clear example of the privatization of public education. Furthermore, and probably most significant, government began to fund using competitive measures—whether outcomes measures of institutional productivity or input measures for lowest cost—in order to control college behaviors and actions. Thus, Rural Valley College as an evolving, developing, and growing institution in the early 1990s was required to accept and abide by government policy if maintenance of growth was to be preserved in the latter part of the 1990s. Government policy included furthering privatization of college services and increasing productivity.

The fourth set of behaviors influenced by the provincial government was labor relations. In the 1990s, these moved from the local level to the provincial level, suggesting a system-wide approach to both personnel relations and to labor. It suggested as well that an industrial model of state control over production in education and training was evolving in the province so that the government could have more control over the economy. Thus, in controlling labor relations, the government could to a greater extent control labor unrest and work stoppages, not only costly to the economy but also a negative incentive for international investors.

The provincial government served as an intermediary force, buffering the college from direct confrontation with global forces of change and translating those forces into its own political agenda. This political agenda contained several social goals, such as increasing access to postsecondary education and training, and several economic goals, such as reducing the burden on government for postsecondary system expansion. These goals were not necessarily compatible, or at least they provided tensions and conflicts to those institutions that were coping with these goals. Conditions at Rural Valley College demonstrated the tensions between institutional growth and lower levels of government fiscal support.

Although the college adapted through choices that were consistent with government priorities, adaptation was stimulated primarily by government initiatives and secondarily by growth. Thus, the external environment, largely in the form of the provincial government, heavily influenced college actions, and internal change, conceptualized as growth, required the college to adjust its structures and processes, such as its acquisition of resources, its hiring of 100 new full-time faculty, and its development of programs. Set against these adaptation approaches were the traditional patterns of institutional behaviors and shared values of institutional members.

College members in asserting the importance of their college's traditional mission of service to community and their autonomy to make decisions as a collegial institution, formed an alliance in opposition to a government they viewed as hostile: "We feel they owe us more than they give us." This alliance united disparate groups, aiding college members in working together not only to maintain their traditional mission of serving the community by maintaining and expanding access but also to adjust to new institutional structures and processes without dysfunctional conflict. Their strong culture, a collegial pattern of behaviors since the college's inception, was sustained through presidential leadership, at least until 1998 when a new president filled the role.

Relations between employees and administrators had a positive history, largely attributed to the labor relations environment at the college. This resulted in considerable unified action on the part of college members. In contrast to labor and management relations, personal relationships among several administrators exhibited friction and value difference, and increasingly made coordinated action more difficult. During the 1990s, the personal value system of the president—belief in autonomy, informal relations, liberal education—drove college strategy and functioned to balance the various opposing values of administrators.

Strategy at Rural Valley College contained contradictory ideas: to develop into a four-year degree-granting institution while maintaining the purposes of a community college and acquire resources to sustain growth and development. These strategies were not without their impediments. The development of a hybrid institution, merging a functioning community college with the concept of a university or four-year college, involved clashes with differing expectations and value systems. For example, while the community college promotes egalitarianism, the university champions expertise; and while the community college's mission is expansive and multifaceted, the university's traditional mission is threefold: teaching, research, and service. Moreover, community college faculty are both theoretically and empirically unlike university faculty, including their level of education, their social class, and their value systems.[17]

Strategy also involved the pursuit and acquisition of resources by college members, a response both to perceived government deterioration in funding and to government policy and funding incentives for institutions to rely less upon government and more upon the private sector. One notable contradiction here was that government froze tuition fees for a three-year period, nullifying the student as an ever expanding source of non-government funding. Rural Valley College enlarged its contract services activities, its international education behaviors which until 1997 led to increasing student numbers, and its partnerships with school districts and civic government in order to acquire more resources. But these actions served largely to offset and not supplement provincial government funding grants, and by 1996–1997 the college found itself with less revenue than in 1995–1996, although about $4 million more than in 1993–1994. And because of government alterations to funding—moving base grant funding money to competitive one-time funding—the college could not rely upon either competitive funding for more than a year or upon "earned revenues" from contracts as ongoing sources of funds. Thus, the acquisition of non-base funding was not compatible with the functioning of an educational enterprise, especially one that offered four-year degree programs, because educational behaviors required a stable context over an extended time period, and the sources to support those endeavors were transitory and unstable.

The mission of the college was not only undergoing change but also receiving serious and wide-ranging reflection by institutional members. Divergent views on the college's mission, and indeed upon the college's identity, while apparent since the development of the college as a university-college surfaced as the major college issue in the latter part of the 1990s. On the one hand the college had developed into a new form of postsecondary institution, driven most recently by faculty in the four-year degree programs and their students. This new form emphasized many of the values, traditions, and behaviors of a university. These supported the advances of a senate-type body, the central role of disciplines, growth in academic areas, particularly the liberal arts, and the diminution of pre-college programming such as adult basic education. Furthermore, faculty in the four-year degree program areas questioned the value of a union as constituted to serve their interests. Present systems and structures did not necessarily fit either four-year degree program areas or an expanding institution.

On the other hand the intent of faculty and administrators to maintain and preserve community college values and purposes was forceful among a large proportion of organizational members. Particularly acute among faculty in non-four-year degree program areas, among faculty located on other than the main campus, and among long-term administrators and staff, was the desire to remain a college devoted to its communities, with emphasis upon the development of the whole student not just cognitive and intellectual development.

Thus, from this perspective, the mission of Rural Valley College was conflicted, and numerous exercises from strategic planning to budget allocation were identity debates and perceived as identity decisions. Nonetheless, the college was not a fractious environment; instead, it had become more tolerant of diverse views and diverse cultures than in the past. Its new role as a baccalaureate institution and the influx of new faculty from cosmopolitan environments enlarged the community served by the college and altered both the approach to education services and the content of programs and the curricula in general. This development was surprising to the extent that in the communities served by the college, Christian fundamentalism not liberal or socialist thinking was prominent.

College personnel were, however, engaged in an institutional identity shift. Faculty and administrators at RVC while expressing the general view that the purposes of the institution were not altering indicated that significant structural changes occurred in the past decade with a variety of alterations anticipated. Institutional alterations arose, most prominently, from the establishment of four-year degree programs and from legislative changes to governance, especially the formalization of a senate-type body and related decision-making and recommending bodies. Government funding behaviors, initially supportive of degree programming in the early 1990s, became antagonistic by the later part of the mid-1990s as significant growth—approximately 100 percent of fulltime equivalency students in a decade—was no longer propelled or even sustained by the provincial government. The government cited international economies and markets as causes of government restraint—for example, the forestry and lumber industry entered a steady decline in the 1990s with resultant job losses and decreasing government revenues,[18] a pattern echoing the 1980s which led to permanent job losses, especially in government service.[19]

While organizational members, especially long-serving members, struggled with maintaining traditional community college principles and behaviors, Rural Valley College evolved into a new category of institution. New structures, including programs and decision-making, and new employees, principally university-socialized faculty, precipitated several fundamental changes to the institution. Yet, simultaneous with the evolution of Rural Valley to a four-year institution emphasizing liberal arts, government behaviors in the mid and late-1990s pushed the institution closer to the marketplace. This pressure to pursue non-government revenues and to emphasize work-force training and skill development, even in baccalaureate degree programs, not only moved the college closer to the needs of business and industry but also altered college purposes to give priority to training for employment. The provincial government thus acted as an economic globalizing force, moving the mission of the college to not just to a higher education level but to a work-force training focus.

North Mountain College: The Business and Industry School

Two vehicles serving a global environment influenced North Mountain College: these included the provincial government and local business and industry. The provincial government, through its policies and funding behaviors, directed and coerced the college to respond and adjust to its neoconservative approach to the economy and increasingly neoconservative approach to social programs: debt and deficit reduction, less reliance of the public sector upon government, protection of business interests, privatization, and a market-oriented economy; as well, privatization of social programs such as education and health, work without welfare, and individual responsibility not government dependence. Local business and industry while instrumental in government policy and behaviors were internationally focused, largely because of their products and competitors. These interests also influenced North Mountain College, as the college adapted its programming and its operations to suit business and industry. Thus, NMC responded through specialized work-force training in its programming and productivity and efficiency in its operations.

The use of electronic technology, ever increasing both in practice and in rhetoric, was a primary vehicle to enact both of these responses. While students at NMC were not all, or even in large numbers, necessarily trained in the use of electronic technology, they were exposed to it through instruction and through college services. Work at NMC underwent significant alteration through the increasing use of electronic technology, in such areas as information management and communications. Through these alterations, NMC was more businesslike and corporate in its functioning. But neither education nor productivity were stimulated solely by electronic technology.

Education and training were affected by ideology, evident in government policy, business practices, and college administrative behaviors and articulations. The establishment of the four-year applied degrees programs was a noteworthy example. These programs were intended to suffice as high level training for a "competitive economy," they served the needs of business and industry, they satisfied government expectations, and they increased both the status and the profile of the college in the community. While in 1997, they constituted approximately 5 percent of college credit enrollments (even with a nursing program that is part of a four-year degree program at another institution, they constituted only 10 percent of enrollments), they occupied a substantial part of the college's attention and its evolving identity; they served as a contested area, a subject of conflict, between faculty and administration and among faculty groups; and they were promoted by college managers as a model of college preferences for arts and sciences education. These programs represented the reliance of the college upon business and industry not only for attracting students to the college and ultimately student placements for employment but also for industry approval of postsecondary education programming, thus acquiring the favor of this sector as well as some of their resources. The four-year applied programs furthered the vocationalizing tendency of postsecondary education—educating and training for jobs—and they further stratified postsecondary institutions and their students, to the extent that traditional programs and skills in the vocations were not as valued. These four-year programs stressed employability of graduates and had selective entry; they claimed to train for a profession, as opposed to a trade or vocation, or even an occupation. But they were neither liberal arts and sciences programs nor even traditional professional schooling such as engineering or law. They are suggestive of the lower end of Reich's new professional class—symbolic analysts[20]—likely those who support these analysts in a clerical or technical capacity.

Although a number of factors contributed to the college's approach to adaptation, the college, largely through its administrative group, exhibited a highly rational and strategic response to environmental stimuli, whether those were government decreases in funding or changing workplace requirements. College decision-making behaviors entailed the elaborate use of committees and advisory bodies. These served numerous purposes, largely strategic. For example, they reinforced not only strategy but also the rationale for strategy; they suggested group acceptance of strategy; and they served to coordinate labor, especially work committed to fulfill strategy. Overall, these committees and bodies indicated high levels of consultation on decisions during decision-making and prior to implementation.

College administrators were constantly adapting the institution to the environment so that no opportunity for resource acquisition was lost. Thus, what was referred to as "the flavor of the month," in response to the behaviors of the president to adopting a new approach or a new idea, was one interpretation of the college adjusting to trends—in work, in pedagogy, in programming—that might yield returns, largely fiscal. NMC performed at a high level in government accountability measures. In enrollments, the college continued to grow even in the face of serious government cutbacks to the institution. And in revenues, the college courted and received the favors of business, industry, and the community, generating, for example, over $10 million in a fundraising campaign during the late 1990s. Thus, the international pursuits and image, the embrace of electronic technologies, the emphasis upon outcomes based learning, and the redefinition of a two-year institution into a four-year institution were all part of the strategic approach of the institution's leaders, including its governing board members, not just for survival but for growth.

The college was nonetheless heavily reliant upon the provincial economy, an economy that experienced serious boom and bust cycles. In the 1990s, government fiscal restraint was attributed to the government's attack on debt and deficit. As a consequence, the government's grants to North Mountain College fell by close to 20 percent over a three-year period. Furthermore, the Japanese economy faltered in mid-1990s, and the college's strategies to pursue revenues through international education, especially in Japan and other Asian countries, were affected.

Although there was considerable debate among college employees about the value and outcomes of the numerous strategies in effect at NMC, there was wide agreement about what these strategies were at the college. Strategies at the institutional level included the alteration of college operations so that college behaviors were more businesslike—that is, directed to outcomes and quantitative productivity—and changes to curriculum and instruction so that efficiency, productivity, and market responsiveness were emphasized. In both college operations and in education, electronic technologies were increasingly used as "drivers of change" (in the language of organizational managers) and a means to achieve efficiency, as well as for their utility as conveyors of a sophisticated image of the institution as technologically fit. There was widespread agreement that the college's management positioned the institution closer to the marketplace and modeled corporate behaviors.

In spite of these corporate behaviors, the college maintained its tradition of an elaborate committee structure, associated with higher education institutions, with their characteristics of "loose-coupling"[21] and unregulated and dynamic participation of employees in decision-making. At North Mountain College, the committee structure was both a vestige of academic governance and a quality-control device. These committees were used by management to control and coordinate work: principally by the president and the academic vice-president to manage institutional strategy; primarily by other senior managers to ensure consistency and efficiency; and commonly by faculty for information exchange and the maintenance of group identity. For every administrative position, there was either a committee or an advisory body: thus, the president had an executive committee; the academic vice president had a deans' council; and the administrative vice president had a vice-president's advisory council. Deans oversaw councils for department and program heads; programs had advisory bodies; and departments, programs, and academic divisions had several committees. At the institutional level, an academic council served as the chief academic advisory body, comprised of institutional representatives, including students. This body advised the college's board of governors, which itself had several committees to advise the board as a whole. While this structure was not dissimilar from those at other academic institutions, North Mountain College administrative leaders utilized these structures strategically so that official or managerially sanctioned information and college management goals and work priorities were communicated in a fairly consistent way in every venue.

Although the college management, the faculty, and the staff lamented the intrusion of the provincial government into the management of the institution, the college's official responses to government initiatives and policy had a strategic cast. First, college management used government policy to change the organization in such ways as increasing class sizes for greater productivity and in moving the college closer to the marketplace both to attract students and to garner private sector revenues. Second, the college management responded positively to government policy and incentives to increase the use of electronic technologies both in work and in instruction: in so doing, the college gained favor and revenues from the government, pursued its goal of greater efficiency through the use of labor-saving technologies, and fostered an external image of a sophisticated institution. Third, the college management took advantage of the government's initiative to establish four-year degree programs at selective colleges in the province. NMC strenuously lobbied government and on achieving approval to offer four-year programs, embarked on a marketing campaign to promote the institution as a high-quality undergraduate institution, placing it in competition with other four-year degree granting institutions, principally the local university. Thus, college managers used government to their best advantage, furthering administrative interests and securing greater control over institutional behaviors.

North Mountain College altered its mission in the 1990s in several significant areas. Most prominent was the alteration from a traditional community college, with two-year diploma programs as the highest level of academic attainment, to a four-year college, combining attributes of a traditional community college and a baccalaureate degree institution. Although numerous faculty and administrators did not identify changes in the 1990s as more than an elaboration of the existing mission, North Mountain College evolved into a four-year college, with emphasis upon applied rather than academic education, and serving vocational aspirations of students and employment needs of local business and industry.

The college furthered its image and reputation as an adaptable, market-sensitive, globally oriented institution through the increasing use of electronic technology, both in instruction and management, through programmatic changes, through striving for and achieving greater productivity, and through less reliance upon government grants for operations. These behaviors assisted the college in the generation of revenues and corresponded with increasing enrollments.

Altering structures included large increases in work for faculty, staff, and especially administrators, and faster-paced work for all. Organizational management structures altered to address growth and the requirement of external responsiveness. But these alterations were minor modifications to existing structures and did little to alleviate the problem of lack of efficiency that change was intended to address.

At issue here was the management's approach to institutional work. Managers expected themselves, each other, and faculty and staff to become increasingly more productive, "doing more with less" and "working to exhaustion" to fulfill a number of institutional aspirations. These included greater autonomy from government, the accommodation of ever-increasing growth, and responsiveness to marketplace demands. Thus, the mission of the college altered, substantially, from an institution that provided a supermarket approach to programming and services to the local community to an institution that serves both society's economic producers and the labor for economic production.

The provincial government played a substantial role in altering college mission. Although the provincial government's share of contributions to college operations diminished considerably in the mid-1990s, the government required the college to conform to its expectations. These expectations were driven by a business-industrial and global nexus,[22] which pushed the college further toward an emphasis upon productivity and work-force preparation, which included the credentialing of business and industry workers up to the baccalaureate level. In embracing the ethos and requirements of a globally competitive economic environment, North Mountain College detached itself from its mission of educational access and a comprehensive curriculum for all adult learners. College programming advanced toward skills development for employment, the vocationalization of curriculum, and away from academic preparation and academic studies in the liberal arts tradition.

In addition to the provincial government and local business and industry, the college president, in concert with other college managers and the governing board of the college, was also responsible for the alterations to mission and structures. In his articulations, external activities, especially in international venues, and his leadership behaviors, the college president enacted a strategy that led to substantial growth, programmatic change, organizational productivity, and responsiveness to the needs and interests of business and industry.

North Mountain College exhibited characteristics of several kinds of organization, including a professional bureaucracy, a rational bureaucracy, a corporation, and labor-management factory or business, among other types. This variety was both emblematic of a shifting institutional identity—for example, from a two-year to a four-year college—and a likely outcome of numerous influences upon the institution over the past decade. Certainly, the institution's history as a liberal arts college was instrumental in the academic milieu of the institution; but the institution's location and its proximity to an internationally competitive business community helped to push the college to both a corporate image and businesslike behaviors. The faculty at the institution were part of a certified bargaining unit, and from time to time, especially during the mid-1990s, the institution lost some of its academic and bureaucratic identity and gained a more overt political structure. Although managerial strategy directed the college in the 1990s, the multiple organizational contexts and organizational types of the institution acted as foils for strategy. They proved to be increasingly less effective against a force that was supported by the provincial government and the leadership of local business and industry.

North Mountain College was suggestive of one kind of emerging postmodern and globalizing organization, demonstrating tensions between its modern role as a comprehensive, government-funded public institution and a postmodern market-oriented, work-force preparatory four-year school, serving economic needs. Its context was important to the extent that business and industry had substantial influence upon both the college and the provincial government, whose policies reflected economic concerns and economic quality-of-life improvements. Connected to international economies—for capital, for markets, and for products—and influenced by a global economy for standards of work-force skills and productivity, local business and industry placed both the provincial government and North Mountain College in a global context. Thus, NMC was required to look businesslike, international, technologically fit, and market-relevant in order to gain credibility with local business and industry.

Altered Patterns of Organizational Behavior

Patterns of behavior that one would find in community colleges in the 1970s and 1980s were evident in the 1990s, but added to these was an emerging set of patterns, surfacing and becoming institutionalized as a consequence of globalization and responses to globalization. The preservation of institutional identity—that is, the identity of a traditional community college that responds to the needs of its local community, that emphasizes teaching and learning, that offers comprehensive and accessible education and training programs—was present, but only in part. Added to these preservation behaviors was a set of behaviors that promoted alteration to this identity, favoring practices and goals imitative of businesses and corporations in some cases and modeling university behaviors in others. The pursuit of growth, while still a pattern of behavior, altered from a primary focus upon the expansion of mission or greater inclusion of the underserved[23] to an avenue for revenue. In our seven colleges, the balance was tipped in the 1990s to favor training over education, the business community over the social community, and corporatism over collegiality. Globalization played a crucial role in these alterations. Both institutional and government responses to globalization molded each institution, differentiating one from another.

CHAPTER 8

WHAT REMAINS BEHIND: THE COMMUNITY COLLEGE IN THE TWENTY-FIRST CENTURY

The argument and discussion to this point suggest that the community college is a different institution at the close of the twentieth century, altered from previous decades along several dimensions. These alterations are explained as consequences, in large part, of organizational responses to global forces. The forces include not only the global economy but also the global flows of immigration and communications. Moreover, global forces are also mediated by the state, and thus government responses to global pressures constitute a component of global forces that affect institutions. Both global forces and community college responses to these have yielded an institution I refer to as globalized—that is, an institution that reflects the globalizing process in its organizational actions and perpetuates or advances globalization through its actions. On the one hand, the 1990s constituted a period of considerable organizational change, with alterations to community colleges' structures and processes. On the other hand, during the 1990s, the institution of the community college began to embark on a path of significant change, altering its mission and its identity as an institution.

Organizational Change

Levy and Merry[1] develop a conceptual framework for organizational change premised upon the concept of second-order, fundamental, and enduring change. Four categories of change are used in their framework: paradigmatic change, mission and purpose change, cultural change, and change in functional processes, including structures, management, technology, decision-making and communication patterns. In using this framework for community colleges in the 1990s, I applied these categories to the seven cases.

Paradigm

Paradigmatic change refers to alteration to the assumptions of those who are stakeholders and influencers of the organization. This change also suggests that the organizational world-view has altered: that organizational members define their institution differently and regard their institutional context as altered over time.

For community colleges, several assumptions remained in the 1990s relatively unchanged from the 1980s. These assumptions included the majority of traditional community college principles,[2] such as access to postsecondary education opportunities and a comprehensive curriculum.

Nonetheless, several organizational assumptions altered in the 1990s. These included new assumptions adopted and former assumptions discarded or modified. For example, the assumption about the primary role of the institution altered in the 1990s. In the 1970s and 1980s, the role of the community college could be said to be largely social and educational.[3] But by the end of the 1980s and the beginning of the 1990s, according to the literature, this role began to shift to an economic one.[4] This shift is evident empirically in the 1990s.[5] "Preparation for jobs," "competing in a global economy," "the engine of the economy," "skills development," "economic renewal for local communities," "academic upgrading," and "training" and "credentialing a competitive workforce" were among the many similar characterizations of the institution, both its goals and roles.[6] Furthermore, college members acknowledged a dramatically different environment from the 1980s, and this environment was economically driven:

> There is more technology, more distance education: it is training versus classical education. The pressures of business will define our goals. Money drives.... [We are being shown] how faculty are no longer necessary.... [We have] canned programs online. Technology is available to serve more students, but there is no discussion on what it does for students. Faculty bury their heads; morale is not good.
> (Faculty union president, Suburban Valley Community College)

> There are fast changes in the college.... There are lots of assumptions about what and why we do things, but we don't check these. We pride ourselves in how we are organized and set up, but we don't check. Changes are on-

going: change feeds upon itself. There are rising pressures for change, for example, student demand. There is tension between our responsibility as social and political citizens and economic citizenship.

(Department chair, Social Sciences, Rural Valley College)

The affluent days of the 1980s and early '90s are not to be seen again. . . . Present fashion of entrepreneurship: can [higher education] drive the economy? But [higher education institutions] are not entrepreneurial, not their job. The economy forces [the institution] to examine practices and to think about the future.

(Governing board member, Pacific Suburban Community College)

We are using a training factory approach: offer what is marketable. We are a free-market organization, and people are added or taken away. We are not preserving fields as we should. . . . We operate on a market model. . . . The provincial government has put all its eggs in the basket of creating employment. The college is moving closer to a business.

(Faculty member and governance committee executive,
East Shoreline College)

We are going through a watershed in education. There is a changing workplace. The needs of students do include fundamental intellectual skills. . . . We build in all programs academic development, career preparation, experiential learning, which is a fusion of work and learning, and a set of skills for the new economy. . . . There is rapidity of change and enormous proliferation of information.

(President, North Mountain College)

Employer demands are tougher: they want skills and decision-making, critical thinking. . . . We are changing technology, with distance learning, on-line courses, and registration. This takes time. . . . We are working with employers. We need different services for different companies. Faculty training is required.

(Faculty, English as a Second Language, City South Community College)

The college is committed to [the mission] statement but not borne out in reality. Mission claims we are student-centered, but we are not student-centered. Economic survival is our real mission. [We are part of the marketplace:] we sell the place; we are almost exploitative, the opposite of student-centered.

(Faculty member, Counseling, City Center College)

The primary role of these institutions was perceived as driven by government as well as by business and industry and student demand.

The prevalence of electronic technology in everyday life and cognizance of both this prevalence and the necessity of its use formed another assumption present at these institutions. Unlike the 1980s, when electronic technologies were gradually accepted as part of both administrative work and instruction, in the 1990s these colleges embraced electronic technologies as critical elements of both work and education. From student registration to financial accounting, from organizational communications to classroom- and non-classroom-based instruction, electronic technologies were viewed as indispensable.

A third assumption that altered from previous decades was the curricular role of community colleges, particularly in the baccalaureate degree area. This assumption was evident largely in the Canadian institutions, in Alberta and British Columbia. This altered assumption and its consequences challenged the traditional definition of a community college. At the institutions in Alberta and British Columbia, organizational members, especially administrators and faculty responsible for baccalaureate programs, no longer viewed their institution as a two-year college. In Alberta, North Mountain College administrators referred to their college as an "undergraduate institution." In British Columbia, East Shoreline College administrators and faculty alike talked about their institution as a university. At Rural Valley College in British Columbia, organizational members were confused about and questioned the college's identity as either a community college or a university. In the United States, focus upon the provision of the baccalaureate degree at community colleges in several states, including, for example, Arizona and Florida, neglected to acknowledge the potential and even likelihood of altering the structure of higher education in the United States and the historical niche of the community college.[7]

Fourth and finally, as an example of the assumptions about the role of the institution, is contract training. In both countries, contract training became much more than an ancillary activity, increasing in both practice and in promotion.[8] These actions, too, reflected changing assumptions about the curricular role and function of community colleges.

Mission and Purpose

Mission and purpose refer to intentionality of organizational members and other stakeholders with respect to organizational actions and outcomes. Three areas in which mission and purpose altered include fiscal resources, organizational identity, and social activism. College members, especially administrators, pursued fiscal resources more deliberately and aggressively than in the past; college officials praised and valued entrepreneurial behaviors of organizational members and organizational units. College administrators endeavored to increase enrollments not because mission expansion motivated such action but rather because student numbers were economic commodities. Government funding in one way or another was tied to enrollments—a drop in these, for example, equaled a drop in government fiscal allocations.

College members devoted more time to organizational image and status within the education sector than in the past. Suburban Valley Community College expended considerable energy in fostering an external image and in reinforcing that image internally among organizational members. The message from organizational members at Suburban Valley Community College was that the institution was an innovative, high-tech, and university transfer-oriented institution, superior to all competitors. North Mountain College administrators, board members, and some faculty promoted their institution as a superior "undergraduate institution," characterized by sophisticated programming and technology. Institutional prestige is pursued on a national basis for U.S. community colleges through a selective national organization. The League for Innovation in the Community College, which has fewer than two dozen member colleges, is touted as "an educational consortium of leading community colleges in the United States and Canada dedicated to experimentation and innovation."[9] League members view themselves as exemplars of the progressive spirit of the community college, making them images for emulation. Member institutions claim that electronic technology use enhances and to some extent drives innovation, claiming that League colleges have the reputation of being at the forefront of "transforming teaching and learning through technology."[10]

Finally, colleges gave considerable attention to multiculturalism and diversity. Hiring practices, curricula, and extracurricular activities reflected this change in purpose from largely passive in the previous decades to active in the 1990s. For example, City South Community College formalized a curricular requirement that associate's degree students complete a cultural studies course. Special units or structures, such as First Nations centers, meditation rooms, and affirmative action committees, were either created where they previously did not exist or were enlarged and formalized where they did exist in the past. With large numbers of minority students in the United States and increasing numbers of students who are immigrants or second-generation immigrants in both countries attending community colleges, practices and structures were modified to address student needs.

Culture

Cultural changes refer to beliefs, norms, and values of organizational members. It is difficult to identify a single collective culture, and it may be more appropriate to view an organization as comprised of various cultures, some ideographic, unique and expressive of a singular ethos, and others holographic, expressive of the attributes of a larger, institutional culture. Colleges exhibited several alterations in both members' and the corporate institution's articulated beliefs, norms, and values, although these were in transition. For example, there was more emphasis upon pluralism among various units within the institutions and little discussion about uniformity or, as one department chair noted for the earlier period of the 1970s and 1980s, "one big family." The belief was that the institutions had grown into larger and more complex organizations necessitating some fragmentation of units and independent actions from those units.

Norms altered, especially with respect to institutional work. Organizational members characterized their work by their efforts and time commitments. Administrators customarily worked on weekends as well as claiming work days of 12 to 14 hours. Faculty, too, characterized themselves and their colleagues as burdened with large student numbers and heavy marking loads. For those faculty participating in distance education or using electronic technology for delivery, there were claims of additional time commitments to course development and preparation.

Norms related to student learning also altered. In the 1990s, new diction for describing the instructional process and educational outcomes became standard. Diction included "skills development," "employability skills," "outcomes based curriculum," "outcomes based assessment," "learner centered," "job ready," and "value added." The diction used to describe intellectual, moral, social, and personal development—a prevalent description in earlier decades[11]—was not evident.

Values altered, most notably shifting from an institutional framework to a corporate one. Faculty looked like and characterized themselves more as labor than in the past; administrators looked more like managers of companies. This corporate framework coincided with an economic agenda: to secure resources, increase productivity, and achieve growth. The reliance upon numerous means to achieve these ends altered institutions, especially those such as North Mountain College, Suburban Valley Community College, and East Shoreline College. These colleges became more corporate, more businesslike, and less like a local college of the 1970s. Chief executive officers may have lamented the "corporate takeover," but they have accepted it nonetheless.[12]

The corporate approaches and image of community colleges shielded these institutions from engulfment by the demographic fluctuations of the local population. Although community colleges responded to community needs in previous decades, those responses were largely functional: they served traditional needs of student development, job preparation, and community development. The actions of these institutions were consistent with dominant national ideologies—for example, in the United States community colleges were reflections of the social belief in upward social and economic mobility. New immigrants to either Canada or the United States were socialized to their country through these institutions: in Canada, mainly through English or French language training; in the United States, through English language training and socialization in the American way.

In the 1990s, new immigrants from non-English speaking countries and from non-Western countries altered the ethnic and linguistic demographics of both countries. Immigration from Asia in both countries and from Mexico in the United States during the 1980s and 1990s altered a long-standing historical pattern, and the presence of Asians and their second generation offspring suggested considerable pressure upon institutions in these Western oriented countries. Although community colleges accommodated Asian immigrants and second generation North Americans of Asian ancestry, the social and cultural values of organizational members did not alter from Occidentalism to Orientalism. Institutions toned down the emphasis upon a Judeo-Christian heritage, but the cultural biases and institutional practices of the West—such as the value placed upon individualism and the rational and bureaucratic approaches to managing institutions—remained intact.

Thus students at community colleges in the 1990s, while ethnically different from previous decades, were treated more and more like commercial customers in a capitalistic enterprise. They continued to be learners in the Western tradition, even though there were efforts to down-grade traditional forms of teaching and to promote a learner-centered education. Community colleges continued to teach and offer curricula that adhered to the same principles of earlier decades. Whether the subject was biology, business, computing, or psychology and whether the program was adult basic education or nursing, the cultural paradigm of the West prevailed, from empiricism to scientific management.

Functional Processes

Functional processes include structures, management, technology, decision-making, and communication patterns. Changing structures were evident in the development of new units, such as international education and distance education; the enlargement of others, such as contract training and language institutes; the establishment of formal committees, such as senates and strategic planning committees; and the diminution or eradication of instructional areas, such as specific vocational programs and remedial and developmental education. Vocational programs deteriorated or disappeared. Specific programs such as secretarial or office management were particularly vulnerable. Remedial programs were shifted, sometimes to non-base budget categories, or components were dropped from the curricula altogether. Overall, remediation attained a lesser institutional priority in the 1990s. Community education was profit-oriented. Thus, programming shifted to revenue-generating content, with business and computer training as ascendant. Contract training and international education expanded, becoming major units of influence at community colleges.

Dramatic structural changes occurred as a result of legislation, reorganizations or restructurings, and budget shortfalls. At Rural Valley College and East Shoreline College, for example, the legislated mandate to provide baccalaureate degrees altered curricular structures and added a substantial program area to these college. At North Mountain College, government cutbacks on annual budget allocations were responsible for an altered administrative structure and change to several program areas. At City South Community College, a mid-1990s restructuring altered administrative structures and educational units, changing as well relationships between units and their members.

Management changed at these institutions, in style, in associations to other organizational levels and with external organizations, and in their relationships with collective bargaining units. The corporate management model of the colleges invariably led to a president's cabinet, if this did not exist before 1990. This corporate body became more removed from core operations such as instruction, more strategic in its approach, and more connected to a larger system—whether that system was a district office or a government office. Managers at whatever level devoted more and more of their time to managing information and finances and less time to people, even though managers continued to meet face-to-face in committee meetings with other managers, selected faculty and staff, and sometimes students.

Most pronounced was the alteration to management and union relationships. In several institutions—North Mountain, Suburban Valley, and City Center—relationships grew increasingly strained over the decade. In other institutions—Rural Valley, City South, and Pacific Suburban—the relationship altered in nature: at Rural Valley a more formal relationship developed in the late 1990s; at City South and Pacific Suburban, the role of the system union-management relationship dominated and superseded local relationships. Greater formality between the parties, except for Pacific Suburban, struggles over compensation and job security, with less attention to language concessions in collective bargaining, and greater influence of government fiscal allocations upon bargaining characterized union-management relations in the 1990s.

Also evident in management alterations was the influence of external stakeholders—district offices, government agencies, and government departments—in managers' work. The district chancellors at Suburban Valley and City South and the system president at Pacific Suburban appeared to be the chief executive officers of the respective college, with the local college president acting as a chief operating officer. At Rural Valley, East Shoreline, City Center, and North Mountain, college managers appeared from time to time to be at the mercy of government policy and funding behaviors.

As noted previously, new technologies and the increased use of computers altered both work and education significantly at these institutions. While e-mail, fax, and voice mail were used in the 1980s, in the 1990s these undergirded institutional internal and external communications. Computers, used in colleges in the 1980s, were ubiquitous in the 1990s. Work that was enhanced by computers in the 1980s, such as written communications and financial accounting, was unimaginable without computers and computer systems in the 1990s. Online student registration replaced in-person, paper-oriented registration and even telephone registration for courses.

In instruction, online and Web-based instruction as well as interactive video began to replace traditional classroom instruction, albeit marginally. The ascendancy of the Internet in the 1990s, the development of the Web, and improvements in video communications made previously used technologies obsolete. Faster computers, new communication and information processing systems, and new capabilities in moving information became necessities in the late 1990s as institutions devoted time and resources to "keep up" with external requirements and marketplace standards in electronic technologies.

The 1990s could be characterized by two contradictory trends in decision-making: greater employee participation and corporate-style management. Employee participation varied among the institutions, and these variations correlated with government legislation, collective bargaining agreements, and presidential preferences. In British Columbia, government legislation in the mid-1990s mandated an employee role in decision-making, requiring a form of shared governance for institutions. By the early 1990s, California's 1988 legislation regarding employee participation in decision-making was interpreted statewide and implemented with considerable variation among the state's community college districts. At Suburban Valley Community College, employee participation was problematic, combining a plethora of committees and institutional bodies ensuring employee involvement in the decision process with a rigid and entrenched union-management forum. In this forum, management rights were sufficient to enable management, particularly district office management, to exercise its authority in decision-making.

Corporate-style management, then, eroded the practice of employee participation, showing participation as an exercise in voice, not a critical component in decision-making, especially in the absence of legislative requirements for shared authority. Most employee groups took a practical and realistic view of participation in decision-making: they readily acknowledged their powerlessness in institutional decisions. Only in two colleges—East Shoreline College and Rural Valley College—and both in British Columbia were faculty convinced of their shared role in some institutional decisions, such as program content and student evaluation.

The rhetoric of participatory governance grew in the 1990s, but except in the case of the British Columbia colleges, there was little evidence of the practice. As a consequence of increasing external demands, a more complex institutional environment, and institutional conformity to business and industry, college management, especially senior management, exercised its legal authority more blatantly. In collective bargaining, for example, management pursued and achieved increased managerial control in significant areas, such as contracting out of services and technological change. This managerialism—that is, executive control over organizational behaviors—was consistent with the expectation of the state for greater productivity and increased efficiency. As traditionally human service organizations, community colleges were neither productivity- nor efficiency-minded.[13] Their characteristic of "loose-coupling," and "organizational slack," in which outcomes do not usually connect with intentions and in which organizational control is diffuse, mitigates against a rational choice organization that is profit-oriented.[14]

With institutional growth, both in size and complexity, and with the availability of electronic technology, communication patterns altered in notable ways. Growth resulted in the proliferation of organizational units and in the diversity of organizational interests and members' needs. Colleges increasingly moved away from their condition of "one big family" in the 1970s and even in the 1980s; employees increasingly interacted primarily with unit members, especially in those colleges in which physical facility and employee growth were evident. Committee operations and meetings, college newsletters, and e-mail broadcasts became principal forms of institution-wide communications. Interpersonal communications relied more and more upon voice mail and e-mail.

The use of voice mail and electronic mail as standard communication tools led to what was viewed as more frequent and informal communications. Memoranda and formal person-to-person meetings, the tools of earlier decades, were less in evidence in the 1990s. Electronic technologies permitted speed in communications, not possible previously. E-mail interaction could accomplish in a day what took one to two weeks in previous decades. This compression of time, relative to the past, affected the pace and quality of institutional work.

Technological change also affected patterns of communication, and networks of communications (for instance, user groups) replaced formal lines of communication. For example, union executive members, academic managers, and department heads could and did form Listservs, or a select group of receivers and senders, for e-mail messages. Such a Listserv would ensure that only that group would receive communications and all the members of the group would receive every communication sent by any group member to another group member.

Somewhat inconsistent with the proliferation of electronic communications was a reported rise in committee meetings. Indeed, at several colleges, meetings dominated administrative work. At two colleges, managers noted that their principal role was to "attend meetings." These meetings had several functions, some symbolic or sensemaking, some for purposes of managerial coordination of work, and some to discuss and decide upon processes. With few exceptions, committee meetings were not decision-making venues; instead, they were forums for communication.

Institutional Change

Institutional change suggests a historical departure from the patterns of institutional behaviors and identity associated with specific "institutional fields."[15] Steven Brint and Jerome Karabel argue that institutional change—indeed, transformation—occurred for community colleges in the 1960s, with a dramatic shift from a liberal arts orientation to a vocational one.[16] I extend this transformation further, although I am not convinced that the one in the 1960s that Brint and Karabel identified was either lasting or universal. Furthermore, the evidence of a liberal arts orientation for community colleges is limited and confined to the early 1900s, applicable to approximately 200 existing institutions, of which only 70 were public ones in 1921.[17]

The evidence from the 1990s indicates that significant cultural change occurred in community colleges, altering "repertoires,"[18] those behaviors that manifest the values and beliefs of a collective—in this case—those of community college practitioners. The "practitioners' culture" of the decades prior to the 1990s, identified by Dennis McGrath and Martin Spear, became more of a subculture in the 1990s, practiced more by long-serving organizational members.[19] Formerly a "consensus culture,"[20] by the beginning of the 1990s and more evident by the mid-1990s, the "practitioners' culture" gave way to business and corporate cultures, in which economic and system values prevailed. The observation and articulation within community colleges of a globally competitive environment, economic in nature and capitalistic in ideology, opened the doors to more business-oriented practices and a corporate style of management. The former mission of community colleges, while vibrant in rhetoric, was becoming obsolete.

The New Mission of the Community College

The lines of discourse on the mission of the community college in the latter half of the twentieth century were several. One strand included a curricular focus, with particular stress upon three domains: academic, vocational, and remedial, with some emphasis upon community education.[21] Another strand encompassed the purposes of the institution: individual and community development; social and economic mobility of the individual, and social stratification and social reproduction.[22] The educational and training role of the community college served as another strand: the institution as a pipeline to baccalaureate degrees,[23] as a job preparation site,[24] and as a place for potential success and failure in society.[25] James Ratcliff encompasses most of the three strands in his concept of "seven streams" of historical development of the community college.[26] Similar to other scholars and practitioners, Ratcliff did not or could not apprehend the emergence of a new community college mission.[27]

By the final decade of the twentieth century, curricular discussions shifted from curricula as inputs to curricula as outputs in the form of outcomes. With the concept of a learning college[28] emerging as a beacon of change, the purposes of the institution decidedly moved from individual and community betterment to economic ends: development sites for work-force preparation. The emphasis upon the economic role of the community college, however, was attenuated by programming that included socially beneficial activities such as service learning, in which community needs were addressed by student projects, demonstrating that the community college was a good corporate citizen.

Although community college organizational members claimed that the mission of their institution was unchanged in the 1990s from the previous decade, organizational behaviors suggested otherwise. While maintaining many of the facets and characteristics of their former mission as well as much of the rhetoric associated with this former mission, community college leaders including chancellors, presidents, board members, and administrators generally embraced a liberal technological philosophy of education,[29] and other institutional members including faculty and support staff adopted the norms of a global economy. These norms assume for example that free markets and global competition are aligned with democracy and economic and social benefits worldwide, and that globalization is irreversible.[30] Given the acceptance of these norms by institutional members, it is not surprising that the community college adapted to a global economy and that the mission of the community college became oriented to economic concerns and to the requirements of the private sector.

This liberal view of a technological society assumes that education is instrumental and that the technology is part of a global economy in which advanced education is best oriented to skills development and marketplace relevance. This view fits into the "high skills/high wages" concept of education and employment. In recent literature on the community college,[31] this liberal technological perspective was promoted in the 1990s. To what extent did practice follow along these lines? Did community colleges alter their mission, and if so, in what directions?

Organizational members at seven community colleges—in excess of 400 individuals—addressed these questions. They compared the present decade to the previous one and articulated considerable change to college mission. Furthermore, institutional documents were also analyzed to determine the alteration to mission. Tables 8.1 to 8.7 display these views, exhibiting specific alterations to each college's mission and the perceived determinants of these alterations.

These observed behaviors suggest that in the 1990s, the mission of the community college had less emphasis on education and more on training; less emphasis upon community social needs and more on the economic needs of business and industry; less upon individual development and more upon work-force preparation and retraining. Even though there was the addition of baccalaureate degree programs in several community colleges in the Canadian provinces of Alberta and British Columbia, there was little or no articulation of the evolution or emergence of a liberal arts

Table 8.1 Suburban Valley Community College

Mission Alterations	Determinants
Greater focus upon learner, customers, and consumer needs	To meet learner needs, to fit conceptions about market demands
Curtailing adult basic education; underplaying ESL	To preserve image as leader in education and as a prestigious institution
Emphasis upon high-tech, multiculturalism, internationalism	To meet student needs; to attract students; to meet community expectations
More businesslike; more productivity-oriented; less emphasis upon lower skills and more on technology	Need to attract students and increase enrollments; to deal with funding constraints
Remediation for underprepared students; serving working adults (especially increased use of distance education)	Increase enrollments, meet student needs, meet employers' needs
Survival, increase productivity, innovation	Combat funding shortfalls, limits, and decline in enrollments
Decrease community focus	Loss of non-credit programs because of need for resource acquisition; focus upon requirements of business and industry
Confused mission; mission under review	"Like rats running in a maze"—too much work, too many contributors to change; deterioration of labor-management relations

college. The emphasis upon multiculturalism and attention to diverse students were acknowledgments of changing population demographics and the requirement of community colleges to respond to the changing marketplace, which was influenced by immigration flows. The responsiveness to this population had economic motives in that government funding was enrollment driven or rationalized. In short, the mission of the community college by the end of the twentieth century was more suited to the rhetoric of the global economy and to its demands.

The new mission of the community college was a departure from that of previous decades, in which community implied all facets and interests of local populations. Pointedly, the evidence suggests that community college mission shifted in the 1990s from serving local communities to serv-

Table 8.2 East Shoreline College

Mission Alterations	Determinants
Broadening of mission to include baccalaureate degree programs	Provincial government legislation; organizational members' lobbying and developmental work; local demand
Contraction of vocational trades program	Decreased demand; changing workplace requirements
Increase in international outlook	Increased opportunities for revenues, for student placements, for faculty development
More provincially managed: more centralized in managerial decisions; follows provincial goals	Establishment of provincial collective bargaining structure; more provincial government direction through policy and funding; provincial government strategic plan
Privatization: establish an international secondary school	Revenue needs to support college growth
Marketplace orientation	Respond to private and public sector demands; increase revenues; provincial government strategic plan

ing the economy, specifically serving the interests of capital by producing labor and reducing public sector spending. The new mission, however, is not so easily simplified. There is complexity in the ambiguous nature of a mission that claims to serve local needs. This complexity involves, for example, the outcomes of instruction and the extent to which education and training are responses to learning needs or to the values of business and industry, and the expectations of government, whereby education and training are more of inculcation of acceptable behaviors to serve employers, rather than the needs of individual learners. At Suburban Valley Community College, a palpable tension was present within the college between the drive to increase enrollments in order to capture greater state funds and the desire to maintain a high-profile image as an innovative, prestigious institution. This tension could be seen in the conflicts over staffing the technology facility and in hiring full time faculty for the arts and sciences. Some organizational members attempted to calm the tensions by promoting technology as the vehicle of access, the means of improving student

Table 8.3 City South Community College

Mission Alterations	Determinants
Broadening, to accommodate more diverse students; less emphasis upon vocational, more on basic skills and adult education including English as a Second Language	Decline in vocational program enrollments; changing local demographics; new immigrants; new college leadership
Expand technological emphasis and increase use of information technologies	Adjust to environment by developing programs that lead to employment; achieve greater efficiencies; capture new enrollments through distance and online instruction
Focus upon student as customer	Changing needs, demographics of student population; welfare-to-work students; increase in part-time working adults, new high school graduates and problem students
Confused mission, going through transition	Restructuring action of 1995; decline in enrollments; lack of academic focus and decline of vocational programs; formalization of task force on mission
Fluctuating job training function	Changing workplace; state economic boom and bust cycles; changing leadership; declining revenues
Multicultural focus	State board mandate for actions on diversity issues; changing student population; new college leadership; and actions of faculty

learning, and a strategy to increase enrollments and thereby gain the needed fiscal resources to support education. North Mountain College, similar to Suburban Valley, pursued recognition as an advanced postsecondary institution with emphasis upon high-level skills and the use of technology, reflecting a mission of serving the local community but an upwardly mobile class within that community. Its tacit mission was to meet the economic needs of business and industry.

These examples suggest that a new vocationalism gained prominence in the community college mission. Unlike the reputed vocationalism of the

Table 8.4 Pacific Suburban Community College

Mission Alterations	Determinants
Greater attention to students as customers	Decreasing enrollments; increased awareness of multiculturalism and diverse needs of students; more adult students
Drifting away from local community	Few structures within college that connect to community; not required in the past
Marketplace orientation	Loss of government revenues
Commodification of education and training	Generate revenues by contract training; selling of program by distance education
Narrowing mission: no longer "everything to everyone"	Drop low-performing areas; eliminated secretarial science
Increasing emphasis upon multiculturalism	Sensitivity to student and community needs; increased enrollments; faculty value system

Table 8.5 City Center College

Mission Alterations	Determinants
Further and greater emphasis upon basic education, language training, remediation, and developmental education	Loss of third campus and its instructional areas and personnel; local community needs; government funding
Emphasis upon student increases	Meet provincial standards and expectations; retain student enrollments; student demographics change to include more "problem" students
Increasing focus upon economic survival, with greater attention to the marketplace	"Trying to do something so we don't lay people off"; fiscal constraints drive along with government "underfunding"

Table 8.6 Rural Valley College

Mission Alterations	Determinants
Baccalaureate degree granting; "moving toward a university model"; "redefining what it is to be a university-college"; "becoming traditional college" in the community	Provincial government legislation; college request to government ministry; local demand; new faculty
"Losing community"; not as responsive to local needs	Establishment and development of college as university-college, i.e., four-year degree granting
"Still a community college, will never be a four-year university"	Internal divisions, e.g., between community college values and university values; faculty educational backgrounds limited; organizational members' value system
Marginalization of college areas, such as trades, ESL, office administration, and non–university-college programs; creation of new subculture—university-college and community college	Limited resources; decisions to support degree programs

1960s to the 1990s identified by scholars such as Brint and Karabel and Clowes and Levin, the new vocationalism addressed the needs of the middle class and the engines of the economy.[32] It was more in line with the prescriptions of Robert Reich for work in the twenty-first century, the preparation of symbolic analysts—research scientists, design engineers, software engineers, public relations executives, investment bankers, lawyers, and real estate developers at the high salaried end and technical support staff at the lower-salary end.[33] The goals of community college education and training shifted in the 1990s to these vocations, either by preparing students for work and further education or by programming options and the curricular emphasis upon "new economy skills," "employability skills," and "applied skills."

The new vocationalism was but one-half of the new community college mission. The second followed the pattern of previous decades—that of an institution that is responsive. In the decade of the 1990s, community colleges became more overtly connected to the marketplace and to the ideologies of the neoliberal state. This meant that community college be-

Table 8.7 North Mountain College

Mission Alterations	Determinants
Four-year degree granting, "undergraduate college," but distinct from a university	Government policy; public demand for higher credentials; college management aspirations
Respond to the marketplace, "new economy skills" and "applied skills"	Government mandate; management strategy; presidential vision and authority; local business and industry requirements
Emphasis upon global and international	Generate revenue; presidential strategy to raise profile of college
"Removal of remediation programs" to non-credit, self-funded	Government cutbacks; need to generate revenue; movement of institution to higher status
Emphasis upon job preparation, electronic technology, and high level skills and away from traditional liberal arts and sciences, away from "second chance" institution image	Government policy; business and industry requests; management strategy

haviors resembled those of private business and industry, pursuing competitive grants, relying more and more on the private sector for its revenues, privatizing services and education, securing contracts with both the private and public sectors, and simply "economizing"—that is, letting financial rationales take precedence over others. The institution's mission actually encompassed the acquisition of resources and the prudent ministering of its own financial resources.

Community Colleges in the Twenty-First Century: Trajectories of Change

The new vocationalism in the community college has affected both education and work and will shape the institution in the twenty-first century just as the access mission and the vocational mission shaped the institution in the twentieth century.[34] At the beginning of the twenty-first century, there are at least three distinctive institutional identities for the community college. The first is what the institution seems to be, what actions it appears to take and with what intentions. The second is what the institution ought to be, how it should act and with what motives, according to observers, such as scholars, external influences, including business, government, and national bodies. The third institutional identity is what the institution actually does, what actions it takes and based upon those actions what intentions can be inferred. These three identities suggest several trajectories of development for the community college in the twenty-first century.

Perceptions and social imaginings of the community college have long suggested that the community college is an institution providing terminal education—that is, education and training that does not lead to further education,[35] or an institution that impedes students in their pursuit of higher education.[36] These perceptions are based upon assumptions that community colleges are singularly educational institutions and an intended integral part of the linear structure of education, fitting between the high school and university or four-year college.[37] Both Kevin Dougherty and David Larabee refer to the community college as "the contradictory college," indicating that its functioning is counter to its claims: for example, that instead of equalizing opportunity for its students, the institution inhibits student economic and social mobility. One implication of this understanding of the community college is that the institution will continue to suffer from problems of identity because of its incompatible practices—open access and marketplace responsiveness, such as training for the local economy. Without intervention, such as institutional transformation to a single purpose, for example to "branch campus" status of a four-year college,[38] the institution will remain an inferior postsecondary educational institution, both contradictory and in crisis.

Ambitions for the community college to become a different institution, unlike its more traditional image, for example, as a transfer institution,[39] portrayed the institution as on the threshold of greatness, as already possessing transcendent qualities but in need of a critical mass to push the institution forward. One ambition was the community college as the savior of the U.S. economy.[40] Another and more popular ambition presented the community college as the educational leader in student learning.[41] These imaginings, such as the community college as the "learning college," are more like ghosts of the future, rhetorical constructions of what might be, and are based upon anecdotal evidence and the aspirations of power elites in the community college movement and optimistic community college practitioners. There is both a light side and a dark side to the implications of the learning college. The light side envisions independent learners pursuing knowledge and skills with the guidance of professionals and the support of advanced technology. The dark side envisions a further stratified higher education system where the poor, the disadvantaged, and minority populations are served by "distance," either in the form of professionals with whom they have little personal contact or in the form of machinery and electronics that reflect a standardized approach to schooling. This "systematized technological bitting"[42] will further disadvantage community college students, especially in their pursuit of baccalaureate degrees.

The third institutional identity of the community college is derived from what the institution actually does, what actions the organization takes and what intentions can be inferred. One variant is the traditional community college of Arthur Cohen and Florence Brawer;[43] a second is the entrepreneurial college of Norton Grubb and associates;[44] and a third is my view of the globalized institution. The trajectory of institutional change for Cohen and Brawer is predicated upon the past patterns of institutional development. In such areas as curriculum and organization and management, Cohen and Brawer see few changes occurring, even with the proliferation of electronic technology. Their perspective on the future is "more of the same"—that is, the same but more of it. Community colleges will continue to provide educational services to an expanding population. To some extent, Cohen and Brawer homogenize the actions of community colleges in the 1980s and 1990s with those of the past: they do not acknowledge the severe pressures and complementary responses of institutions toward privatization; they ignore the rising number of students educated by distance. Yet, their assessment is based upon the foundation of historical development, noting that many similar issues confronted the institution in earlier parts of the twentieth century, such as the tension between the vocational and the transfer function.[45]

Grubb and associates detect the presence of a college within a college in their conceptualization of the entrepreneurial college. In their research, they discover new, entrepreneurial functions of community colleges, with a new culture, new rules, and new regulations that sustain a market orientation of the institution. These new functions are driven by greater demand for training, by immigration, and by pressures for economic development. The implication of this concept for Grubb and associates is that it will increase in size and in influence within the institution. Yet, they see that the entrepreneurial college will become independent from the rest of the college, not that the entrepreneurial college may dominate and that the entrepreneurial function might become the main one for the institution. In a later publication, Grubb contradicts his assertion that the entrepreneurial emphasis is new.[46] But he confuses entrepreneurialism in community colleges with responsiveness, claiming that more than any other institution community colleges are responsive to local communities and to changing economic and demographic conditions, indicating that this makes optional "the entrepreneurial spirit."

The final trajectory of change for the community college is toward my concept of a globalized institution. This is the institution that advances globalization, acting as a conduit for the globalization process. Implications of globalization are connected conceptually to space and time, to the compression of space and to the relative diminution of time. Places are closer to each other; actions occur more rapidly. For the community college, this suggests that the definition of community, usually having the connotation of the local, will alter and the institution will respond to a broader base of constituents, losing its local community orientation. The globalization process is not only a boundary-spanning process but also a set of behaviors that breaks down boundaries. This suggests for the community college that traditional institutional boundaries, such as the identity of the community college as a two-year institution,[47] will become obsolete.

Furthermore, this is also the institution that exemplifies the globalization process and its effects upon organizations. Globalization is also concerned with the reordering of time and space in social life and in social interactions: distance and time are no longer constraints.[48] Globalization entails disjunctive and even contradictory tendencies. These include greater centralization of decision-making in organizations and decentralization in the supervision of work, as well as the pursuit of homogenization in production and the tolerance of heterogeneity in work processes. As a globalized institution, the community college has been subject to workplace disruptions and dislocations, with a corporate ideology behind production and with emphasis upon quantitative outcomes, realized by technological improvements and an altered curriculum that stresses "employability skills," so that the economy can be served. Not only are students and their learning outcomes viewed in economic terms, but the institution has become a business enterprise. This suggests that for the twenty-first century, community colleges will function more on a model compatible with business norms: a fluid organization, with little reverence for academic traditions, little evidence of a dominant professional class of faculty and more evidence of a professional managerial class, greater reliance upon technology and less upon full-time labor. A systems approach to the infrastructure of organizations will take care of operations, and thus the need for a large cadre of professional educators will diminish.

This trajectory of change is a conglomerate of the dark sided view of O'Banion's learning college, Grubb's entrepreneurial college, and Cohen and Brawer's traditional college. The institution will continue to maintain its traditional functions, some with less vigilance, others through technological change; add new functions; and enlarge its community or clientele, becoming more fragmented in its operations and more confused in its identity. It will no longer be a two-year college, ironically matching its rhetoric of a lifelong learning institution with practice because it will have no limits to its curricula and none to its credentials. Indeed, the current movement to outcomes-based assessment suggests that the issue of credentials may be moot in the coming decades, except for those who require baccalaureate or post-baccalaureate status. Like Cohen and Brawer's traditional college, the globalized institution will be the same institution, even more so.

After Globalization

Globalization, like postmodernism, is not kind to the remnants and memories of the past. Assaults on globalization in the 1990s were in part responses to preserve individual and community identities and in part interest-group reactions to economic globalization and its irreverence for specific causes, such as the preservation of the environment, the provision of fair labor practices, and the protection of jobs. Intense social unrest in North America in reaction to the Canada - U.S. Free Trade Agreement, to the North American Free Trade Agreement, and to the World Trade Organization manifested the conflict between positions on the social understanding of globalization. This social understanding frames globalization as global capitalism, sometimes in the form of multinational corporations, sometimes as Americanization, and sometimes as McDonaldization. The more benign and even munificent face of globalization—for example, "the global village" of McLuhan or the global identity of the human species—is lost in social consciousness when globalization as global capitalism is the predominant frame of understanding.

The "one needful thing"[49] is often that which is neglected or absent. In the case of the community college, that one needful thing is attention to student and community needs for a more diverse form of education, a form that is not a mere consequence of economic priorities. This includes personal enrichment programs, recreational activities, and even liberal education, which has long been eroded, forgotten, but from time to time alluded to by those who study the institution.[50] Because institutions can and do interpret and respond to global forces in different ways, dependent upon institutional history and institutional power, community colleges can sustain or revitalize education that informs the mind and develops the person, even in the face of global pressures including the pressures from business, industry, and the state to become globally competitive and mechanisms for economic development.

The community college, as an adaptable institution, is less restricted in its choices than other educational institutions. It is largely unfettered by tradition or by its own bureaucracy, and it is free in many ways to pursue a virtuous and historically idealized path in which students as people, not as economic entities, are paramount to institutional purposes. This will require less emphasis upon the economic domain of globalization and more upon the cultural domain, absent a corporatist, global ideology. This will require less attention to economic outputs and more to human development, relationships, and achievements.

APPENDIX

RESEARCH METHODS FOR "MISSION AND STRUCTURE: THE COMMUNITY COLLEGE IN A GLOBAL CONTEXT"

This book addresses the impacts of globalization on community colleges in the period of the 1990s. It is based upon a comparative study of influences of globalization and globalizing trends on community colleges in the United States and Canada, undertaken from 1996 to 1999. The Social Sciences and Humanities Research Council of Canada funded that study. The study, called "Mission and Structure: The Community College in a Global Context," was an examination of external forces acting upon seven institutions during the decade of the 1990s and the responses of those institutions, including their organizational adaptation and institutional changes to mission and structures. As a scholarly qualitative field study, "Mission and Structure: The Community College in a Global Context" adopted principles and practices of credible research, ensuring that findings were both valid and reliable.

Validity is generally viewed as the accuracy of data and the reasonableness of findings and conclusions. Reliability is represented as a question of replicability, on the one hand the extent to which the same methods used over again at the same sites would yield the same data and findings and on the other hand whether the findings and conclusions can be generalized or applied to other sites not represented in the study. In qualitative field research, however, the concepts of validity and reliability become somewhat problematic. To some extent, the difficulty with applying concepts of validity and reliability, drawn from quantitative research, is that in qualitative field research the purpose of research is not necessarily to discover factual or objective truths, however defined, and the assumption is certainly not that there is either another identical site or that the same site will be unchanged if investigated again. Furthermore, in field research, the researcher is a principal instrument, and thus to assume that another researcher would gather the same data or arrive at the same findings is to expect researcher duplicability or objectivity, assumptions that seem to lack an empirical basis.

The above, however, is not meant to suggest that qualitative field research should be idiosyncratic, or what Miles and Huberman view as "mystification."[1] Data in qualitative research should be authentic, not manufactured; it should be representative of a sample set, whether individuals or groups or sites, and meaningful. Findings and conclusions should be credible and coherent.

In "Mission and Structure: The Community College in a Global Context," a multisite and broad-based research design was used to gather data. Data collection occurred not only at each site but also for the organizational context of each site, for the legal jurisdictions of all sites, and over time. In using four distinct data sources, including interview, document, observational, and institutional survey data, and in collecting large quantities of data, as well as relying upon stratified data sampling, the study adhered to the suggestion of scholars who advise multiple strategies for data collection, both comprehensive collection of data and research strategies to capture meaning from sites.[2]

Findings were grounded in data and the result of a process of lengthy researcher engagement with sites. Furthermore, theoretical frameworks guided the research and analytical frameworks guided data analysis, indicating that the idiosyncratic and the wholly personal were held in check. A number of techniques to disconfirm evidence and observations were applied, including member checking,[3] as were strategies to collect and analyze data almost simultaneously,[4] especially during interviewing. Additionally, the advice of Eisenhardt[5] was followed in using multiple researchers, including multiple data collectors and data analyzers. These strategies helped to ensure credible findings.

Coherency relied upon the connections between data, findings, and conclusions. Here, theoretical and analytical frameworks, particularly globalization theory and organization theory, served as security guides. Data were analyzed using consistent frameworks; findings were derived from the use of three analytical frameworks (that is, globalization theory, organization adaptation theory, and higher education literature). Conclusions were achieved by relating findings to initial research questions and to questions that arose during investigation. That is, conclusions addressed not only changes that occurred during the study period but also predictions or speculations about community colleges in the coming decades. The thread of understanding moved thus from the past to the present to the future.

The Study

A qualitative, multiple case study design was used in "Mission and Structure: The Community College in a Global Context" because of several factors that made case study appropriate for the research questions and given the comprehensive scope of the topic.[6] The use of field methods—including document analysis, interviews, informal conversations, observations, and the use of informants—is one suggested way to understand organizational life and organizational behaviors.[7] Furthermore, investigation of multiple sites or cases was deemed to be particularly appropriate for the understanding of different institutional contexts.[8] Demands on resources and personnel in extensive examination of sites and limitations of time limited the sample size—with approximately 1,200 U. S. community colleges and 125 Canadian colleges, even to achieve a high level of statistical confidence would require more colleges visited than would be feasible. The purpose here was not to achieve statistical generalizations but rather theoretical soundness.[9]

In refining the design, I narrowed the focus to a geographical area—the Pacific/Western Region. This narrowing was intended to capture the concept of international and global economics and trade within what is referred to as the Pacific Rim; to identify and follow the development of international cultural connections consistent with this region; and to follow along the lines of a previous investigation on the effects of external forces of change on community colleges in the Western United States and Canada.[10] Furthermore, I assumed that globalizing forces would be more evident in or near large population centers (that is, Western cities), especially those with relatively large immigrant populations or those that depend upon international trade. I concluded that I would need to understand not only the colleges but also their communities, however defined. Several sites (that is, colleges) made up the multiple cases, and the use of more than one site permitted comparisons and offered additional possibilities for generalization and even theory construction.

The formal aspect of the investigation began in April 1996. The investigative strategy was to study multiple sites in depth through interviews and informal conversations with college personnel and students, through the review and analysis of institutional documents, and through observations. In addition, each college was surveyed and asked to provide quantitative information on budgets, students, programs, and graduate employment placements. To complement this multicase study, the research involved the review and analysis of government documents pertinent to higher education policy, specifically policy that was directed to or might affect community colleges.

Site Selection

The choice of sites followed two basic patterns. The first was along the lines of theoretical or purposeful sampling. The second was associated with site access. Purposeful sampling consists of choosing a sample of a population (in this case, community colleges) that fits characteristics of the study's purpose and that may conform to working hypotheses. Thus, colleges possessing characteristics that suggested connections to globalization and internationalization were chosen as part of the sample pool. This included those colleges with reputations for international projects and programs; those colleges that served diverse populations; and those colleges reputed to be innovative, especially in their use of electronic technology. It also included those colleges that were in jurisdictions in which influential policy bodies promoted change along marketplace—both domestic and international—lines; those colleges in geographical areas in which there was considerable international activity, in finance, business, industry, and culture; and those colleges in which college officials possessed high profiles in national and international educational forums or reputations as participants in international education activities.

Additionally, in order to provide cases that were not identical to each other and reflected as a whole a variety of other sites, the sample pool was further refined to include different organizational systems. This included, for example, colleges that were part of a multicollege district, colleges that were part of a larger educational system, and colleges that were independent—that is, having their own governing board. It also included colleges in different political jurisdictions (that is, the United States and Canada on one level and different states and provinces on another), and of differing sized institutions, especially because of the widely held view of organizations that size is related to complexity and that differences among organizations can be a factor of size differences primarily. Thus, the sample pool was limited conceptually.

The second pattern was associated with site access. From the sample pool, colleges in which there was known opportunity for access because of my familiarity of a college official who might be able to provide uncontested access were the initial choices. Six colleges were initially identified from a larger list. The total list was comprised of 15 colleges, including several institutions within a multicollege district. One of the six was dropped from the list because I became aware of internal upheaval and the impending departure of the college president. Another college was added in its place—a college within the same geographical region—because of the interest and willingness of the college president to participate. Another college was eventually dropped from the list because of a laborious process to achieve college agreement to participate. This college was replaced by a college in a different geographical region, but only after I had exhausted possibilities of replacement with another college in that region. The final choice of replacement in this example was based not only upon access but also upon the conceptual appropriateness of the college's character as an innovative institution that was reputed to be involved in using new educational technologies.

Ultimately, seven colleges were selected with the assumption that at least one college might drop out after the investigation began. In this event, there would be at least six colleges. Four to eight is a reasonable number of sites for multicase study research.[11] Given the duration of the study, a loss of at least one college was a prudent assumption. Nonetheless, all seven colleges remained as study sites: three U.S. and four Canadian colleges.

Investigative Strategy

The investigative strategy was to study multiple sites in depth through interviews and informal conversations with college personnel and students, through the review and analysis of institutional documents, and through observations. A group of researchers undertook site visits—from three to five investigators at one site at the same time. The use of a group approach assisted not only in data collection but also in analysis during collection. The multiple viewpoints, the discussion of individual on-site observations, and the confirming and disconfirming of preliminary hunches all contributed to a richer and more accurate understanding of the site.[12]

The collection and analysis of other related data augmented the study of multiple sites. These data included state/province legislation, policy, and higher education, labor, and finance reports. Also included were national (U.S. and Canada) federal policies and policy reports. Other government agency documents (local or regional) on the economy, labor markets, or population demographics were collected and reviewed.

In addition to existing public documents, each college was surveyed and asked to provide quantitative information on budgets, students, programs, and graduate employment placements. This survey was intended to provide a comparative guide for the sites as well as a quantitative measure against which qualitative assessments could be compared within sites. That is, when college members refer consistently to specific dates for budget reductions and to reduced program enrollments, the survey data were compared to the perceptions of college members. This not only provided for a validity check but also enhanced the investigators' understanding of participant perceptions.

The multisite investigation was both cross-sectional and longitudinal. The first site visit, lasting between four and five days, was on the one hand an extensive examination involving interviews, conversations, and observations, using the concept of organizational change over a five-year period as an analytical tool to gain understanding of the present. Thus, from this exploration, observations, findings and conclusions were derived. On the other hand, a second site visit at each college, from between 12 and 18 months subsequent to the first, permitted a longitudinal analysis, enabling the research to address observable change over time, as well as check on the validity of initial observations.

Procedures: Interviews and Observation

Colleges that agreed to participate in the study were sent formal documents on the investigation, including an agreement to have their college included in the study, an agreement that was signed by the chief executive officer of the institution, and a copy of an interview consent form used later in on-site interviews. Arrangements were made for site visits, and a team of researchers was established, including U.S. and Canadian members. Of these members, three were university professors and six were doctoral students in university programs. The research team was involved in the first set of site visits, and the principal investigator, with just one other team member, completed the second set of site visits.

For the first set of site visits, the research team spent from four to five days at each site. During this time, team members conducted individual and group interviews. At each institution, the following college personnel were interviewed: president or chief executive officer, president's assistant or secretary, chief business officer, chief academic officer, chief student services officer, chief human resources/personnel officer, samples of mid-level administrators (deans, directors), samples of full-time faculty and part-time faculty, faculty union president, support staff union president, and one to two board members (if available, the board chair was interviewed). Additionally, if a college was part of a multicollege district, the district chancellor was interviewed. As well as formally arranged interviews, more informal interviews and conversations were held with administrators, faculty (full-time and part-time), support staff, and students.

Formal interviews were taped recorded, unless objected to or inappropriate because of location (for example, one interview was conducted over lunch in a restaurant). Objections to tape recording, which were few, occurred only during small portions of individual interviews. Interview notes were recorded by hand. Interview questions were developed and pilot tested prior to site visits. Pilot testing occurred at a site that was not part of this investigation. Questions were both specific and open-ended and invited interviewees to explain and elaborate on their responses. Following site investigations, the principal investigator reviewed data collected at each site and subsequently wrote a detailed case study report, combining description with observation and the generation of concepts that would serve as analytical frames for the understanding of behaviors and actions at each site. The case study write-up aided in making sense of the enormous quantity of data collected during site visits.[13] At the stage of interview data analysis, another two research assistants were added to the research team, and their role was to transcribe interview data from tape recordings and interview notes onto a data display sheet organized around the interview questions.

A second set of site visits followed the first set by 12 to 18 months, all lasting from two to three days at each site, with only the principal investigator on site for all site visits, and a collaborator present at a majority of sites. During these site visits, the principal investigator and collaborator interviewed faculty and administrators as well as one or two support staff, using follow-up questions derived from the questions and responses in the first round of interviews. In addition, for those colleges connected to larger systems or multicollege districts, officials of these larger organizations were interviewed. The purpose of the second site visits was to explore a limited number of questions in greater depth and to ascertain the extent of institutional change over a one-year period, relative to the changes identified in the previous five years. Questions addressed changes to missions and structures over a one- to two-year period. Those interviewed included both individuals who were interviewed previously and those not interviewed previously. Interview responses were recorded by hand.

In all, interviews were conducted over a two-year period at seven colleges in the United States and Canada, in the states of California, Hawaii, and Washington and the provinces of Alberta and British Columbia. Approximately 60 individuals were involved in interviews, formally or informally, at each college, for a total of approximately 430 people interviewed, with the majority of formal interviews lasting from 50 minutes to 2 hours.

During both site visits, as the principal investigator, I also used a participant observation approach to data collection and analysis.[14] I kept a journal that included notes from meetings, interviews, and observations of institutional environments and interactions. Meetings included groups reporting to the president, groups reporting to other senior managers, college employee meetings, and governing board meetings. As well, I made notes on my ongoing analysis of data and the generation of observations and working hypotheses. Subsequent to site visits, I wrote detailed case histories combining analyses of observations, documents, and interviews as well as historical and social analysis.

The seven colleges in this study were given fictitious names, consistent with the agreement with each college president to maintain relative anonymity of institutions. The seven colleges were named City Central College (CCC); City South Community College (CSCC); East Shoreline College (ESC); North Mountain College (NMC); Pacific Suburban Community College (PSCC); Rural Valley College (RVC); and Suburban Valley Community College (SVCC).

Procedures: Document Collection and Analysis

The data sources included federal (Canada and the United States) departments, agencies, and commissions, state and provincial government departments and agencies, and individual colleges and college districts.

Document data included institutional documents, government documents, and institutional survey data. Institutional documents were comprised of college catalogues (calendars in Canada), annual reports, collective agreements, policies, institutional reports, program/course schedules, and institutional communications (for example, memoranda); they also included material such as student newspapers and informational brochures gathered during site visits. Government documents comprised legislation, policies, policy discussion papers, and reports. Institutional surveys provided data on institutional budgets, student enrollments, and student graduation placements. Data also included regional and local demographic figures related to jurisdictions served by each community college.

Data Analysis

In order to determine the ways and the extent to which globalizing forces affected and influenced community colleges, I employed several analytical frameworks to understand organizational behaviors. Principal among these was globalization theory, which provided me with a number of categories for analysis. These included the categories of change in organizations and institutions, such as increasing speed of production facilitated by the use of electronic technologies, alterations in labor as a consequence of productivity and efficiency of operations, and restructuring of organization and work in order to increase managerial flexibility and control as well as organizational productivity or efficiency or both. Particular to the postsecondary educational sector, categories of change included less public sector funding for public institutions, increasing associations with and connections to the private sector, and increasing state intervention into the governance and operations of the institution.

Analytical frameworks were developed not only from globalization theory but also from organizational theory, as well as recent applications of globalization to higher education.[15] The goal of these frameworks was to identify patterns and themes that helped to explain the effects of globalizing forces and how the globalization process affected college behaviors.

Interview, document, observational, institutional questionnaire, and government document data were analyzed using an analytical framework drawn from globalization literature. Data were coded according to the categories noted in Figure A.1, drawn from globalization literature (for instance, internationalization, public sector funding constraints, and commodification). Procedures for coding and then drawing conclusions followed the advice of Miles and Huberman.[16]

Category	Abbreviation Code
A. Internationalization (students, curriculum, delivery)	[I]
B. Work-force training	[WT]
C. Electronic technology—real-time communications	[ET]
D. Labor alterations (e.g., additional work)	[LA]
E. Productivity and efficiency	[P/E]
F. Public sector funding constraints	[LPS]
G. Restructuring	[R]
H. State intervention	[SI]
I. Private sector interaction	[PR]
J. Partnerships	[PA]
K. Extenal competition	[C]
L. Homogenization	[HOM]
M. Commodification	[COM]

Figure A.1 Globalization Categories

Furthermore, national and state and provincial policy document data underwent a second iteration of coding and thus another analysis process. First, documents were categorized according to their jurisdiction: Federal Canada, Federal U.S., state, or province. Second, documents were categorized according to their source, and these categories included government, government affiliate, non-government body, non-government organization, institution, and private. And finally, documents were categorized by type, including legislation, policy, research, and report. Policy included formal policy, policy discussion, policy background, policy draft, review of legislation, and review of policy. Analysis then proceeded to include coding, using a modified pattern of globalization categories discussed previously, as noted in Figure A. 2 (Categories for Government Policy Document Analysis).

After pattern coding, content analysis of the extracted data included counting of coded data by category and the identification and explanation of specific themes. Counting ensured that there was a substantial quantity of data for the established patterns. Thematic analysis led to a clearer understanding of the meaning of the patterns.

Observational data were analyzed both during site visits at each college and following site visits for all colleges. During site visits, I recorded my observations and subsequently began to conceptualize these data working toward hypotheses and theory building, not unlike the approach recommended by Glaser and Strauss.[17] Observational data were thus treated in two distinct ways. On the one hand, observational data served as evidence of the presence of patterns related to concepts consistent with those drawn from globalization literature and theory. On the other hand, observational data were coded using categories derived from globalization theory, as

Internationalization (students, curriculum, delivery)	[I]
Public sector funding constraints	[LPS]
Private sector interaction	[PR]
Electronic technology—real-time communications	[ET]
Productivity and efficiency	[P/E]
External competition	[C]
Restructuring	[R]
Partnerships	[PA]
Work-force training	[WT]
Marketplace	[MRK]

Figure A.2 Categories for Government Policy Document Analysis

noted in Figure A.1, and used in conjunction with other categories of data (for instance, interviews).

In addition to a globalization analytical framework for data analysis, I employed an analytical framework drawn from organization theory. Interview and observational data were also coded according to the categories established by Cameron[18] to explain organizational adaptation. These theoretical perspectives provide descriptive power with respect to the relative strength of internal organizational influence and external environmental influence over organizational actions. These categories comprise at least four distinct theoretical perspectives on adaptation and are labeled Population Ecology, Life Cycles, Strategic Choice, and Symbolic Action (See Figure A.3). Furthermore, I added a fifth category to Cameron's framework—Accidentalism—to cover a perspective missing in adaptation literature. This fifth category avoids the internal/external dichotomy implied by the other four categories, and suggests that chancelike events might influence organizational actions.

Finally, interview and journal data were coded thematically, relying upon patterns identified as those connected to college mission and college structure changes, such as mission alteration that favors higher level programming in instruction and structural changes to institutional decision-making. These themes and patterns were then used to explain alterations to institutional mission and structures.

Thus, one set of coded data was connected to globalization behaviors; a second set, to organizational adaptation; and a third set, to changing missions and structures. For example, the use of performance indicators for organizational outcomes, such as growth or diminution of student numbers, the practice of pay for administrative performance, government funding based upon competitive grants, changes to legislation, such as adding a role for college employees to governance processes, were coded "state intervention" and categorized as one component of the globalizing of organizational behaviors.

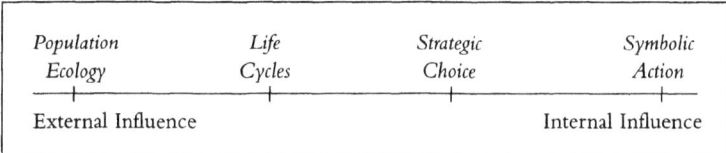

Figure A.3 Organizational Adaptation Continuum

NOTES

Introduction

1. John Diekhoff, *Democracy's College: Higher Education in the Local Community* (New York: Harper and Brother Publishers, 1950).
2. Ian Mitroff, *Stakeholders of the Mind* (San Francisco: Jossey-Bass, 1984). By stakeholders, I include specifically governing board members; government and agency officials in departments responsible for community colleges; community members and community groups; politicians at the local, regional, and national levels; local business and industry leaders; and professionals, such as university faculty, and professional bodies that accredit or judge college programs, among other influencers contributing to institutional responses to global forces.

Chapter 1

1. Arthur Cohen and Florence Brawer, *The American Community College* (San Francisco: Jossey-Bass, 1996); John Dennison and Paul Gallagher, *Canada's Community Colleges* (Vancouver: University of British Columbia Press, 1986); and John Frye, *The Vision of the Public Junior College, 1900–1940* (New York: Greenwood Press, 1992).
2. James Ratcliff, "Seven Streams in the Historical Development of the Modern Community College," in *A Handbook on the Community College in America*, ed. George Baker III (Westport CT, 1994), 3–16.
3. Arthur Cohen and Florence Brawer, *The American Community College* (San Francisco: Jossey-Bass, 1996), quoting Kent Phillipe, ed., *National Profile of Community Colleges: Trends and Statistics* (Washington, D.C.: American Association of Community Colleges, 1995).
4. Ibid.; Dennis McGrath and Martin Spear, *The Academic Crisis of the Community College* (Albany: State University of New York Press, 1991); and Richard Richardson, Jr., Elizabeth Fisk, and Morris Okun, *Literacy in the Open-Access College* (San Francisco: Jossey-Bass Publishers, 1983).
5. McGrath and Spear, *The Academic Crisis of the Community College;* Richardson, Jr., Fisk, and Okun, *Literacy in the Open-Access College;* and John

Roueche and Suanne Roueche, *Between a Rock and a Hard Place* (Washington, D.C.: Community College Press, 1993).
6. National Commission on Excellence in Education, *A Nation at Risk: The Imperative for Educational Reform* (Washington, D.C.: U.S. Department of Education, April 1983).
7. George Keller, *Academic Strategy: The Management Revolution in American Higher Education* (Baltimore: The Johns Hopkins University Press, 1983).
8. John E. Roueche and George A. Baker III, *Access and Excellence* (Washington, D.C.: The Community College Press, 1987).
9. William Deegan and Dale Tillery, "The Process of Renewal: An Agenda for Action," in *Renewing the American Community College,* eds. William Deegan, Dale Tillery and Associates (San Francisco: Jossey-Bass Publishers, 1985), 303–324; Cohen and Brawer, *The American Community College;* and Earl Seidman, *In the Words of the Faculty* (San Francisco: Jossey-Bass Publishers, 1985).
10. Darrel Clowes and Bernard Levin, "Community, Technical and Junior Colleges: Are They Leaving Higher Education?" *The Journal of Higher Education* 60, no. 3 (1989): 349–355; K. Patricia Cross, "Determining Missions and Priorities for the Fifth Generation," in *Renewing the American Community College,* eds. William Deegan, Dale Tillery, and Associates (San Francisco: Jossey-Bass Publishers, 1985), 34–50; Ken Kempner, "The Community College as a Marginalized Institution" (unpublished paper, presented at annual meeting of Association for the Study of Higher Education, Boston, 1991); McGrath and Spear, *The Academic Crisis of the Community College;* Richard Richardson and Louis Bender, *Fostering Minority Access and Achievement in Higher Education* (San Francisco: Jossey-Bass Publishers, 1987); Mary Ann Roe, *Education and U.S. Competitiveness: The Community College Role* (Austin, Texas: IC2 Institute, University of Texas at Austin, 1989); Roueche and Baker, *Access and Excellence;* and Lois Weis, *Between Two Worlds: Black Students in an Urban Community College* (Boston: Routledge and Kegan Paul, 1985).
11. Marilyn Amey and Susan Twombly, "Re-visioning Leadership in Community Colleges," *The Review of Higher Education* 15, no. 2 (Winter 1992): 125–150; George Baker and Associates, *Cultural Leadership: Inside America's Community Colleges* (Washington, D.C.: The Community College Press, 1992); Joanne Cooper and Ken Kempner, "Lord of the Flies Community College: A Case Study of Organizational Disintegration," *The Review of Higher Education* 16, no. 4 (Summer 1993): 419–437; Thomas Fryer Jr., and John Lovas, *Leadership in Governance* (San Francisco: Jossey-Bass Publishers, 1991); Richard Richardson, "Responsible Leadership: Tipping the Balance Toward Institutional Achievement," in *Community College Leadership for the '80s,* eds. John Roueche and George Baker III (Washington, D.C.: American Association of Community and Junior Colleges, 1983); John Roueche, George Baker III, and Robert Rose, *Shared Vision* (Washington, D.C.: The Community College Press, 1989); and George Vaughan, *The*

NOTES 197

    Community College Presidency (New York: American Council on Education/Macmillan, 1986).
12. National Center for Educational Statistics, *Digest of Education Statistics, 1994*, U.S. G.P.O.
13. In 1980, part-time faculty comprised 56 percent of the total faculty numbers; by 1991 they comprised 65 percent nationally; see Kent Phillipe, ed., *National Profile of Community Colleges: Trends and Statistics* (Washington, D.C.: American Association of Community Colleges, 1995).
14. John Dennison and Paul Gallagher, *Canada's Community Colleges* (Vancouver: University of British Columbia Press, 1986).
15. John Dennison and John Levin, *Canada's Community College in the Nineteen Eighties* (Willowdale, Ontario: Association of Canadian Community Colleges, 1989).
16. Statistics Canada Report 81–222; Canada, Department of the Secretary of State, *Profile of Higher Education in Canada* (Ottawa: Ministry of Supply and Services, 1991). Enrollment figures are not reliable, in part because much of the enrollment figures in the 1970s and 1980s reflected full-time students.
17. Dennison and Levin, *Canada's Community College in the Nineteen Eighties*.
18. Amir Levy and Uri Merry, *Organizational Transformation: Approaches, Strategies, and Theories* (New York: Praeger, 1986).
19. John Levin, "Mission and Structure: The Community College in a Global Context" (Center for the Study of Higher Education, The University of Arizona, Tucson, Arizona, 1999).
20. Saskia Sassen, *The Global City* (Princeton: Princeton University Press, 1991).
21. Arjun Appadurai, "Disjunctures and Difference in the Global Cultural Economy," in *Global Culture: Nationalism, Globalization and Modernity*, ed. Mike Featherstone (Newbury Park, CA: Sage Publications, 1990), 295–310; Stanley Aronowitz and William Di Fazio, *The Jobless Future: Sci-Tech and the Dogma of Work* (Minneapolis: University of Minnesota Press, 1994); Mike Featherstone, "Global Culture: An Introduction," in *Global Culture*, ed. Mike Featherstone (Newbury Park, CA: Sage Publications, 1990); Anthony Giddens, *The Consequences of Modernity* (Stanford: Stanford University Press, 1990); Roland Robertson, *Globalization: Social Theory and Global Culture* (London: Sage Publications, 1992); Gary Teeple, *Globalization and the Rise of Social Reform* (New Jersey: Humanities Press, 1995); and Malcom Waters, *Globalization* (New York: Routledge, 1996).
22. David Held, Anthony McGrew, David Goldblatt, and Jonathan Perraton, *Global Transformations* (Stanford: Stanford University Press, 1999), 1.
23. Appadurai, "Disjunctures and Difference," 295–310; Aronowitz and Di Fazio, *The Jobless Future;* William Bridges, *Job Shift* (Reading, MA: Addison-Wesley, 1994); Martin Carnoy, Manuel Castello, Stephen Cohen, and Fernando Cardoso, *The New Global Economy in the Information Age* (University

Park: The Pennsylvania State University, 1993); Manuel Castells, "The Informational Economy and the New International Division of Labor," in *The New Global Economy in the Information Age,* eds. Martin Carnoy, Manuel Castells, Stephen Cohen, and Fernando Cardosa (University Park: The Pennsylvania State University, 1993),15–43; Jeremy Rifkin, *The End of Work* (New York: G. P. Putnam's Sons, 1995); and Don Tapscott, *The Digital Economy Promise and Peril in the Age of Networked Intelligence* (New York: McGraw Hill, 1996).
24. Tapscott, *The Digital Economy.*
25. Aronowitz and DiFazio, *The Jobless Future;* Castells, "The New Informational Economy"; Richard Lipsey, "The Case for Trilateralism," in *Continental Accord: North American Economic Integration,* ed. Steven Globerman (Vancouver: The Fraser Institute, 1991), 89–123; and Tapscott, *The Digital Economy.*
26. Steven Vallas, *Power in the Workplace: The Politics of Production at AT&T* (Albany: State University of New York Press, 1993).
27. Appadurai, "Disjunctures and Differences," 296.
28. Waters, *Globalization.*
29. George Ritzer, *The McDonaldization Thesis: Explorations and Extensions* (Thousand Oaks, CA: Sage Publications, 1998).
30. Waters, *Globalization.*
31. Robertson, *Globalization.*
32. Paul Di Maggio and Walter Powell, "The Iron Cage Revisited: Institutional Isomorphism and Collective Rationality in Organizational Fields," *American Sociological Review* 48 (1983): 147–160.
33. Aronowitz and Di Fazio, *The Jobless Future;* Jan Currie and Janice Newson, *Universities and Globalization,* with an introduction by Jan Currie (Thousand Oaks: Sage Publications, 1998), 1–13; John Levin, "Missions and Structures: Bringing Clarity to Perceptions about Globalization and Higher Education in Canada," *Higher Education* 37, no. 4 (1999): 377–399; Larry Leslie and Sheila Slaughter, "The Development and Current Status of Market Mechanisms in the United States Postsecondary Education," *Higher Education Policy* 10 (March/April 1997): 238–252; Janice Newson, "NAFTA and Higher Education in Canada" (unpublished paper, York University, Toronto, Ontario, 1994); Sheila Slaughter, "Who Gets What and Why in Higher Education? Federal Policy and Supply-Side Institutional Resource Allocation" (presidential address, Association for the Study of Higher Education annual meeting, Memphis, Tennessee, 1997); and Sheila Slaughter and Larry Leslie, *Academic Capitalism, Politics, Policies, and the Entrepreneurial University* (Baltimore: The Johns Hopkins University Press, 1997).
34. Amir Levy and Uri Merry, *Organizational Transformation: Approaches, Strategies, and Theories* (New York: Praeger, 1986).
35. Henry Mintzberg, *Power In and Around Organizations* (Englewood Cliffs, N.J.: Prentice-Hall, Inc., 1983).

36. Kim Cameron, "Organizational Adaptation and Higher Education," *The Journal of Higher Education* 55, no. 2 (1984): 122–144.
37. Ibid.
38. Lloyd Sandelands and Robert Drazin, "On the Language of Organizational Theory," *Organization Studies* 10, no. 4 (1989): 457–478.
39. Steven Brint and Jerome Karabel, "Institutional Origins and Transformations: The Case of American Community Colleges," in *The New Institutionalism*, eds. Walter Powell and Paul DiMaggio (Chicago: The University of Chicago Press, 1991), 337–360; and DiMaggio and Powell, "The Iron Cage Revisited."
40. Stuart Albert and David Whetten, "Organizational Identity," *Research in Organizational Behavior* 7 (1985): 263–295; Brint and Karabel, "Institutional Origins"; and John Meyer and Brian Rowan, "Institutionalized Organizations: Formal Structure as Myth and Ceremony," *American Journal of Sociology* 83 (1977): 340–363.
41. Martin Carnoy, *The State and Political Thought* (Princeton: Princeton University Press, 1984); and Theyda Skocpol, "Bring the State Back In: Strategies in Current Research," in *Bring the State Back In*, eds. Peter Evans, Deithrich Reuschemeyer, and Theyda Skocpol (New York: Cambridge University Press, 1985), 3–37.
42. Ibid., 250.
43. Carnoy, *The State and Political Thought*.
44. Sheila Slaughter, *The Higher Learning and High Technology* (Albany: State University of New York, 1990).
45. Kevin Dougherty, *The Contradictory College* (Albany: State University of New York Press, 1994).
46. Slaughter, *The Higher Learning and High Technology*.
47. Slaughter and Leslie, *Academic Capitalism*.
48. Jeffrey Pfeffer and Gerald Salancik, *The External Control of Organizations: A Resource Dependence Perspective* (New York: Harper and Row, 1978).
49. Brint and Karabel, "Origins and Transformations"; Clowes and Levin, "Community, Technical, and Junior Colleges: Are They Leaving Higher Education?"; John Dennison, *Challenge and Opportunity* (Vancouver: The University of British Columbia Press, 1995); John Dennison and Paul Gallagher, *Canada's Community Colleges*; Dougherty, *The Contradictory College*; Richardson, Fisk, and Okun, *Literacy in the Open Access College*; and Roueche and Baker, *Access and Excellence*.
50. John Dewey, *Democracy and Education* (New York: The Free Press, 1966).
51. Henry Giroux, *Border Crossings: Cultural Workers and the Politics of Education*. (New York: Routledge, 1992).
52. Martin Carnoy, *The State and Political Thought*.
53. Andre Frank, "Reorient World History and Social Theory" (unpublished paper, Montreal, Quebec, 1994); and Roland Robertson, *Globalization: Social Theory and Global Culture*.

54. Appadurai, "Disjunctures and Difference," 295–310.
55. Aronowitz and Di Fazio, *The Jobless Future;* Bridges, *Job Shift;* and Rifkin, *The End of Work.*
56. Castells, "The Informational Economy," 15–43; Scott Lash and John Urry, *Economies of Signs and Space* (Thousand Oaks, CA: Sage Publications, 1994); and Saskia Sassen, *The Global City* (Princeton: Princeton University Press, 1991).
57. John Ralston Saul, *The Unconscious Civilization* (Concord, Ontario: House of Anansi Press, 1995); and Teeple, *Globalization and the Decline of Social Reform.*
58. Richard Barnet and John Cavanagh, *Global Dreams: Imperial Corporations and the New World Order* (New York: Simon & Schuster, 1994); Jeremy Brecher, "Global Village or Global Pillage," *The Nation* 257 (December 6, 1993): 685–688; Stewart Clegg and John Gray, "Metaphors of Globalization," in *Postmodern Management and Organization,* eds. David Boje, Robert Gephart, and Tojo Thatchenkery (Thousand Oaks, CA: Sage Publications, 1996), 293–307; Gordon Laxer, "Social Solidarity and Global-Capitalism," *The Canadian Review of Sociology and Anthropology* (August 1995): 287–312; Ralston Saul, *The Unconscious Civilization;* and Teeple, *Globalization and the Decline of Social Reform.*
59. Thomas Friedman, *The Lexus and the Olive Tree* (New York: Farrar, Straus Giroux, 1999); Gregory Millman, *The Vandal's Crown: How Rebel Currency Traders Overthrew the World's Central Banks* (New York: The Free Press, 1995); Robert Reich, *The Work of Nations* (New York: Vintage Books, 1992); Sassen, *The Global City;* and Tapscott, *The Digital Economy.*
60. Frank, "Reorient World History and Social Theory"; E. Fuat Keyman, *Globalization, State, Identity, and Deference* (New Jersey: Humanities Press, 1997); Robertson, *Globalization;* and Waters, *Globalization.*
61. Aronowitz and Di Fazio, *The Jobless Future;* Maude Barlow and Heather-Jane Robertson, "Homogenization of Education," in *The Case Against the Global Economy,* eds. Jerry Mandes and Edward Goldsmith (San Francisco: The Sierra Club, 1996), 60–70; Currie, *Universities and Globalization;* Jane Kenway, "Fast Capitalism, Fast Feminism, and Some Fast Food for Thought," paper presented at the Annual Meeting of the American Educational Research Association, San Diego, April 1998; Simon Marginson, *Educating Australia: Government, Economy, and Citizen since 1960* (Melbourne: Cambridge University Press, 1997); Newson, "NAFTA and Higher Education in Canada"; Ritzer, *The McDonaldization Thesis;* and Daniel Schugurensky and Kathy Higgins, "From Aid to Trade: New Trends in International Education in Canada," in *Dimensions of the Community College: International, Intercultural, and Multicultural,* eds. Rosalind Raby and Norma Tarrow (New York: Garland Publishing, 1996), 53–78.
62. Aronowitz and Di Fazio, *The Jobless Future;* Currie, *Universities and Globalization;* Kenway, "Fast Capitalism"; Newson, "NAFTA and Higher Education in Canada"; and Ritzer, *The McDonaldization Thesis.*

63. Noel Gough, "Globalization and Curriculum: Theorizing a Transnational Imaginary," paper presented at the Annual Meeting of the American Educational Research Association, San Diego, 1998, 6.
64. Appadurai, "Disjunctures and Difference," 295–310.
65. Cameron, "Organizational Adaptation," 122–144; DiMaggio and Powell, "The Iron Cage Revisited"; Henry Mintzberg, *Power In and Around Organizations* (Englewood Cliffs, NJ: Prentice-Hall, Inc., 1983); and Levy and Merry, *Organizational Transformation*.
66. Appadurai, "Disjunctures and Difference"; Barnet and Cavanagh, *Global Dreams;* Manuel Castells, *The Rise of the Network Society* (Cambridge, Mass: Blackwell Publishers, 1996); Clegg and Gray, "Metaphors of Globalization"; Janice Dudley, "Globalization and Education Policy in Australia," *Universities and Globalization,* eds. Jan Currie and Janice Newson (Thousand Oaks, CA: Sage Publications, 1998), 21–43; Friedman, *The Lexus and the Olive Tree;* Lash and Urry, *Economies of Signs and Space;* and Waters, *Globalization*.
67. Frank, "Reorient World History and Social Theory"; Friedman, *The Lexus and the Olive Tree;* and Robertson, *Globalization*.
68. Bridges, *Job Shift;* Manuel Castells, "The Informational Economy"; Reich, *The Work of Nations;* and Rifkin, *The End of Work*.
69. Friedman, *The Lexus and the Olive Tree*.
70. Castells, *The Rise of the Network Society;* Clegg and Gray, "Metaphors of Globalization"; and Reich, *The Work of Nations*.
71. Aronowitz and Di Fazio, *The Jobless Future;* Bridges, *Job Shift;* Clegg and Gray, "Metaphors for Globalization"; and Rifkin, *The End of Work*.
72. Aronowitz and DiFazio, *The Jobless Future;* Bridges, *Job Shift;* and Castells, *The Rise of the Network Society*.
73. Howard Palmer and Tamari Palmer, *Alberta: A New History* (Edmonton: Hurtig Publishers, 1990); Peter Schrag, *Paradise Lost: California's Experience, America's Future* (New York: New York Press, 1998); and Veronica Strong-Boag, "Society in the Twentieth Century," *The Pacific Province,* ed. Hugh Johnstone (Vancouver: Douglas & McIntyre, 1996), 273–312.
74. Robert Gephart, Jr., "Management Social Issues and the Postmodern Era," in *Postmodern Management and Organization,* eds. David Boje, Robert Gephart, and Toje Thatchenkery (Thousand Oaks: Sage Productions, 1996), 21–44.
75. Dudley, "Globalization," 21–43; Marginson, *Educating Australia;* Ralston Saul, *The Unconscious Civilization;* and Ritzer, *The McDonaldization Thesis*.
76. John Diekhoff, *Democracy's College: Higher Education in the Local Community* (New York: Harper and Brother Publishers, 1950).
77. Robert Barr and John Tagg, "From Teaching to Learning: A New Paradigm for Undergraduate Education," *Change* (November/December 1995): 13–25; and Michael Dolence and Donald Norris, *Transforming Higher Education: A Vision for Learning in the 21st Century* (Ann Arbor, MI: Society for College and University Planning, 1995).

Chapter 2

1. Howard London, *The Culture of a Community College* (New York: Praeger Publishers, 1978); Dennis McGrath and Martin Spear, *The Academic Crisis of the Community College* (Albany: State University of New York Press, 1991); Richard Richardson, Jr., Elizabeth Fisk, and Morris Okun, *Literacy in the Open-Access College* (San Francisco: Jossey-Bass Publishers, 1983); Robert Rhoads and James Valadez, *Democracy, Multiculturalism, and the Community College* (New York: Garland Publishing, 1996); and Lois Weis, *Between Two Worlds: Black Students in an Urban Community College* (Boston: Routledge and Kegan Paul, 1985).
2. Kathleen Shaw, Robert Rhoads, and James Valdez, "Community Colleges as Cultural Texts: A Conceptual Overview," in *Community Colleges as Cultural Texts*, ed. Kathleen Shaw, James Valdez, and Robert Rhoads (Albany: State University of New York Press, 1999), 3.
3. John Frye, "Educational Paradigms in the Professional Literature of the Community College," in *Higher Education: Handbook of Theory and Research*, Vol. X, ed. John Smart (New York: Agathon Press, 1994), 181–224.
4. Dennis McGrath and Martin Spear, *The Academic Crisis of the Community College*.
5. See, for example, Joanne Cooper and Ken Kempner, "Lord of the Flies Community College: A Case Study of Organizational Disintegration," *The Review of Higher Education* (Summer 1993): 419–437; John Levin, "Success Community College: An Examination of Organizational Change," *The Canadian Journal of Higher Education* vol. 25, no. 1 (1995): 19–39; John Levin, "Limits to Organizational Change in the Community College," *Community College Journal of Research and Practice* vol. 20, no. 20 (1996): 185–197; and Starr Owen, "An Interpretive Approach to Leadership: Developing a Theme from a Case Study," in *Educational Leadership: Challenge and Change*, ed. Erwin Miklos and Eugene Ratsoy (Edmonton: Department of Educational Administration, University of Alberta, 1992), 259–284.
6. Michael Andrews, Edward Holdaway, and Gordon Mowat, "Postsecondary Education in Alberta since 1945," in *Higher Education in Canada*, ed. Glen Jones (New York: Garland Publishing, 1997), 59–92; Jean Barman, *The West Beyond the West: A History of British Columbia* (Toronto: University of Toronto Press, 1991); John Belshaw and David Mitchell, "The Economy since the Great War," in *The Pacific Province*, ed. Hugh Johnstone (Vancouver: Douglas & McIntyre, 1996), 313–342; Gavan Daws, *Shoal of Time: A History of the Hawaiian Islands* (Honolulu: University of Hawaii Press, 1974); Michael Howlett and Keith Brownsley, "Public Sector Politics in a Rentier Resource Economy," in *The Provincial State*, eds. Michael Howlett and Keith Brownsley (Mississauga, Ontario: Copp Clark Pitman, 1992), 264–295; John Levin, "Mission and Structure: The Community College in

a Global Context" (A Report on a Research Investigation, The Center for the Study of Higher Education, University of Arizona, Tucson, 1999); Howard Palmer and Tamari Palmer, *Alberta: A New History* (Edmonton: Hurtig Publishers, 1990); Larry Pratt, "The Political Economy of Province Building: Alberta's Development Strategy, 1971–1981," in *Essays on the Political Economy of Alberta,* ed. David Leadbeater (Toronto: New Hogtown Press; 1984), 194–222; Province of Alberta, "New Directions for Adult Learning in Alberta" (Edmonton: Minister of Alberta Advanced Education and Career Development, 1996); *Charting a New Course: A Strategic Plan for the Future of British Columbia's Colleges* (Victoria, British Columbia: Ministry of Education, Skills, and Training, 1996); Richard Rice, William Bullough, and Richard Orsi, *The Elusive Eden: A New History of California* (New York: Alfred Knopf, 1988); Roger Sale, *Seattle: Past to Present* (Seattle: University of Washington Press, 1976); Peter Schrag, *Paradise Lost: California's Experience, America's Future* (New York: New York Press, 1998); Carlos Schwantes, *The Pacific Northwest: An Interpretive History* (Lincoln: University of Nebraska Press, 1996); Carlos Schwantes, "Wage Earners and Wealth Makers," in *The Oxford History of the American West,* eds. Clyde Milner O'Connor and Martha Sandweiss (New York: Oxford University Press, 1996), 431–467; Michael Shires, *The Future of Public Undergraduate Education in California* (Santa Monica, CA: Rand, 1996); Peter Smith, "A Province Just Like Any Other," in *The Provincial State,* eds. Michael Howlett and Keith Brownsley (Mississauga, Ontario: Copp Clark Pitman, 1992), 242–264; Kevin Starr, *Endangered Dreams: The Great Depression in California* (New York: Oxford University Press, 1996); and Veronica Strong-Boag, "Society in the Twentieth Century," in *The Pacific Province,* ed. Hugh. Johnstone (Vancouver: Douglas & McIntyre, 1996), 273–312.

7. Arthur Cohen and Florence Brawer, *The American Community College* (San Francisco: Jossey-Bass, 1996); and John Dennison and John Levin, *Canada's Community College in the Nineteen Eighties* (Willowdale, Ontario: Association of Canadian Community Colleges, 1989).

8. Gareth Morgan, *Images of Organization* (Thousand Oaks, CA: Sage Publications, 1997); and Edgar Schein, *Organizational Culture and Leadership* (San Francisco: Jossey-Bass Publishers, 1985).

9. Joanne Martin and Debra Meyerson, "Organizational Cultures and the Denial, Channeling and Acknowledgment of Ambiguity," in *Managing Ambiguity and Change* eds. Louis Pondy, Richard Boland, and Howard Thomas (New York: John Wiley & Sons, 1988), 93–125.

10. George Baker and Associates, *Cultural Leadership: Inside America's Community Colleges* (Washington, D.C.: The Community College Press, 1992); Dennis McGrath and Martin Spear, *The Academic Crisis of the Community College* (Albany: State University of New York Press, 1991); Starr Owen, "Organizational Culture and Community Colleges," in *Challenge and Opportunity,* ed. John Dennison, (Vancouver, B.C.: UBC Press, 1995), 141–168; Richard

Richardson and Louis Bender, *Fostering Minority Access and Achievement in Higher Education* (San Francisco: Jossey-Bass Publishers, 1987); John Roueche and Suanne Roueche, *Between a Rock and a Hard Place: The At-Risk Student in the Open Door College* (Washington: The Community College Press, 1993); and George Vaughan, *The Community College Presidency* (New York: American Council on Education/Macmillan, 1986).
11. John Frye, "Educational Paradigms in the Professional Literature of the Community College," in *Higher Education: Handbook of Theory and Research*, Vol. X, ed. John Smart, 181–224 (New York: Agathon Press, 1994).
12. Steven Brint and Jerome Karabel, "Institutional Origins and Transformations: The Case of American Community Colleges," in *The New Institutionalism*, eds. Walter Powell and Paul DiMaggio (Chicago: The University of Chicago Press, 1991); Kevin Dougherty, *The Contradictory College* (Albany: State University of New York, 1994); and Lois Weis, *Between Two Worlds: Black Students in an Urban Community College* (Boston: Routledge and Kegan Paul, 1985).
13. Peter Schrag, *Paradise Lost: California's Experience, America's Future* (New York: New York Press, 1998).
14. Jean Barman, *The West Beyond the West: A History of British Columbia* (Toronto: University of Toronto Press, 1991).
15. Ibid.
16. Dennis McGrath and Martin Spear, *The Academic Crisis of the Community College* (Albany: State University of New York Press, 1991).
17. Michael Andrews, Edward Holdaway, and Gordon Mowat. "Postsecondary Education in Alberta since 1945."
18. Henry Mintzberg, *The Structuring of Organizations—A Synthesis Of Research* (Englewood Cliffs, NJ : Prentice-Hall, Inc., 1979).
19. Jeffrey Pfeffer and Gerald Salancik, *The External Control of Organizations: A Resource Dependence Perspective* (New York: Harper and Row, 1978).

Chapter 3

1. Richard Barnet and John Cavanagh, *Global Dreams: Imperial Corporations and the New World Order* (New York: Simon & Schuster, 1994).
2. William Bridges, *Job Shift* (Reading, MA: Addison-Wesley Publishing Company, 1994); Martin Carnoy, Manuel Castello, Stephen Cohen, and Fernando Cardoso, *The New Global Economy in the Information Age* (University Park: The Pennsylvania State University, 1993); Manuel Castells, "The Informational Economy and the New International Division of Labor," in *The New Global Economy in the Information Age*, eds. Martin Carnoy, Manuel Castells, Stephen Cohen, and Fernando Cardoso (University Park: The Pennsylvania State University, 1993), 15–43; and Don Tapscott, *The Digital Economy: Promise and Peril in the Age of Networked Intelligence* (New York: McGraw-Hill, 1996).

3. Daniel Schugurensky and Kathy Higgins, "From Aid to Trade: New Trends in International Education in Canada," in *Dimensions of the Community College: International, Intercultural and Multicultural,* eds. Rosalind Raby and Norma Tarrow (New York: Garland Publishing, 1996), 53–78.
4. Simon Marginson, *Educating Australia: Government, Economy and Citizen since 1960* (Melbourne: Cambridge University Press, 1997).
5. Robert Barr and John Tagg, "From Teaching to Learning—A New Paradigm for Undergraduate Education," *Change* (November/December, 1995): 13–25; and Michael Dolence and Donald Norris, *Transforming Higher Education: A Vision for Learning in the 21st Century* (Ann Arbor, MI: Society for College and University Planning, 1995).
6. Richard Edwards and Robin Usher, "Globalization, Diaspora Space and Pedagogy," paper presented at the annual meeting of the American Educational Research Association, San Diego, April 1998.
7. K. Smith, "Philosophical Problems in Thinking about Organization Change," in *Change in Organizations,* ed. Paul Goodman (San Francisco: Jossey-Ba   lishers, 1982), 316–374.
8. Amir Levy and Uri Merry, *Organizational Transformation: Approaches, Strategies, and Theories* (New York: Praeger, 1986), 288.
9. Richard Alfred and Patricia Carter, "Inside Track to the Future," *Community College Journal* 66, no. 4 (February/March, 1996): 10–19; Stanley Aronowitz and William Di Fazio, *The Jobless Future: Sci-Tech and the Dogma of Work* (Minneapolis: University of Minnesota Press, 1994); Jan Currie, "Introduction," *Universities and Globalization,* eds. Jan Currie and Janice Newson (Thousand Oaks, CA: Sage Publications, 1998), 1–13; Janice Dudley, "Globalization and Education Policy in Australia," in *Universities and Globalization,* eds. Jan Currie and Janice Newson (Thousand Oaks, CA: Sage Publications, 1998), 21–43; John Levin, "Missions and Structures: Bringing Clarity to Perceptions about Globalization and Higher Education in Canada," *Higher Education* 37, no. 4 (June, 1999): 377–399; Larry Leslie and Sheila Slaughter, "The Development and Current Status of Market Mechanisms in United States Postsecondary Education," *Higher Education Policy* 10 (March/April 1997): 239–252; Simon Marginson, *Educating Australia* (Melbourne: Cambridge University Press, 1997); Janice Newson, "NAFTA and Higher Education in Canada" (unpublished manuscript, York University, Toronto, Ontario, 1994); George Ritzer, *The McDonaldization Thesis: Explorations and Extensions* (Thousand Oaks, CA: Sage Publications, 1998); Daniel Schugurensky and Kathy Higgins, "From Aid to Trade," (New York: Garland Publishing, 1996), 53–78; Sheila Slaughter, "Who Gets What and Why in Higher Education? Federal Policy and Supply-side Institutional Resource Allocation," presidential address, Association for the Study of Higher Education annual meeting, Memphis, TN, 1997; and Sheila Slaughter and Larry Leslie, *Academic Capitalism: Politics, Policies, and the Entrepreneurial University* (Baltimore: The Johns Hopkins University Press, 1997).

10. While Canadian and U.S. dollars are not of equal worth on international money markets, they may reflect other equalities such as buying power in their own countries. For example, in Canada, health care costs are borne much more by government than by private citizens. Thus, considerably less private income in Canada is expended upon health care. In my discussion, I am comparing data and behaviors over time, and therefore my interest is either within sites or among all sites, not between sites. Therefore, I have decided to refer to these currencies without converting them into an equivalent value.
11. Statistics Canada, "Operating Income of Community Colleges by Source of Funds and by Province, Fiscal Years Ending in 1991" (Ottawa, Ontario, 1999); Statistics Canada, "Operating Income of Community Colleges by Source of Funds and by Province, Fiscal Years Ending in 1997" (Ottawa, Ontario, 1999); and U.S. Department of Education, National Center for Education Statistics, *Higher Education General Information Survey* (HEGIS) "Financial statistics of Institutions of Higher Education," Table 54–1, 1998.
12. Statistics Canada, "Operating Income of Community Colleges by Source of Funds and by Province, Fiscal Years Ending in 1991" (Ottawa, Ontario, 1999); and Statistics Canada, "Operating Income of Community Colleges by Source of Funds and by Province, Fiscal Years Ending in 1997" (Ottawa, Ontario, 1999).
13. Statistics Canada, "Operating Income of Community Colleges by Source of Funds and by Province, Fiscal Years Ending in 1991" (Ottawa, Ontario, 1999); Statistics Canada, "Operating Income of Community Colleges by Source of Funds and by Province, Fiscal Years Ending in 1997" (Ottawa, Ontario, 1999); and U.S. Department of Education, National Center for Education Statistics, *Higher Education General Information Survey* (HEGIS) "Financial Statistics of Institutions of Higher Education," Table 54–1, 1998.
14. Peter Schrag, *Paradise Lost: California's Experience, America's Future* (New York: The New Press, 1998); Carlos Schwantes, *The Pacific Northwest: An Interpretive History* (Lincoln: University of Nebraska Press, 1996); Carlos Schwantes, "Wage Earners and Wealth Makers," in *The Oxford History of the American West,* eds. Clyde Milner, Carol O'Connor, and Martha Sandweiss (New York: Oxford University Press, 1996), 431–467.
15. Norton Grubb, Norena Badway, Denise Bell, Debra Bragg, and Maxine Russman, *Workforce, Economic and Community Development: The Changing Landscape of the Entrepreneurial Community College* (Berkeley: National Center for Research in Vocational Education, The University of California, 1997).
16. Barr and Tagg, "From Teaching to Learning"; and Michael Dolence and Donald Norris, *Transforming Higher Education.*
17. John Dennison and John Levin, *Canada's Community Colleges in the Nineteen Eighties: Renewal and Responsiveness* (Toronto: Association of Canadian Community Colleges, 1989), and John Levin, "Missions and Structures:

Bringing Clarity to Perceptions about Globalization and Higher Education in Canada," *Higher Education* vol. 37, no. 4 (June 1999): 377–399.
18. Michael Andrews, Edward Holdaway, and Gordon Mowat, "Postsecondary Education in Alberta Since 1945," in *Higher Education in Canada*, ed. Glen Jones (New York: Garland Publishing, Inc. 1997), 59–92; John Belshaw and David Mitchell, "The Economy Since the Great War," in *The Pacific Province*, ed. Hugh Johnstone (Vancouver: Douglas & McIntyre, 1996), 313–342; Michael Howlett and Keith Brownsley, "Public Sector Politics in a Rentier Resource Economy," in *The Provincial State*, eds. Michael Howlett and Keith Brownsley (Mississauga, Ontario: Copp Clark Pitman, 1992), 264–295; Carlos Schwantes, *The Pacific Northwest: An Interpretive History*; Peter Schrag, *Paradise Lost: California's Experience, America's Future* (New York: New York Press, 1998); Carlos Schwantes, "Wage Earners and Wealth Makers," in *The Oxford History of the American West*, eds. Clyde Milner, Carol O'Connor, and Martha Sandweiss (New York: Oxford University Press, 1996), 431–467; Peter Smith, "A Province Just Like Any Other," in *The Provincial State*, eds. Michael Howlett and Keith Brownsley (Mississauga, Ontario: Copp Clark Pitman, 1992), 242–264; and Veronica Strong-Boag, "Society in the Twentieth Century," in *The Pacific Province*, ed. Hugh Johnstone (Vancouver: Douglas & McIntyre, 1996), 273–312.

Chapter 4

1. Arjun Appadurai, "Disjuncture and Difference in the Global Cultural Economy"; Manuel Castells, *The Rise of the Network Society* (Cambridge, MA: Blackwell Publishers, 1996), p. 201.
2. Appadurai, ibid.; Mike Featherstone, "Global Culture: An Introduction," in *Global Culture: Nationalism, Globalization and Modernity*, ed. Mike Featherstone (Newbury Park, CA., 1990), 1–14; and Saskia Sassen, *The Global City* (Princeton: Princeton University Press, 1991).
3. Scott Lash and John Urry, *The End of Organized Capitalism* (Oxford: Polity Press, 1987); and Malcom Waters, *Globalization* (New York: Routledge, 1996).
4. George Ritzer, *The McDonaldization Thesis: Explorations and Extensions* (Thousand Oaks, CA: Sage Publications, 1998).
5. Johann Arnason, "Nationalism, Globalization and Modernity," in *Global Culture: Nationalism, Globalization and Modernity*, ed. Mike Featherstone (Newbury Park, CA., 1990), 207–236; and Roland Robertson, *Globalization: Social Theory and Global Culture* (London: Sage Productions, 1992).
6. Featherstone, "Global Culture: An Introduction."
7. John Ralston Saul, *The Unconscious Civilization* (Concord, Ontario: House of Anansi Press, 1995).
8. Noam Chomsky, *Profit Over People: Neoliberalism and Global Order* (New York: Seven Stories Press, 1999).

9. Gary Teeple, *Globalization and the Rise of Social Reform* (New Jersey: Humanities Press, 1995), 5.
10. Robertson, *Globalization: Social Theory and Global Culture*.
11. Robert Gephart, Jr., "Management, Social Issues, and the Postmodern Era," in *Postmodern Management and Organizational Theory*, eds. David Boje, Robert Gephart, and Tojo Thatchenkery (Thousand Oaks, CA.: Sage Publications, 1996), 21–44.
12. Simon Marginson, *Educating Australia: Government, Economy, and Citizen since 1960* (Melbourne: Cambridge University Press, 1997); and Ritzer, *The McDonaldization Thesis: Explorations and Extensions*.
13. Stanley Aronowitz and William Di Fazio, *The Jobless Future: Sci-Tech and the Dogma of Work* (Minneapolis: University of Minnesota Press, 1994); and Sheila Slaughter and Larry Leslie, *Academic Capitalism, Politics, Policies, and the Entrepreneurial University* (Baltimore: The Johns Hopkins University Press, 1997).
14. Daniel Bell, *The Coming of Post-Industrial Society: A Venture in Social Forecasting* (New York: Basic Books, 1973), 348–349; and Edward Schaffer, "The University in Service to Technocracy," *Education Theory*, vol. 30, no. 1 (Winter 1980): 47–52.
15. Anthony Carnavele and Donna Desrochers, "Community Colleges in the New Economy," *Community College Journal*, April/May, vol. 67, no. 5, 1997, 26–33; Melanie Griffith and Ann Connor, *Democracy's Open Door: The Community College in America's Future* (Portsmouth, NH: Boynton/Cook Publishers, 1994); Mary Ann Roe, *Education and U.S. Competitiveness: The Community College Role* (Austin, Texas: IC2 Institute, University of Texas at Austin, 1989); and Daniel Schugurensky and Kathy Higgins, "From Aid to Trade: New Trends in International Education in Canada," in *Dimensions of the Community College: International, Intercultural and Multicultural*, eds. Rosalind Raby and Norma Tarrow (New York: Garland Publishing, 1996), 53–78.
16. Henry Mintzberg, *Power In and Around Organizations* (Englewood Cliffs, NJ: Prentice Hall, Inc., 1983).
17. Ralston Saul, *The Unconscious Civilization*.
18. Henry Mintzberg, *Mintzberg on Management: Inside Our Strange World of Organizations.* (New York: The Free Press, 1989).
19. George Baker and Associates, *Cultural Leadership: Inside America's Community Colleges.* (Washington, D.C.: The Community College Press, 1993); Griffith and Connor, *Democracy's Open Door: The Community College in America's Future;* Janet Knowles, "A Matter of Survival: Emerging Entrepreneurship in Community Colleges in Canada," in *Challenge and Opportunity*, ed. John Dennison (Vancouver, B.C.: University of British Columbia Press, 1995), 184–207; Roe, *Education and U. S. Competitiveness: The Community College Role;* and John Roueche, Lynn Taber, and Suanne Roueche, *The Company We Keep: Collaboration in the Community College* (Washington, D.C.: American Association of Community Colleges, 1995).

20. Tom Peters and Robert Waterman, *In Search of Excellence* (New York: Warner Books, 1982).
21. Richard Alfred and Patricia Carter, "Inside Track to the Future," *Community College Journal*, February/March, vol. 66, no. 4 (1996): 10–19; and George Baker and Vaughn Upshaw, "A Team Approach to Institutional Quality: Toward a Model," in *Team Building for Quality*, eds. George Baker and Associates (Washington, D.C.: Community College Press, 1995), 1–25.
22. Arthur Cohen and Florence Brawer, "The Changing Environment: Contexts, Concepts, and Crises," in *Managing Community Colleges*, eds. Arthur Cohen and Florence Brawer (San Francisco: Jossey-Bass Publishers, 1994), 5–21.
23. Paul Gallagher, "Promise Fulfilled, Promise Pending," in *Challenge and Opportunity: Canada's Community Colleges at the Crossroads*, ed. John Dennison (Vancouver: University of British Columbia Press, 1995), 256–274.
24. Cohen and Brawer, *The American Community College*; Dennison and Gallagher, *Canada's Community Colleges*.
25. Linda Thor, Carol Scarafiotti, and Laura Helminski, "Managing Change: A Case Study in Evolving Strategic Management," in *Organizational Change in the Community College: A Ripple or a Sea Change?*, ed. John Stewart Levin (San Francisco: Jossey-Bass Publishers, 1998), 57.
26. Ibid., 59.
27. Robert Gordon, "Partnerships at Humber College," in *The Company We Keep: Collaboration in the Community College*, ed. John Roueche, Lynn Taber, and Suanne Roueche (Washington, D.C.: Community College Press, 1995), 125.
28. Paul Gianini and Sandra Sarantos, "Academic Rhetoric Versus Business Reality," in *The Company We Keep: Collaboration in the Community College*, 205–226.
29. Ibid., 220.
30. Steven Johnson, "Organizational Structures and the Performance of Contract Training Operations in American Community Colleges," unpublished doctoral dissertation, The University of Texas, 1995, 5.
31. Norton Grubb, Norena Badway, Denise Bell, Debra Bragg, and Maxine Russman, *Workforce, Economic and Community Development: The Changing Landscape of the Entrepreneurial Community College* (Berkeley: National Center for Research in Vocational Education, The University of California, 1997).
32. Ken Meier, "The Community College Mission and Organizational Behavior," unpublished paper, The Center for the Study of Higher Education, Tucson, Arizona, 1999.
33. Daniel Schugurensky and Kathy Higgins, "From Aid to Trade: New Trends in International Education in Canada."
34. Leo Driedger, *Multi-Ethnic Canada: Identities and Inequalities* (Toronto: Oxford University Press, 1996), 58–59; Employment and Immigration Canada, *Immigration Statistics*, 1980, Table 3; Ibid., 1981, Table 3; Statistics

Canada, *Annual Demographic Statistics,* 1993, Catalogue no. 91–213; Ibid., 1998, Catalogue no. 91–213; Ibid., 1993, Catalogue no. 91–213, Table 4.3; and U.S. Department of Commerce, *Statistical Abstract of the United States,* (Washington, D.C.: Bureau of the Census, 1998), 11; Ibid., 1996, 11; Ibid., 1995, 11; Ibid., 1995, 11; Ibid., 1994, 11; Ibid., 1993, 11; Ibid., 1992, 11; Ibid., 1991,10; Ibid., 1990, 10; Ibid., 1989,10; Ibid., 1989, 10; Ibid., 1987, 11; Ibid., 1986, 86; Ibid., 1985, 86; Ibid., 1981,126.

35. Ernest Pascarella and Patrick Terenzini, "Studying College Students in the 21st Century: Meeting New Challenges," *The Review of Higher Education,* vol. 21, no. 2 (Winter 1998): 151–165.
36. *The Chronicle of Higher Education Almanac,* August 27, 1999, 24.
37. Dinesh D'Souza, *Illiberal Education: The Politics of Race and Sex on Campus* (New York: Free Press, 1991); Susan Faludi, *Backlash: The Undeclared War Against American Women* (New York: Crown, 1991); Henry Giroux, *Border Crossings: Cultural Workers and the Politics of Education* (New York: Routledge, 1992); Robert Rhoads and James Valadez, *Democracy, Multiculturalism and the Community College* (New York: Garland Publishing, 1996); and William Tierney, *Building Communities of Difference: Higher Education in the 21st Century* (Westport, CT: Bergin and Garvey, 1993).
38. Included are Japan, Korea, Taiwan, Hong Kong, China, Macao, Singapore, Malaysia, the Philippines, and in one college, India.
39. Daniel Schugurensky and Kathy Higgins, "From Aid to Trade: New Trends in International Education in Canada."
40. Henry Giroux, *Border Crossings: Cultural Workers and the Politics of Education;* Diane Ravitch, "Multiculturalism," *The American Scholar* (Winter 1990):337–354; Robert Rhoads and James Valadez, *Democracy, Multiculturalism, and the Community;* and William Tierney, *Building Communities of Difference: Higher Education in the 21st Century.*
41. Douglas Baker, "Aboriginal Education in Community Colleges," in *Challenge and Opportunity,* ed. John Dennison (Vancouver, B.C.: University of British Columbia Press, 1995), 208–219.
42. California Department of Finance, Research Unit, "Race/Ethnic Estimates by County," 1998; U.S. Bureau of the Census, "U.S. Counties," Censtats, 1996; U. S. Bureau of the Census, "Estimates of the Population of Counties and Demographic Components of Population Change: Annual Time Series, July 1, 1990 to July 1, 1997," PE-62, CO 97–6, 1997; U. S. Census Bureau, "Estimates of the Population of States: Annual Time Series, July 1, 1990 to July 1, 1998 and Demographic Components of Population Change," *Annual Time Series,* Block 1, 1998; Washington State, Employment Security Department, 1998; and Washington State, "Washington Selected Economic Data," Office of Financial Management, 1998.
43. The Financial Post Data Group, *Canadian Markets* (Toronto, 1991, 1993, 1994); and Statistics Canada, *Annual Demographic Statistics,* Catalogue no. 91–913, 1998.

44. Roland Robertson, *Globalization: Social Theory and Global Culture.*
45. Mike Featherstone, "Global Culture: An Introduction," in *Global Culture: Nationalism, Globalization and Modernity,* ed. Mike Featherstone (Newbury Park, CA: Sage Publications, 1990), 1–14; and Anthony Giddens, *The Consequences of Modernity* (Stanford: Stanford University Press, 1990).
46. Anthony Smith, "Towards a Global Culture?," in *Global Culture: Nationalism, Globalization and Modernity,* ed. Mike Featherstone (Newbury Park, CA: Sage Publications, 1990), 171–191; and Malcom Waters, *Globalization* (New York: Routledge, 1996).
47. Arjun Appadurai, "Disjuncture and Difference in the Global Cultural Economy."
48. Roland Robertson, *Globalization: Social Theory and Global Culture.*
49. Gordon Laxer, "Social Solidarity and Global Capitalism," *The Canadian Review of Sociology and Anthropology* (August 1995): 287–312; George Ritzer, *The McDonaldization Thesis: Explorations and Extensions* (Thousand Oaks, CA: Sage Publications, 1998).
50. Mike Featherstone, "Global Culture: An Introduction," 2.
51. Giddens, *The Consequences of Modernity;* E. Fuat Keyman, *Globalization, State, Identity, and Deference* (New Jersey: Humanities Press, 1997); and David Morley and Kevin Robins, *Spaces of Identity: Global Media, Electronic Landscapes and Cultural Boundaries* (New York: Routledge, 1995).
52. Appadurai, "Disjuncture and Difference in the Global Cultural Economy"; and David Held, Anthony McGrew, David Goldblatt, and Jonathan Perraton, *Global Transformations: Politics, Economics and Culture* (Stanford: Stanford University Press, 1999).
53. Jan Currie, "Introduction," in *Universities and Globalization,* eds. Jan Currie and Janice Newson (Thousand Oaks: Sage Publications, 1998), 1–13; Noel Gough, "Globalization and Curriculum: Theorizing a Transnational Imaginary," paper presented at the Annual Meeting of the American Educational Research Association, San Diego 1998; Jane Kenway, "Fast Capitalism, Fast Feminism, and Some Fast Food for Thought," paper presented at the Annual Meeting of the American Educational Research Association, San Diego April 1998; Daniel Schugurensky and Kathy Higgins, "From Aid to Trade: New Trends in International Education in Canada"; and Sheila Slaughter and Larry Leslie, *Academic Capitalism, Politics, Policies, and the Entrepreneurial University* (Baltimore: The Johns Hopkins University Press, 1997).
54. Ronald Inglehart, *Culture Shift in Advanced Industrial Society* (Princeton: Princeton University Press, 1990).
55. Neil Nevitte, Miguel Basañez, and Ronald Inglehart, "Directions of Value Change in North America," in *North America Without Borders,* eds. Stephen Randall, Herman Konrad, and Sheldon Silverman (Calgary: The University of Calgary Press), 247.
56. Appadurai, 1990.

57. Karen Cárdenas, "Technology in Today's Classroom: It Slices and It Dices, but Does It Serve Us Well?," *Academe*, May-June, 1998, 27–29; Stephen Erhmann, "Asking the Right Questions: What Does Research Tell Us about Technology and Higher Education?," *Change*, vol. 27, no. 2 (1995): 20–27; Steven Gilbert and Kenneth Green, "Great Expectations: Content, Communication Productivity, and the Role of Information Technology in Higher Education," *Change*, vol. 27, no. 2 (1995): 8–18; and John Levin, "Is the Management of Distance Education Transforming Instruction in Colleges?" *The Quarterly Review of Distance Education* (in press).
58. Manuel Castells, *The Rise of the Network Society* (Cambridge, MA: Blackwell Publishers, 1996).
59. Paul Levinson, *Digital McLuhan: A Guide to the Information Millennium* (New York: Routledge, 1999).
60. Steven Brint and Jerome Karabel, *The Diverted Dream: Community Colleges and the Promise of Educational Opportunity in America, 1900–1985* (New York: Oxford University Press, 1989); Kevin Dougherty, *The Contradictory College* (Albany: State University of New York Press, 1994); and Fred Pincus, "How Critics View the Community College's Role in the Twenty-First Century," in *A Handbook on the Community College in America*, ed. George Baker III (Westport, CT: Greenwood Press, 1994), 624–636.
61. Robertson, *Globalization: Social Theory and Global Culture*, 8.

Chapter 5

1. Anne Balsmo, "Myths of Information: The Cultural Impact of New Information Technologies," in *The Information Revolution*, eds. Alan Porter and William Read (Greenwich, CT: Ablex, 1998), 225–235; Martin Carnoy, Manuel Castells, Stephen Cohen, and Fernando Cardoso, *The New Global Economy in the Information Age* (University Park: The Pennsylvania State University, 1993); Manuel Castells, *The Rise of the Network Society* (Cambridge, MA: Blackwell Publishers, 1996); and Robert Chodos, Eric Hamovitch, and Rae Murphy, *Lost in Cyberspace?* (Toronto: James Lorimer and Company, 1997).
2. David Morley and Kevin Robins, *Spaces of Identity: Global Media, Electronic Landscapes and Cultural Boundaries* (New York: Routledge, 1995).
3. Roland Robertson, *Globalization: Social Theory and Global Culture* (London: Sage Publications, 1992).
4. Ian Miles, "The Information Society: Competing Perspectives on the Social and Economic Implications of Information and Communication Technologies," *Information and Communication Technologies: Visions and Realities*, ed. William Dutton (New York: Oxford University Press, 1996), 37–52.
5. Robert Kozma and Jerome Johnston, "The Technological Revolution Comes to the Classroom," *Change* (January/February 1991): 10–23.

6. Robert Barr and John Tagg, "From Teaching to Learning—A New Paradigm for Undergraduate Education," *Change* (November/December 1995): 13–25.
7. Michael Skolnik, "Higher Education in the 21st Century," *Futures* 30, no. 7 (1998): 635–650.
8. Karen Cárdenas, "Technology in Today's Classroom: It Slices and It Dices, but Does it Serve Us Well?," *Academe* (May-June 1998): 27–29; Don Doucette, "Transforming Teaching and Learning Through Technology," in *Teaching and Learning in the Community College,* ed. Terry O'Banion (Washington, D.C.: The American Association of Community Colleges, 1995), 201–227; John Levin, "Is the Management of Distance Education Transforming Instruction in Colleges?" *The Quarterly Review of Distance Education* (in press); and Jamie Merisotis, "The 'What's-the-Difference?' Debate," *Academe* (September-October 1999): 47–51.
9. Sir John Daniel, "Why Universities Need Technology Strategies," *Change* (July-August, 1997): 11–17; Stephen Erhmann, "Asking the Right Questions: What Does Research Tell Us about Technology and Higher Education?," *Change* 27, no. 2 (1995): 20–27; Rick Garrett, "Computer-Assisted Instruction in 2-Year Colleges: Technology for Innovative Teaching," *Community College Journal of Research and Practice* 19 (1995): 529–536; Steven Gilbert and Kenneth Green, "Great Expectations: Content, Communication Productivity, and the Role of Information Technology in Higher Education," *Change* 27, no. 2 (1995): 8–18; Kozma and Johnston, "The Technological Revolution Comes to the Classroom," 10–23; Terry O'Banion, "Teaching and Learning: A Mandate for the Nineties," in *Teaching and Learning in the Community College,* ed. Terry O'Banion (Washington, D.C.: The American Association of Community Colleges, 1995), 3–20; and David Snyder, "High Tech and Higher Education: A Wave of Creative Destruction is Rolling Toward the Halls of Academe," *Horizon* 4, no. 5 (1996): 1–7.
10. Stanley Aronowitz and William Di Fazio, *The Jobless Future: Sci-Tech and the Dogma of Work* (Minneapolis: University of Minnesota Press, 1994); Anthony Carnavele and Donna Desrochers, "Community Colleges in the New Economy," *Community College Journal* 67, no. 5 (1997): 26–33; Kevin Robins and Frank Webster, *Times of Technoculture* (New York: Routledge, 1999); and Skolnik, "Higher Education in the 21st Century," 635–650.
11. George Ritzer, *The McDonaldization Thesis: Explorations and Extensions* (Thousand Oaks: Sage Publications, 1998).
12. Arthur Cohen and Florence Brawer, *The American Community College* (San Francisco: Jossey-Bass, 1996); John Dennison and Paul Gallagher, *Canada's Community Colleges* (Vancouver: University of British Columbia Press, 1986); John Dennison and John Levin, *Canada's Community College in the Nineteen Eighties* (Willowdale, Ontario: Association of Canadian Community Colleges, 1989); Lynn Taber, "Chapter and Verse: How We

Came to Be Where We Are," in *The Company We Keep: Collaboration in the Community College,* eds. John Roueche, Lynn Taber, and Suanne Roueche (Washington, D.C.: American Association of Community Colleges, 1995), 25–37.
13. Steven Brint and Jerome Karabel, *The Diverted Dream: Community Colleges and the Promise of Educational Opportunity in America, 1900–1985* (New York: Oxford University Press, 1989); and John Frye, *The Vision of the Public Junior College, 1900–1940* (New York: Greenwood Press, 1992).
14. Don Doucette, "Transforming Teaching and Learning Using Information Technology," *The College Board Review,* no. 167 (Spring 1993): 24.
15. Rich Gross, "Defining the New Mandate for Distance Learning in the 21st Century," *Community College Journal* (October/November, 1995): 28–33.
16. Don Doucette, "Transforming Teaching and Learning Through Technology," 201.
17. Province of Alberta, Alberta Advanced Education and Career Development, "Encouraging Excellence and Rewarding Success in Alberta's Public Adult Learning System" (Edmonton, Alberta: December, 1996); Province of Alberta, Alberta Advanced Education and Career Development, "Vision for Change: A Concept Paper for the Development of a Virtual Learning System" (Edmonton, Alberta: September 25, 1995); Province of Alberta, Alberta Advanced Education and Career Development, "A Proposal for Performance-Based Funding. Promoting Excellence in Alberta's Public Adult Learning System" (Edmonton, Alberta: November 1995); Province of Alberta, Alberta Advanced Education and Career Development, "New Directions for Adult Learning in Alberta: Adult Learning Access through Innovation" (Edmonton, Alberta: October, 1994); Province of Alberta, Alberta Advanced Education and Career Development, "Enhancing Alberta's Adult Learning System through Technology. Policy, Guidelines and Procedures for the Learning Enhancement Envelope" (Edmonton, Alberta: undated); and Province of Alberta, "Framework for Technology Integration in Education. A Report of the MLA Implementation Team on Business Involvement and Technology Integration" (Edmonton, Alberta: Alberta Education Cataloguing in Publication Data, March, 1996).
18. Province of British Columbia, Ministry of Education, Skills and Training, "Charting a New Course" (Victoria, B.C.: September 13, 1996); Province of British Columbia, British Columbia Labour Force Development Board, "Training for What?" (Victoria, B.C.: Ministry of Skills, Training, and Labour, 1995); and Province of British Columbia, B.C. Human Resources Development Project, "Report of Steering Committee" (Victoria, B.C.: November 1992).
19. Province of British Columbia, Ministry of Skills, Training and Labor, "Opportunities in Post Secondary Education and Training" (Victoria, B.C.: undated); "The Report of the Post-Secondary Policy Forum on Distributed Learning Environments." (Victoria, BC: 1995).

20. "Telecommunications Infrastructure Model Master Plan and Guidelines Appendix A," ORSA Consulting Engineers, Inc., Fullerton California, for The California State University, 1995; "California Community Colleges Telecommunication Technology Infrastructure," Certification Document Materials, November 1996; State of California, State Legislature, "Education Code and Government Code including AB 1497 Chap. 1214 of the Statutes of 1991 and SB 3512 Chap. 805 of the 1994 Statutes," Economic Development Program Codes and New Legislation, Revised, November 18 1996; and State of California, Commission on Innovation, "Choosing the Future: An Action Agenda for Community Colleges," Report of Commission on Innovation to the Board of Governors of the California Colleges, Sacramento, CA: October 1993.
21. State of California, State Legislature, "Education Code and Government Code including AB 1497 Chap. 1214 of the Statutes of 1991 and SB 3512 Chap. 805 of the 1994 Statutes," Economic Development Program Codes and New Legislation, Revised, November 18, 1996.
22. State of Hawaii, "Chapter 304, University of Hawaii," The Statues of the State of Hawaii, 1996, Honolulu, HI, 1996; State of Hawaii, Governor Benjamin Cayento, "Restoring Hawaii's Economic Momentum," Governor's Report, Honolulu, HI: 1996; The University of Hawaii Community Colleges, "Annual Report 1993–94," Honolulu, HI: The Office of the Chancellor for Community Colleges, 1995; The University of Hawaii Community Colleges, "Facing the Future: On the Edge of a New Millennium, Annual Report 1994–1995," Honolulu, HI: Office of the Chancellor for Community Colleges, 1996; The University of Hawaii, Board of Regents, "Policy Section 4–2, Part D Distance Learning," June 19, 1998; and The University of Hawaii, The Board of Regents and Office of the President, "Mission," November, 1997.
23. State of Washington, Higher Education Coordinating Board, "The Challenge for Higher Education: 1996 State of Washington Master Plan for Education," Olympia, WA: 1996; State of Washington, Workforce Training and Education Board, "Workforce Training: Supply, Demand, and Gaps," Olympia, WA: 1996; State of Washington, State Board for Community College Education (SBCE)/State of Washington Information Services and Enrollment Planning (SWSEP), "Fall Enrollment & Staffing 1995," Olympia, WA: 1996; and State of Washington, State Board for Community College Education (SBCE)/State of Washington Information Services and Enrollment Planning (SWSEP), "Academic year report 1992–93," Olympia, WA: 1993.
24. Manuel Castells, *The Rise of the Network Society.*
25. Ibid.; Daniel Cornfield, "Workers, Managers, and Technological Change," in *Workers, Managers, and Technological Change,* ed. Daniel Cornfield (New York: Plenum Press, '1987), 3–24; Ian Miles, "The Information Society: Competing Perspectives on the Social and Economic Implications of In-

formation and Communication Technologies," 37–52; Gary Rhoades, *Managed Professionals: Unionized Faculty and Restructuring Academic Labor* (Albany: SUNY Press, 1998); Kevin Robins and Frank Webster, *Times of Technoculture;* and Robert Thomas and Thomas Kochan, "Technology, Industrial Relations, and the Problem of Organizational Transformation," in *Technology and the Future of Work,* ed. Paul Adler (New York: Oxford University Press, 1992), 210–231.

26. Cornfield, "Workers, Managers, and Technological Change," 3–24; Ian McLoughlin and Jon Clark, *Technological Change at Work* (Philadelphia: Open University Press, 1994); and Steven Vallas, *Power in the Workplace: The Politics of Production at AT&T* (Albany: State University of New York Press, 1993).
27. Aronowitz and Di Fazio, *The Jobless Future: Sci-Tech and the Dogma of Work;* William Bridges, *Job Shift* (Reading, MA: Addison Wesey, 1994); and Jeremy Rifkin, *The End of Work* (New York: G.P. Putnam's Sons, 1995).
28. Castells, *The Rise of the Network Society;* Manuel Castells, "The Informational Economy and the New International Division of Labor," in *The New Global Economy in the Information Age,* eds. Martin Carnoy, Manuel Castells, Stephen Cohen and Fernando Cardosa (University Park: The Pennsylvania State University, 1993),15–43; and McLoughlin and Clark, *Technological Change at Work.*
29. Aronowitz and Di Fazio, *The Jobless Future: Sci-Tech and the Dogma of Work;* Castells, *The Rise of the Network Society;* and Robins and Webster, *Times of Technoculture.*
30. Aronowitz and Di Fazio, *The Jobless Future: Sci-Tech and the Dogma of Work;* Manuel Castells, *The Rise of the Network Society;* McLoughlin and Clark, *Technological Change at Work;* Don Tapscott, *The Digital Economy Promise and Peril in the Age of Networked Intelligence* (New York: McGraw Hill, 1996); and Rifkin, *The End of Work.*
31. See Castells, *The Rise of the Network Society.*
32. Ibid., p. 1.
33. Ibid.
34. Castells, *The Rise of the Network Society.*
35. Sheila Slaughter and Larry Leslie, *Academic Capitalism. Politics, Policies, and the Entrepreneurial University* (Baltimore: The Johns Hopkins University Press, 1997).
36. David Leslie and E.K. Fretwell Jr., *Wise Moves in Hard Times* (San Francisco: Jossey Bass, 1996).
37. Ibid., p. 26
38. Ibid., p. 18.
39. Bridges, *Job Shift;* Robins and Webster, *Times of Technoculture;* Robert Thomas and Thomas Kochan, "Technology, Industrial Relations, and the Problem of Organizational Transformation," 210–231; and Steven Vallas, *Power in the Workplace: The Politics of Production at AT&T.*

40. Rhoades, *Managed Professionals: Unionized Faculty and Restructuring Academic Labor*.
41. Cynthia Hardy, *The Politics of Collegiality: Retrenchment Strategies in Canadian Universities* (Buffalo: McGill-Queen's University Press, 1996), 184.
42. Jack Schuster, Daryl Smith, Kathleen Corak, and Myrtle Yamada, *Strategic Governance: How to Make Big Decisions Better* (Phoenix, AZ: American Council on Education and Oryx Press, 1994); David Dill, "The Management of Academic Culture: Notes on the Management of Meaning and Social Integration," *Higher Education* 11 (1982): 303–320, made this observation an earlier time during the economic rise of Japan and the publicity over Japanese managerial practices. Dill and others assumed that Japan's economic success was connected to its practice of collegial decision-making. However, economic performance of Japan in the 1990s as well as new understandings about Japanese practices would lead one to revise Dill's assumptions.
43. Aronowitz and Di Fazio, *The Jobless Future: Sci-Tech and the Dogma of Work*; and Rifkin, *The End of Work*.
44. Rhoades, *Managed Professionals: Unionized Faculty and Restructuring Academic Labor*, 199.
45. John Levin, "What's the Impediment? Structural and Legal Constraints to Shared Governance in the Community College," *The Canadian Journal of Higher Education* XXX, 2 (2000): 87–122.
46. Robins and Webster, *Times of Technoculture*.

Chapter 6

1. The terms *vocationalism* and *commercialism* are adapted here from the work of Jane Kenway, "Fast Capitalism, Fast Feminism and Some Fast Food for Thought," paper presented at the annual meeting of the American Educational Research Association, San Diego, April 1998.
2. Leo Goedegebuure, Frans Kaiser, Peter Maassen, and Egbert De Weert, "Higher Education Policy in International Perspective: An Overview," in *Higher Education Policy*, eds. Leo Goedegebuure, Frans Kaiser, Peter Maassen, Lynn Meek, Frans Van Vught, and Egbert De Weert (New York: Pergamon Press, 1993), 1–12.
3. Edella Schlager and William Blomquist, "A Comparison of Three Emerging Theories of the Policy Process," *Political Research Quarterly* 49, no. 3: 651–672.
4. Daniel Schugurensky and Kathy Higgins, "From Aid to Trade: New Trends in International Education in Canada," in *Dimensions of the Community College: International, Intercultural, and Multicultural*, eds. Rosalind Raby and Norma Tarrow (New York: Garland Publishing, 1996), 53–78.
5. Martin Carnoy, *The State and Political Thought* (Princeton: Princeton University Press, 1984); and Theyda Skocpol, "Bring the State Back In: Strategies in Current Research," in *Bring the State Back In*, eds. Peter Evans,

Deithrich Reuschemeyer, and Theyda Skocpol (New York: Cambridge University Press, 1985), 3–37.
6. Carnoy, *The State and Political Thought*, 250.
7. Carnoy, *The State and Political Thought*.
8. Kevin Dougherty, *The Contradictory College* (Albany: State University of New York Press, 1994).
9. William Coleman and Grace Skogstad, "Policy Communities and Policy Networks: A Structural Approach," in *Policy Communities and Public Policy in Canada*, eds. William Coleman and Grace Skogstad (Mississauga, Ontario: Copp Clark Pitman Limited, 1990), 14–31.
10. Sheila Slaughter, *The Higher Learning and High Technology* (Albany: State University of New York Press, 1990).
11. Goedegebuure, Kaiser, Maassen, and De Weert, "Higher Education Policy in International Perspective: An Overview," 5.
12. Goedegebuure, Kaiser, Maassen, and De Weert, "Higher Education Policy in International Perspective: An Overview," 1.
13. Skocpol, "Bring the State Back In: Strategies in Current Research."
14. Carnoy, *The State and Political Thought*.
15. Carnoy, *The State and Political Thought*, 250.
16. Carnoy, *The State and Political Thought*; Dougherty, *The Contradictory College*; and Skocpol, "Bring the State Back In: Strategies in Current Research."
17. Skocpol, "Bring the State Back In: Strategies in Current Research," 15.
18. Slaughter, *The Higher Learning and High Technology*.
19. Major U.S. federal documents included among others the following: Carl D. Perkins Vocational and Applied Technology Education Act, as amended through July 1995, Washington, D.C.: Government Printing Office, 1995; Commission on Workforce and Community Development, *Responding to the Challenges on Workforce and Economic Development: The Role of America's Community Colleges*, Washington, D.C.: American Association of Community Colleges, 1996; U.S. Department of Education, *National Assessment of Vocational Education*, Washington, D.C.: Office of Education Research and Improvement, 1994; and Workforce and Career Development Act of 1996, Conference Report, H.R. 104–707, 104th Congress, 2nd session, 1996.
20. Report of the Commission on Innovation to the Board of Governors of the California Community Colleges, *Choosing the Future: An Action Agenda for Community Colleges*, Sacramento, California: Board of Governors, California Community Colleges, 1993; State of California, Economic Development Program Codes and New Legislation, Revised, November 18, 1996, *Education and Government Code*, Chapter 1214 and Chapter 805 of State Statutes; and 2005 Task Force of the Chancellor's Consultation Council. Technical Papers, California Policy Analysis and Management Information Services Division, Chancellor's Office, 1997.
21. University of Hawaii Community College 1990–95 Annual Reports, Office of the Chancellor for Community Colleges. Honolulu, HI; and *Uni-*

versity of Hawaii Community Colleges Strategic Plan 1997–2007, Approved by the Board of Regents 1997, Office of Senior Vice President and Chancellor University of Hawaii Community Colleges, Honolulu, HI.
22. Higher Education Coordinating Board, *The Challenge for Higher Education, State of Washington Master Plan for Education,* 1996; Washington State, Government legislation, 1991–1993; and Workforce Training and Education Coordinating Board, *High Skills, High Wages: Washington's Comprehensive Plan for Workforce Training and Education,* Progress report, Olympia, WA, 1995.
23. Minister of Human Resource Development, *Federal and Provincial Support to Post Secondary Education in Canada: A Report to Parliament 1993–94,* Minister of Supply and Services Canada, Ottawa, ON, 1995; and Minister of Human Resource Development, *Federal and Provincial Support to Post Secondary Education in Canada: A Report to Parliament 1994–95,* Minister of Supply and Services Canada, Ottawa, ON, 1996.
24. David Cameron, "The Federal Perspective," in *Higher Education in Canada,* ed. Glen Jones (New York: Garland Publishing, 1997), 9–27; Linda McQuaig, *Shooting the Hippo: Death By Deficit* (Toronto: Penguin Books, 1995); and Personal communication with Tom Austin, Director, Post Secondary Finance, Ministry of Education, Skills, and Training, Province of B.C., 1996.
25. Province of Alberta, *New Directions for Adult Learning in Alberta: Adult Learning Access through Innovation,* Alberta Advanced Education and Career Development, Edmonton, AB, 1994; Alberta Advanced Education and Career Development, *Vision for Change: A Concept Paper for the Development of a Virtual Learning System,* Alberta Advanced Education and Career Development, Edmonton, AB, 1995; Alberta Advance Educational and Career Development, *Business Plan,* Advance Education and Career Development, Edmonton, AB, 1994; and Alberta Advance Educational and Career Development, *Business Plan,* Advance Education and Career Development, Edmonton, AB, 1996.
26. British Columbia Labour Force Development Board, *Training for What?,* Ministry of Skills, Training, and Labour, Victoria, BC, 1995; Government of British Columbia, *College and Institute Amendment Act,* Victoria, BC: Queen's Printer, 1994; and Ministry of Education, Skills and Training *Charting a New Course,* Victoria, BC: Ministry of Education, Skills and Training, 1996.
27. Carnoy, *The State and Political Thought.*
28. Kevin Dougherty, *The Contradictory College.*
29. Leif Hartmark and Edward Hines, "Politics and Policy in Higher Education: Reflection on the Status of the Field," in *Policy Controversies in Higher Education,* eds. Samuel Gove and Thomas Stauffer, (New York: Greenwood Press, 1986), 3–26.
30. See Sheila Slaughter and Larry Leslie, *Academic Capitalism, Politics, Policies, and the Entrepreneurial University* (Baltimore: The Johns Hopkins University Press, 1997).

31. Peter Smith, "A Province Just Like Any Other," in *The Provincial State*, eds. Michael Howlett and Keith Brownsley (Mississauga, Ontario: Copp Clark Pitman, 1992), 242–264.
32. Michael Andrews, Edward Holdaway, and Gordon Mowat, "Postsecondary Education in Alberta since 1945," in *Higher Education in Canada*, ed. Glen Jones (New York: Garland Publishing, 1997), 59–92.
33. Wendy Wheeler, *A New Modernity? Change in Science, Literature and Politics* (London: Lawrence and Wishart, 1999), 11.
34. Dennis McGrath and Martin Spear, *The Academic Crisis of the Community College* (Albany: State University of New York Press, 1991).
35. Arthur Cohen and Florence Brawer, *The American Community College* (San Francisco: Jossey-Bass, 1982), 28; and John Frye, *The Vision of the Public Junior College, 1900–1940* (New York: Greenwood Press, 1992), 4.
36. Steven Brint and Jerome Karabel, *The Diverted Dream: Community Colleges and the Promise of Educational Opportunity in America, 1900–1985* (New York: Oxford University Press, 1989); Thomas Diener, *Growth of an American Invention: A Documentary History of the Junior and Community College Mission* (New York: Greenwood Press, 1986); and John Frye, *The Vision of the Public Junior College, 1900–1940*.
37. Arthur Cohen, *Dateline '79: Heretical Concepts for the Community College* (Beverly Hills: Glencoe Press, 1969), xvi.
38. John Dennison and Paul Gallagher, *Canada's Community Colleges* (Vancouver: University of British Columbia Press, 1986).
39. See Dennison and Gallagher, *Canada's Community Colleges*; and W. Norton Grubb, *Honored But Invisible* (New York: Routledge, 1999).
40. See Arthur Cohen and Florence Brawer, *The American Community* College, 1996; Dennison and Gallagher, *Canada's Community Colleges*; and W. Norton Grubb, *Honored But Invisible*.
41. Arjun Appadurai, "Disjunctures and Difference in the Global Cultural Economy," in *Global Culture: Nationalism, Globalization and Modernity*, ed. Mike Featherstone (Newbury Park: Sage Publications, 1990), 295–310.
42. Manuel Castells, *The Rise of the Network Society* (Cambridge, MA: Blackwell Publishers, 1996).

Chapter 7

1. Peter Schrag, *Paradise Lost: California's Experience, America's Future* (New York: New York Press, 1998).
2. Manuel Castells, *The Rise of the Network Society* (Cambridge, MA: Blackwell Publishers, 1996), 13.
3. David Held and Anthony McGrew, "Globalization and the Liberal Democratic State," *Government and Opposition: The International Journal of Comparative Politics* 23, no. 2 (1993): 261–288.

4. Henry Mintzberg, *The Structuring of Organizations—A Synthesis of Research* (Englewood Cliffs, NJ: Prentice-Hall, Inc., 1979).
5. Hasard Adams, *The Academic Tribes* (New York: Liveright, 1976); Ellen Chaffee and William Tierney, *Collegiate Culture and Leadership Strategies* (New York: American Council on Education and Macmillan Publishing Company, 1988); George Keller, *Academic Strategy: The Management Revolution in American Higher Education* (Baltimore: The Johns Hopkins University Press, 1983); and Starr Owen, "Organizational Culture and Community Colleges," in *Challenge and Opportunity*, ed. John Dennison (Vancouver, B.C.: UBC Press, 1995), 141–168.
6. Henry Mintzberg, *The Structuring of Organizations—A Synthesis of Research*.
7. Stanley Aronowitz and William Di Fazio, *The Jobless Future: Sci-Tech and the Dogma of Work* (Minneapolis: University of Minnesota Press, 1994); William Bridges, *Job Shift* (Reading, MA, 1994); Jan Currie and Janice Newson, *Universities and Globalization*, with an introduction by Jan Currie (Thousand Oaks: Sage Publications, 1998), 1–13; Jane Kenway, "Fast Capitalism, Fast Feminism, and Some Fast Food for Thought," paper presented at the annual meeting of American Educational Research Association San Diego, April 1998; Jeremy Rifkin, *The End of Work* (New York: G.P. Putnam's Sons, 1995); and Don Tapscott, *The Digital Economy Promise and Peril in the Age of Networked Intelligence* (New York: McGraw Hill, 1996).
8. Aronowitz and Di Fazio, *The Jobless Future*; Robert Reich, *The Work of Nations* (New York: Vintage Books, 1992); Rifkin, *The End of Work;* and Tapscott, *The Digital Economy.*
9. Henry Mintzberg, *Mintzberg on Management: Inside Our Strange World of Organizations* (New York: The Free Press, 1989).
10. Bridges, *Job Shift.*
11. Gavan Daws, *Shoal of Time: A History of the Hawaiian Islands* (Honolulu: University of Hawaii Press, 1974).
12. B. C. Stats., "Focus on Mobility and Migration in B.C.," *1996 Census Fast Facts* 16, 1998.
13. B. C. Stats., "Labour Force Survey," *Statistics Canada,* 1998.
14. Arthur Cohen and Florence Brawer, *The American Community College* (San Francisco: Jossey-Bass, 1996); and John Dennison and John Levin, *Canada's Community College in the Nineteen Eighties* (Willowdale, Ontario: Association of Canadian Community Colleges, 1989).
15. Richard Barnet and John Cavanagh, *Global Dreams: Imperial Corporations and the New World Order* (New York: Simon & Schuster, 1994); and Mike Featherstone, "Global Culture: An Introduction," in *Global Culture,* ed. Mike Featherstone (Newbury Park, CA: Sage Publications, 1990).
16. Arjun Appadurai, "Disjunctures and Difference in the Global Cultural Economy," in *Global Culture: Nationalism, Globalization and Modernity,* ed. Mike Featherstone (Newbury Park: Sage Publications, 1990), 295–310.

17. Ken Kempner, "Faculty Culture in the Community College: Facilitating or Hindering Learning," *The Review of Higher Education*, vol. 13, no. 2 (1990): 215–235.
18. Veronica Strong-Boag, "Society in the Twentieth Century," *The Pacific Province*, ed. Hugh Johnstone (Vancouver: Douglas & McIntyre, 1996), 273–312.
19. John Belshaw and David Mitchell, "The Economy since the Great War," in *The Pacific Province*, ed. Hugh Johnstone (Vancouver: Douglas & McIntyre, 1996), 313–342.
20. Robert Reich, *The Work of Nations* (New York: Vintage Books, 1992).
21. Karl Weick, "Educational Organizations as Loosely Coupled Systems," *Administrative Science Quarterly* 21 (1976): 1–19.
22. Michael Howlett and Keith Brownsley, "Public Sector Politics in a Rentier Resource Economy," in *The Provincial State*, eds. Michael Howlett and Keith Brownsley (Mississauga, Ontario: Copp Clark Pitman, 1992), 264–295; and Howard Palmer and Tamari Palmer, *Alberta: A New History* (Edmonton: Hurtig Publishers, 1990).
23. Richard Richardson, Jr., Elizabeth Fisk, and Morris Okun, *Literacy in the Open-Access College* (San Francisco: Jossey-Bass Publishers, 1983); and Robert Rhoads and James Valadez, *Democracy, Multiculturalism, and the Community College* (New York: Garland Publishing, 1996).

Chapter 8

1. Amir Levy and Uri Merry, *Organizational Transformation: Approaches, Strategies, and Theories* (New York: Praeger, 1986).
2. Arthur Cohen and Florence Brawer, *The American Community College* (San Francisco: Jossey-Bass, 1996); and John Dennison and John Levin, *Canada's Community College in the Nineteen Eighties* (Willowdale, Ontario: Association of Canadian Community Colleges, 1989).
3. Quentin Bogart, "The Community College Mission," in *A Handbook on the Community College in America*, ed. George Baker (Westport, CT: Greenwood Press, 1994), 60–73; K. Patricia Cross, "Community Colleges on the Plateau," *Journal of Higher Education* 52, 2 (1981): 113–123; K. Patricia Cross and Elizabeth Fiedler, "Community College Missions: Priorities in the Mid-1980s," *The Journal of Higher Education* 60, 2 (1989): 209–216; and John Dennison and John Levin, *Canada's Community College in the Nineteen Eighties*.
4. John Dennison, "Community College Development in Canada since 1985," in *Challenge and Opportunity*, ed. John Dennison (Vancouver: The University of British Columbia Press, 1995), 13–104; Melanie Griffith and Ann Connor, *Democracy's Open Door: The Community College in America's Future*, (Portsmouth, NH: Boynton/Cook Publishers, 1994); and Mary

Ann Roe, *Education and U. S. Competitiveness: The Community College Role* (Austin: IC2 Institute, University of Texas at Austin, 1989).
5. See John Levin, "Mission and Structure: The Community College in a Global Context," Center for the Study of Higher Education, The University of Arizona, Tucson, Arizona, 1999.
6. Ibid.
7. Steven Brint and Jerome Karabel, "Institutional Origins and Transformations: The Case of American Community Colleges," in *The New Institutionalism,* eds. Walter Powell and Paul DiMaggio (Chicago: The University of Chicago Press, 1991), 337–360; David Larabee, *How to Succeed in School Without Really Learning* (New Haven: Yale University Press, 1997).
8. See Norton Grubb, Norena Badway, Denise Bell, Debra Bragg, and Maxine Russman, *Workforce, Economic and Community Development: The Changing Landscape of the Entrepreneurial Community College* (Berkeley: National Center for Research in Vocational Education, The University of California, 1997); Steven Johnson, "Organizational Structures and the Performance of Contract Training Operations in American Community Colleges," unpublished doctoral dissertation, The University of Texas at Austin, 1995; and Janet Knowles, "A Matter of Survival: Emerging Entrepreneurship in Community Colleges in Canada," in *Challenge and Opportunity,* ed. John Dennison (Vancouver: The University of British Columbia Press, 1995), 184–207.
9. Terry O'Banion and Associates, *Teaching and Learning in the Community College* (Washington D.C.: Community College Press, 1995), 323.
10. Don Doucette, "Transforming Teaching and Learning through Technology," in *Teaching and Learning in the Community College,* eds. Terry O'Banion and Associates (Washington, D.C.: Community College Press, 1995), 201.
11. Arthur Cohen and Florence Brawer, *The American Community College;* and John Dennison and Paul Gallagher, *Canada's Community Colleges* (Vancouver: University of British Columbia Press, 1986).
12. Personal communication from Jerry Young, Chief Executive Officer, Chaffey College, California, November 24, 1999.
13. Yeheskel Hasenfeld, *Human Service Organizations* (Englewood Cliffs, NJ: Prentice-Hall, 1983).
14. See James March and Michael Cohen, *Leadership and Ambiguity: The American College President* (New York: McGraw-Hill Book Company, 1974); Henry Mintzberg, *Power In and Around Organizations* (Englewood Cliffs, NJ: Prentice-Hall Inc., 1983); and Karl Weick, "Educational Organizations as Loosely Coupled Systems," *Administrative Science Quarterly* 21 (1976): 1–19.
15. Steven Brint and Jerome Karabel, "Institutional Origins and Transformations: The Case of American Community Colleges."

16. Steven Brint and Jerome Karabel, *The Diverted Dream: Community Colleges and the Promise of Educational Opportunity in America, 1900–1985* (New York: Oxford University Press, 1989).
17. See John Frye, *The Vision of the Public Junior College, 1900–1940* (New York: Greenwood Press, 1992); and Kent Phillipe, *National Profile of Community Colleges: Trends and Statistics* (Washington, D.C.: American Association of Community Colleges, 1995).
18. Charles Taylor, "Social Imaginaries," presentation at the biennial meeting of the Association for Canadian Studies in the United States, Pittsburgh, PA, November 1999.
19. Dennis McGrath and Martin Spear, *The Academic Crisis of the Community College* (Albany: State University of New York Press, 1991).
20. Joanne Martin and Debra Meyerson, "Organizational Cultures and the Denial, Channeling and Acknowledgement of Ambiguity," in *Managing Ambiguity and Change*, eds. Louis Pondy, Richard Boland, and Howard Thomas (New York: John Wiley and Sons, 1988), 93–125.
21. Arthur Cohen and Florence Brawer, *The American Community College*; John Dennison and Paul Gallagher, *Canada's Community Colleges*; and Dennis McGrath and Martin Spear, *The Academic Crisis of the Community College*.
22. Steven Brint and Jerome Karabel, *The Diverted Dream: Community Colleges and the Promise of Educational Opportunity in America, 1900–1985*; K. Patricia Cross, "Determining Missions and Priorities for the Fifth Generation," in *Renewing the American Community College*, eds. William Deegan, Dale Tillery, and Associates (San Francisco: Jossey-Bass Publishers, 1985), 34–50; John Dennison and Paul Gallagher, *Canada's Community Colleges*; Kevin Dougherty, *The Contradictory College* (Albany: State University of New York Press, 1994); Melanie Griffith and Ann Connor, *Democracy's Open Door: The Community College in America's Future*; and Lois Weis, *Between Two Worlds: Black Students in an Urban Community College* (Boston: Routledge and Kegan Paul, 1985).
23. Kevin Dougherty, *The Contradictory College*.
24. Darryl Clowes and Bernard Levin, "Community, Technical and Junior Colleges: Are They Leaving Higher Education?" *The Journal of Higher Education* 60, no. 3 (1989): 349–355.
25. Richard Richardson, Jr., Elizabeth Fisk, and Morris Okun, *Literacy in the Open-Access College* (San Francisco: Jossey-Bass Publishers, 1983); and John E. Roueche and George A. Baker III, *Access and Excellence* (Washington, D.C.: The Community College Press, 1987).
26. James Ratcliff, "Seven Streams in the Historical Development of the Modern Community College," in *A Handbook on the Community College in America*, ed. George Baker III (Westport, CT: Greenwood Press, 1994), 3–16.
27. Surprisingly, it is Dougherty who detects a new role for the community college. See Kevin Dougherty and Marianne Bakia, "The New Economic

Role of the Community College: Origins and Prospects," occasional paper, Community College Research Center, Teachers College, New York, June 1998.
28. Terry O' Banion, *The Learning College for the 21st Century* (Phoenix, AZ.: American Council on Education and the Oryx Press, 1997).
29. Ronald Manzer, *Public Schools and Political Ideas: Canadian Educational Policy in Historical Perspective* (Toronto: University of Toronto Press, 1994).
30. James Laxer, "Social Solidarity, Democracy and Global Capitalism," *The Canadian Review of Sociology and Anthropology* (August 1995): 287–312.
31. Terry O' Banion, *The Learning College for the 21st Century*.
32. See Steven Brint and Jerome Karabel, *The Diverted Dream: Community Colleges and the Promise of Educational Opportunity in America, 1900–1985*; and Darryl Clowes and Bernard Levin, "Community, Technical and Junior Colleges: Are They Leaving Higher Education?"
33. See Robert Reich, *The Work of Nations* (New York: Vintage Books, 1992); and Robert Reich, "Hire Education," *Rolling Stone*, October 20, 1994: 119–125.
34. See Steven Brint and Jerome Karabel, *The Diverted Dream: Community Colleges and the Promise of Educational Opportunity in America, 1900–1985*; John Dennison and Paul Gallagher, *Canada's Community Colleges;* Richard Richardson, Jr., Elizabeth Fisk, and Morris Okun, *Literacy in the Open-Access College;* and John E. Roueche and George A. Baker III, *Access and Excellence.*
35. John Frye, *The Vision of the Public Junior College, 1900–1940.*
36. Kevin Dougherty, *The Contradictory College.*
37. Ibid.; and David Larabee, *How to Succeed in School Without Really Learning.*
38. Kevin Dougherty, *The Contradictory College.*
39. Arthur Cohen and Florence Brawer, *The American Community College.*
40. Melanie Griffith and Ann Connor, *Democracy's Open Door: The Community College in America's Future.*
41. Terry O'Banion, *The Learning College for the 21st Century.*
42. Ken Meier, personal communication, December 8, 1999; See Richard Richardson, Jr., Elizabeth Fisk, and Morris Okun, *Literacy in the Open-Access College* for an earlier description of "bitting."
43. Arthur Cohen and Florence Brawer, *The American Community College.*
44. Norton Grubb, Norena Badway, Denise Bell, Debra Bragg, and Maxine Russman, *Workforce, Economic and Community Development: The Changing Landscape of the Entrepreneurial Community College.*
45. See John Frye, *The Vision of the Public Junior College, 1900–1940.*
46. W. Norton Grubb, *Honored But Invisible: An Inside Look at Teaching in Community Colleges* (New York: Routledge, 1999).
47. James Ratcliff, "Seven Streams in the Historical Development of the Modern Community College."

48. David Held and Anthony McGregor, "Globalization and the Liberal Democratic State," *Government and Opposition: The International Journal of Comparative Politics* 23, no. 2, 1993: 261–288.
49. See Thomas Carlyle, *Past and Present* (New York: Charles Scribner's Sons, 1918); and Charles Dickens, *The Speeches of Charles Dickens*, ed. K. J. Fielding, 2nd ed. (Hemel Hempstead: Harvester, 1988).
50. See Arthur Cohen and Florence Brawer, *The American Community College;* John Dennison and Paul Gallagher, *Canada's Community Colleges;* Dennis McGrath and Martin Spear, *The Academic Crisis of the Community College;* and Richard Richardson, Jr., Elizabeth Fisk, and Morris Okun, *Literacy in the Open-Access College.*

Appendix

1. Matthew Miles and Michael Huberman, *Qualitative Data Analysis: A Sourcebook of New Methods* (Beverly Hills: Sage Publications, 1984), 20.
2. See Ingrid Connidis, "Integrating Qualitative and Quantitative Methods in Survey Research on Aging: An Assessment," *Qualitative Sociology* 6, no. 4 (Winter 1983): 334–352; Frederick Erickson, "Qualitative Methods in Research on Teaching," in *Handbook of Research on Teaching*, ed. Merlin Wittrock (New York: Macmillan Publishing Company, 1986), 119–161; and Robert Crowson, "Qualitative Research Methods in Higher Education," in *Higher Education: Handbook of Theory and Research*, Volume III, ed. John Smart (New York: Agathon Press, 1987).
3. Miles and Huberman, *Qualitative Data Analysis: A Sourcebook of New Methods.*
4. Robert Burgess, "Methods of Field Research 1: Participant Observation," in *In the Field: An Introduction to Field Research*, ed. Robert Burgess (London: George Allen and Unwin, 1984), 78–100; and Robert Burgess, *Strategies of Educational Research: Qualitative Methods* (London: The Falmer Press, 1985).
5. Kathleen Eisenhardt, "Building Theories from Case Study Research," *Academy of Management Review* 14, no. 4, (1989): 532–550.
6. Bruce Berg, *Qualitative Research Methods for the Social Sciences* (Boston: Allyn and Bacon, 1995); Kathleen Eisenhardt, "Building Theories from Case Study Research"; and Robert Yin, *Case Study Research* (Newbury Park, CA: Sage Publications, 1984).
7. Bruce Berg, *Qualitative Research Methods for the Social Sciences.*
8. Cynthia Hardy, C. *The Politics of Collegiality: Retrenchment Strategies in Canadian Universities* (Buffalo: McGill-Queen's University Press, 1996).
9. Robert Yin, *Case Study Research.*
10. John Levin, "External Forces of Change and the Preservation of Accessibility in the Community College," *The Journal of Applied Research in the Community College* 4, no. 4, (1997): 137–146.
11. Kathleen Eisenhardt, "Building Theories from Case Study Research."

12. Ibid.
13. Ibid.
14. Bruce Berg, *Qualitative Research Methods for the Social Sciences;* and Robert Burgess, "Methods of Field Research 1: Participant Observation."
15. Arjun Appadurai, "Disjunctures and Difference in the Global Cultural Economy," in *Global Culture: Nationalism, Globalization and Modernity*, ed. Mike Featherstone (Newbury Park, CA: Sage Publications, 1990), 295–310; Stanley Aronowitz and William Di Fazio, *The Jobless Future: Sci-Tech and the Dogma of Work* (Minneapolis: University of Minnesota Press, 1994); Kim Cameron, "Organizational Adaptation and Higher Education," *The Journal of Higher Education* 55, no. 2 (1984): 122–144; Manuel Castells, "The Informational Economy and the New International Division of Labor," in *The New Global Economy in the Information Age*, eds. Martin Carnoy, Manuel Castells, Stephen Cohen, and Fernando Cardosa (University Park: The Pennsylvania State University, 1993), 15–43; Paul DiMaggio and Walter Powell, "The Iron Cage Revisited: Institutional Isomorphism and Collective Rationality in Organizational Fields," *American Sociological Review* 48, (1983): 147–160; Amir Levy and Uri Merry, *Organizational Transformation: Approaches, Strategies, and Theories* (New York: Praeger, 1986); Jeffrey Pfeffer and Gerald Salancik, *The External Control of Organizations: A Resource Dependence Perspective* (New York: Harper and Row, 1978); and Sheila Slaughter and Larry Leslie, *Academic Capitalism, Politics, Policies, and the Entrepreneurial University* (Baltimore: The Johns Hopkins University Press, 1997).
16. Miles and Huberman, *Qualitative Data Analysis: A Sourcebook of New Methods.*
17. Barney Glaser and Anselm Strauss, *The Discovery of Grounded Theory: Strategies for Qualitative Research* (Chicago: Aldine, 1967).
18. Kim Cameron, "Organizational Adaptation and Higher Education."

BIBLIOGRAPHY

Adams, Hasard. *The Academic Tribes*. New York: Liveright, 1976.
Albert, Stuart, and David Whetten. "Organizational Identity." *Research in Organizational Behavior* 7 (1985): 263–295.
Alberta Advanced Educational and Career Development. *Business Plan*. Advanced Education and Career Development, Edmonton, Alberta, 1994.
Alberta Advanced Educational and Career Development. *Business Plan*. Advanced Education and Career Development. Edmonton, Alberta, 1996.
Alberta Advanced Education and Career Development. *Vision for Change: A Concept Paper for the Development of a Virtual Learning System*. Alberta Advanced Education and Career Development. Edmonton, Alberta, 1995.
Alfred, Richard, and Patricia Carter. "Inside Track to the Future." *Community College Journal* 66, no. 4 (February/March, 1996): 10–19.
Amey, Marilyn, and Susan Twombly. "Re-visioning Leadership in Community Colleges." *The Review of Higher Education* 15, no. 2 (Winter 1992): 125–150.
Andrews, Michael, Edward Holdaway, and Gordon Mowat. "Postsecondary Education in Alberta since 1945." In *Higher Education in Canada*, ed. Glen Jones. New York: Garland Publishing, 1997, 59–92.
Appadurai, Arjun. "Disjunctures and Difference in the Global Cultural Economy." In *Global Culture: Nationalism, Globalization and Modernity*, ed. Mike Featherstone. Newbury Park, CA: Sage Publications, 1990, 295–310.
Arnason, Johann. "Nationalism, Globalization and Modernity." In *Global Culture: Nationalism, Globalization and Modernity*, ed. Mike Featherstone. Newbury Park, CA.: Sage Publications, 1990, 207–236.
Aronowitz, Stanley, and William Di Fazio. *The Jobless Future: Sci-Tech and the Dogma of Work*. Minneapolis: University of Minnesota Press, 1994.
Austin, Tom. Personal Communication. Director, Post Secondary Finance, Ministry of Education, Skills, and Training, Province of B.C., 1996.
Baker, George, and Associates. *Cultural Leadership: Inside America's Community Colleges*. Washington, D.C.: The Community College Press, 1992.
———, and Vaughn Upshaw. "A Team Approach to Institutional Quality: Toward a Model." In *Team Building for Quality*, eds. George Baker and Associates. Washington, D.C.: Community College Press, 1995, 1–25.
Baker, Douglas. "Aboriginal Education in Community Colleges." In *Challenge and Opportunity*, ed. John Dennison. Vancouver: University of British Columbia Press, 1995, 208–219.

Balsmo, Anne. "Myths of Information: The Cultural Impact of New Information Technologies." In *The Information Revolution,* eds. Alan Porter and William Read. Greenwich, CT: Ablex, 1998, 225–235.

Barlow, Maude, and Heather-Jane Robertson. "Homogenization of Education." In *The Case Against the Global Economy,* eds. Jerry Mandes and Edward Goldsmith. San Francisco: The Sierra Club, 1996, 60–70.

Barman, Jean. *The West Beyond the West: A History of British Columbia.* Toronto: University of Toronto Press, 1991.

Barnet, Richard, and John Cavanagh. *Global Dreams: Imperial Corporations and the New World Order.* New York: Simon & Schuster, 1994.

Barr, Robert, and John Tagg. "From Teaching to Learning: A New Paradigm for Undergraduate Education." *Change* (November/December 1995): 13–25.

B.C. Stats. "Focus on Mobility and Migration in B.C." *1996 Census Fast Facts,* 1998.

———. "Labour Force Survey." *Statistics Canada,* 1998.

Bell, Daniel. *The Coming of Post-Industrial Society: A Venture in Social Forecasting.* New York: Basic Books, 1973, 348–349.

Belshaw, John, and David Mitchell. "The Economy since the Great War." In *The Pacific Province,* ed. Hugh Johnstone. Vancouver: Douglas & McIntyre, 1996, 313–342.

Berg, Bruce. *Qualitative Research Methods for the Social Sciences.* Boston: Allyn and Bacon, 1995.

Bogart, Quentin. "The Community College Mission." In *A Handbook on the Community College in America,* ed. George Baker. Westport, CT: Greenwood Press, 1994, 60–73.

Brecher, Jeremy. "Global Village of Global Pillage." *The Nation* 257 (December 6, 1993): 685–688.

Bridges, William. *Job Shift.* Reading, MA: Addison Wesley, 1994.

Brint, Steven, and Jerome Karabel. *The Diverted Dream: Community Colleges and the Promise of Educational Opportunity in America, 1900–1985.* New York: Oxford University Press, 1989.

———. "Institutional Origins and Transformations: The Case of American Community Colleges." In *The New Institutionalism,* eds. Walter Powell and Paul DiMaggio. Chicago: The University of Chicago Press, 1991, 337–360.

British Columbia Labour Force Development Board. *Training for What?* Victoria, B.C.: Ministry of Skills, Training, and Labour, 1995.

Burgess, Robert. "Methods of Field Research 1: Participant Observation." In *In the Field: An Introduction to Field Research,* ed. Robert Burgess. London: George Allen and Unwin, 1984, 78–100.

———. *Strategies of Educational Research: Qualitative Methods.* London: The Falmer Press, 1985.

"California Community Colleges Telecommunication Technology Infrastructure." Certification Document Materials, November 1996.

California Department of Finance. "Race/Ethnic Estimates by County." Research Unit, 1998.

Cameron, David. "The Federal Perspective." In *Higher Education in Canada*, ed. Glen Jones. New York: Garland Publishing, 1997, 9–27.

Cameron, Kim. "Organizational Adaptation and Higher Education." *The Journal of Higher Education* 55, no. 2 (1984): 122–144.

Cárdenas, Karen. "Technology in Today's Classroom: It Slices and It Dices, but Does it Serve Us Well?" *Academe*, May-June, 1998, 27–29.

Carlyle, Thomas. *Past and Present*. New York: Charles Scribner's Sons, 1918.

Carnavele, Anthony, and Donna Desrochers. "Community Colleges in the New Economy." *Community College Journal* 67, no. 5 (April/May 1997): 26–33.

Carnoy, Martin. *The State and Political Thought*. Princeton: Princeton University Press, 1984.

———, Manuel Castello, Stephen Cohen, and Fernando Cardoso. *The New Global Economy in the Information Age*. University Park: The Pennsylvania State University, 1993.

Castells, Manuel. "The Informational Economy and the New International Division of Labor." In *The New Global Economy in the Information Age*, eds. Martin Carnoy, Manuel Castells, Stephen Cohen, and Fernando Cardosa. University Park: The Pennsylvania State University, 1993, 15–43.

———. *The Rise of the Network Society*. Cambridge, MA: Blackwell Publishers, 1996.

Chaffee, Ellen, and William Tierney. *Collegiate Culture and Leadership Strategies*. New York: American Council on Education and Macmillan Publishing Company, 1988.

Chodos, Robert, Eric Hamovitch, and Rae Murphy. *Lost in Cyberspace?* Toronto: James Lorimer and Company, 1997.

Chomsky, Noam. *Profit over People: Neoliberalism and Global Order*. New York: Seven Stories Press, 1999.

The Chronicle of Higher Education Almanac, August 27, 1999, 24.

Clegg, Stewart, and John Gray. "Metaphors of Globalization." In *Postmodern Management and Organization*, eds. David Boje, Robert Gephart, and Tojo Thatchenkery. Thousand Oaks, CA: Sage Publications, 1996, 293–307.

Clowes, Darrel, and Bernard Levin. "Community, Technical and Junior Colleges: Are They Leaving Higher Education?" *The Journal of Higher Education* 60, no. 3 (1989): 349–355.

Cohen, Arthur. *Dateline '79: Heretical Concepts for the Community College*. Beverly Hills: Glencoe Press, 1969.

———, and Florence Brawer. *The American Community College*. San Francisco: Jossey-Bass, 1996.

———. "The Changing Environment: Contexts, Concepts, and Crises." In *Managing Community Colleges*, eds. Arthur Cohen and Florence Brawer. San Francisco: Jossey-Bass Publishers, 1994, 5–21.

Coleman, William, and Grace Skogstad. "Policy Communities and Policy Networks: A Structural Approach." In *Policy Communities and Public Policy in Canada*, eds. William Coleman and Grace Skogstad. Mississauga, Ontario: Copp Clark Pitman Limited, 1990, 14–31.

Commission on Workforce and Community Development. *Responding to the Challenges on Workforce and Economic Development: The Role of America's Community Colleges*. Washington, D.C.: American Association of Community Colleges, 1996.

Connidis, Ingrid. "Integrating Qualitative and Quantitative Methods in Survey Research on Aging: An Assessment." *Qualitative Sociology* 6, no. 4 (Winter 1983): 334–352.

Cooper, Joanne, and Ken Kempner. "Lord of the Flies Community College: A Case Study of Organizational Disintegration." *The Review of Higher Education* (Summer 1993): 419–437.

Cornfield, Daniel. "Workers, Managers, and Technological Change." In *Workers, Managers, and Technological Change*, ed. Daniel Cornfield. New York: Plenum Press, 1987, 3–24.

Cross, K. Patricia. "Community Colleges on the Plateau." *The Journal of Higher Education* 52, no. 2 (1981): 113–123.

———. "Determining Missions and Priorities for the Fifth Generation." In *Renewing the American Community College*, eds. William Deegan, Dale Tillery, and Associates. San Francisco: Jossey-Bass Publishers, 1985, 34–50.

———, and Elizabeth Fiedler. "Community College Missions: Priorities in the Mid-1980s." *The Journal of Higher Education* 60, no. 2 (1989): 209–216.

Crowson, Robert. "Qualitative Research Methods in Higher Education." In *Higher Education: Handbook of Theory and Research* Vol. III, ed. John Smart. New York: Agathon Press, 1987.

Currie, Jan, and Janice Newson. *Universities and Globalization*. Thousand Oaks, CA: Sage Publications, 1998, 1–13.

Currie, Jan. "Introduction." In *Universities and Globalization*, eds. Jan Currie and Janice Newson. Thousand Oaks, CA: Sage Publications, 1998, 1–13.

Carl D. Perkins Vocational and Applied Technology Education Act, as amended through July 1995. Washington, D.C.: Government Printing Office, 1995.

D'Souza, Dinesh. *Illiberal Education: The Politics of Race and Sex on Campus*. New York: Free Press, 1991.

Daniel, Sir John. "Why Universities Need Technology Strategies." *Change* (July-August 1997): 11–17.

Daws, Gavan. *Shoal of Time: A History of the Hawaiian Islands*. Honolulu: University of Hawaii Press, 1974.

Deegan, William, and Dale Tillery. "The Process of Renewal: An Agenda for Action." In *Renewing the American Community College*, eds. William Deegan, Dale Tillery and Associates. San Francisco: Jossey-Bass Publishers, 1985, 303–324.

Dennison, John, and John Levin. *Canada's Community College in the Nineteen Eighties*. Willowdale, Ontario: Association of Canadian Community Colleges, 1989.

———, and Paul Gallagher. *Canada's Community Colleges*. Vancouver: University of British Columbia Press, 1986.

———. *Challenge and Opportunity*. Vancouver: The University of British Columbia Press, 1995.

———. "Community College Development in Canada since 1985." In *Challenge and Opportunity*, ed. John Dennison. Vancouver: The University of British Columbia Press, 1995, 13–104.

Dewey, John. *Democracy and Education*. New York: The Free Press, 1966.

Dickens, Charles. *The Speeches of Charles Dickens*. Edited by K. J. Fielding, 2nd ed. Hemel Hempstead: Harvester, 1988.

Diekhoff, John. *Democracy's College: Higher Education in the Local Community*. New York: Harper and Brother Publishers, 1950.

Diener, Thomas. *Growth of an American Invention: A Documentary History of the Junior and Community College Mission*. New York: Greenwood Press, 1986.

Dill, David. "The Management of Academic Culture: Notes on the Management of Meaning and Social Integration." *Higher Education* 11 (1982): 303–320.

DiMaggio, Paul, and Walter Powell. "The Iron Cage Revisited: Institutional Isomorphism and Collective Rationality in Organizational Fields." *American Sociological Review* 48 (1983): 147–160.

Dolence, Michael, and Donald Norris. *Transforming Higher Education: A Vision for Learning in the 21st Century*. Ann Arbor, MI: Society for College and University Planning, 1995.

Doucette, Don. "Transforming Teaching and Learning Through Technology." In *Teaching and Learning in the Community College*, ed. Terry O'Banion. Washington, D.C.: The American Association of Community Colleges, 1995, 201–227.

———. "Transforming Teaching and Learning Using Information Technology." *The College Board Review* 167 (Spring 1993): 18–25.

Dougherty, Kevin. *The Contradictory College*. Albany: State University of New York Press, 1994.

———, and Marianne Bakia. "The New Economic Role of the Community College: Origins and Prospects." Occasional paper, Community College Research Center, Teachers College, New York, June 1998.

Driedger, Leo. *Multi-Ethnic Canada: Identities and Inequalities*. Toronto: Oxford University Press, 1996.

Dudley, Janice. "Globalization and Education Policy in Australia. " In *Universities and Globalization*, eds. Jan Currie and Janice Newson. Thousand Oaks, CA: Sage Publications, 1998, 21–43.

Edwards, Richard, and Robin Usher. "Globalization, Diaspora Space and Pedagogy." Paper presented at the annual meeting of the American Educational Research Association, San Diego, April 1998.

Eisenhardt, Kathleen. "Building Theories from Case Study Research." *Academy of Management Review* 14, no. 4 (1989): 532–550.

Employment and Immigration Canada. *Immigration Statistics*, 1980 and 1981.

Erhmann, Stephen. "Asking the Right Questions: What Does Research Tell Us about Technology and Higher Education?" *Change* 27, no. 2 (1995): 20–27.

Erickson, Frederick. "Qualitative Methods in Research on Teaching." In *Handbook of Research on Teaching*, ed. Merlin Wittrock. New York: Macmillan Publishing Company, 1986, 119–161.

Faludi, Susan. *Backlash: The Undeclared War Against American Women.* New York: Crown, 1991.

Featherstone, Michael. "Global Culture: An Introduction." In *Global Culture: Nationalism, Globalization and Modernity,* ed. Mike Featherstone. Newbury Park, CA., 1990, 1–14.

The Financial Post Data Group. *Canadian Markets.* Toronto, 1991, 1993, and 1994.

Frank, Andre. "Reorient World History and Social Theory." Unpublished paper. Montreal, Quebec, 1994.

Friedman, Thomas. *The Lexus and the Olive Tree.* New York: Farrar, Straus Giroux, 1999.

Frye, John. "Educational Paradigms in the Professional Literature of the Community College." In *Higher Education: Handbook of Theory and Research,* Vol. X, ed. John Smart. New York: Agathon Press, 1994, 181–224.

———. *The Vision of the Public Junior College, 1900–1940.* New York: Greenwood Press, 1992.

Fryer, Thomas, Jr., and John Lovas. *Leadership in Governance.* San Francisco: Jossey-Bass Publishers, 1991.

Galbraith, John K. "For Richer for Poorer." *The Manchester Guardian* 161, no. 2 (July 8–14, 1999): 11.

Gallagher, Paul. "Promise Fulfilled, Promise Pending. " In *Challenge and Opportunity: Canada's Community Colleges at the Crossroads,* ed. John Dennison. Vancouver: University of British Columbia Press, 1995, 256–274.

Garrett, Rick. "Computer-Assisted Instruction in 2-Year Colleges: Technology for Innovative Teaching." *Community College Journal of Research and Practice* 19 (1995): 529–53.

Gephart, Robert, Jr. "Management, Social Issues, and the Postmodern Era." In *Postmodern Management and Organizational Theory,* eds. David Boje, Robert Gephart, and Tojo Thatchenkery. Thousand Oaks, CA.: Sage Publications, 1996, 21–44.

Gianini, Paul, and Sandra Sarantos. "Academic Rhetoric Versus Business Reality." In *The Company We Keep: Collaboration in the Community College,* eds. John Roueche, Lynn Taber, and Suanne Roueche. Washington, D.C.: American Association of Community Colleges, 1995, 205–226.

Giddens, Anthony. *The Consequences of Modernity.* Stanford: Stanford University Press, 1990.

Gilbert, Steven, and Kenneth Green. "Great Expectations: Content, Communication Productivity, and the Role of Information Technology in Higher Education." *Change* 27, no. 2 (1995): 8–18.

Giroux, Henry. *Border Crossings: Cultural Workers and the Politics of Education.* New York: Routledge, 1992.

Glaser, Barney, and Anselm Strauss. *The Discovery of Grounded Theory: Strategies for Qualitative Research.* Chicago: Aldine, 1967.

Goedegebuure, Leo, Frans Kaiser, Peter Maassen, and Egbert De Weert. "Higher Education Policy in International Perspective: An Overview." In *Higher Edu-*

cation Policy, eds. Leo Goedegebuure, Frans Kaiser, Peter Maassen, Lynn Meek, Frans Van Vught, and Egbert De Weert. New York: Pergamon Press, 1993, 1–12.

Gordon, Robert. "Partnerships at Humber College." In *The Company We Keep: Collaboration in the Community College*, eds. John Roueche, Lynn Taber, and Suanne Roueche. Washington, D.C.: Community College Press, 1995, 107–127.

Gough, Noel. "Globalization and Curriculum: Theorizing a Transnational Imaginary." Paper presented at the Annual Meeting of the American Educational Research Association, San Diego, 1998.

Government of British Columbia. *College and Institute Amendment Act*. Victoria, B. C.: Queen's Printer, 1994.

Griffith, Melanie, and Ann Connor. *Democracy's Open Door: The Community College in America's Future*. Portsmouth, NH: Boynton/Cook Publishers, 1994.

Gross, Rich. "Defining the New Mandate for Distance Learning in the 21st Century." *Community College Journal* (October/November, 1995): 28–33.

Grubb, W. Norton. *Honored But Invisible: An Inside Look at Teaching in Community Colleges*, New York: Routledge, 1999.

———, Norena Badway, Denise Bell, Debra Bragg, and Maxine Russman. *Workforce, Economic and Community Development: The Changing Landscape of the Entrepreneurial Community College*. Berkeley: National Center for Research in Vocational Education, The University of California, 1997.

Hardy, Cynthia. *The Politics of Collegiality: Retrenchment Strategies in Canadian Universities*. Buffalo: McGill-Queen's University Press, 1996.

Hartmark, Leif, and Edward Hines. "Politics and Policy in Higher Education: Reflection on the Status of the Field." In *Policy Controversies in Higher Education*, eds. Samuel Gove and Thomas Stauffer. New York: Greenwood Press, 1986, 3–26.

Hasenfeld, Yeheskel. *Human Service Organizations*. Englewood Cliffs, NJ: Prentice-Hall, 1983.

Held, David, Anthony McGrew, David Goldblatt, and Jonathan Perraton. *Global Transformations: Politics, Economics and Culture*. Stanford: Stanford University Press, 1999.

Higher Education Coordinating Board. *The Challenge for Higher Education*. State of Washington Master Plan for Education, 1996.

Howlett, Michael, and Keith Brownsley. "Public Sector Politics in a Rentier Resource Economy." In *The Provincial State*, eds. Michael Howlett and Keith Brownsley. Mississauga, Ontario: Copp Clark Pitman, 1992, 264–295.

Inglehart, Ronald. *Culture Shift in Advanced Industrial Society*. Princeton: Princeton University Press, 1990.

Johnson, Steven. "Organizational Structures and the Performance of Contract Training Operations in American Community Colleges." Unpublished doctoral dissertation. Austin: The University of Texas, 1995.

Keller, George. *Academic Strategy: The Management Revolution in American Higher Education*. Baltimore: The Johns Hopkins University Press, 1983.

Kempner, Ken. "The Community College as a Marginalized Institution." Unpublished paper presented at annual meeting of Association for the Study of Higher Education, Boston, 1991.

———. "Faculty Culture in the Community College: Facilitating or Hindering Learning." *The Review of Higher Education* 13, no. 2 (1990): 215–235.

Kenway, Jane. "Fast Capitalism, Fast Feminism, and Some Fast Food for Thought." Paper presented at the Annual Meeting of the American Educational Research Association, San Diego, April 1998.

Keyman, E. Fuat. *Globalization, State, Identity, and Deference.* New Jersey: Humanities Press, 1997.

Knowles, Janet. "A Matter of Survival: Emerging Entreprenuership in Community Colleges in Canada." In *Challenge and Opportunity,* ed. John Dennison. Vancouver: University of British Columbia Press, 1995, 184–207.

Kozma, Robert, and Jerome Johnston. "The Technological Revolution Comes to the Classroom." *Change* (January/February 1991): 10–23.

Larabee, David. *How to Succeed in School Without Really Learning.* New Haven: Yale University Press, 1997.

Lash, Scott, and John Urry. *Economies of Signs and Space.* Thousand Oaks, CA: Sage Publications, 1994.

Laxer, Gordon. "Social Solidarity and Global Capitalism." *The Canadian Review of Sociology and Anthropology* (August 1995): 287–312.

Leslie, David, and E. K. Fretwell, Jr. *Wise Moves in Hard Times.* San Francisco: Jossey-Bass, 1996.

Leslie, Larry, and Sheila Slaughter. "The Development and Current Status of Market Mechanisms in the United States Postsecondary Education." *Higher Education Policy* 10 (March/April 1997): 238–252.

Levin, John. "External Forces of Change and the Preservation of Accessibility in the Community College." *The Journal of Applied Research in the Community College* 4, no. 4 (1997): 137–146.

———. "Is the Management of Distance Education Transforming Instruction in Colleges?" *The Quarterly Review of Distance Education* (in press).

———. "Limits to Organizational Change in the Community College." *Community College Journal of Research and Practice* 20, no. 20 (1996): 185–197.

———. "Mission and Structure: The Community College in a Global Context." A Report. Center for the Study of Higher Education, The University of Arizona, Tucson, Arizona, 1999.

———. "Missions and Structures: Bringing Clarity to Perceptions about Globalization and Higher Education in Canada." *Higher Education* 37, no. 4 (1999): 377–399.

———. "Success Community College: An Examination of Organizational Change." *The Canadian Journal of Higher Education* 25, no. 1 (1995): 19–39.

———. "What's the Impediment? Structural and Legal Constraints to Shared Governance in the Community College." *The Canadian Journal of Higher Education* XXX, no. 2 (2000): 87–122.

Levinson, Paul. *Digital McLuhan: A Guide to the Information Millennium*. New York: Routledge, 1999.

Levy, Amir, and Uri Merry. *Organizational Transformation: Approaches, Strategies, and Theories*. New York: Praeger, 1986.

Lipsey, Richard. "The Case for Trilateralism." In *Continental Accord: North American Economic Integration*, ed. Steven Globerman. Vancouver: The Fraser Institute, 1991, 89–123.

London, Howard. *The Culture of a Community College*. New York: Praeger Publishers, 1978.

Manzer, Ronald. *Public Schools and Political Ideas: Canadian Educational Policy in Historical Perspective*. Toronto: University of Toronto Press, 1994.

March, James, and Michael Cohen. *Leadership and Ambiguity: The American College President*. New York: McGraw-Hill Book Company, 1974.

Marginson, Simon. *Educating Australia: Government, Economy and Citizen Since 1960*. Melbourne: Cambridge University Press, 1997.

Martin, Joanne, and Debra Meyerson. "Organizational Cultures and the Denial, Channeling and Acknowledgment of Ambiguity." *Managing Ambiguity and Change*, eds. Louis Pondy, Richard Boland, and Howard Thomas. New York: John Wiley & Sons, 1988, 93–125.

McGrath, Dennis, and Martin Spear. *The Academic Crisis of the Community College*. Albany: State University of New York Press, 1991.

McLoughlin, Ian, and Jon Clark. *Technological Change at Work*. Philadelphia: Open University Press, 1994.

McQuaig, Linda. *Shooting the Hippo: Death By Deficit*. Toronto: Penguin Books, 1995.

Meier, Ken. "The Community College Mission and Organizational Behavior." Unpublished Paper. The Center for the Study of Higher Education, Tucson, Arizona, 1999.

———. Personal Communication. December 8, 1999.

Merisotis, Jamie. "The 'What's-the-Difference?' Debate." *Academe* (September-October, 1999): 47–51.

Meyer, John, and Brian Rowan. "Institutionalized Organizations: Formal Structure as Myth and Ceremony." *American Journal of Sociology* 83 (1977): 340–363.

Miles, Ian. "The Information Society: Competing Perspectives on the Social and Economic Implications of Information and Communication Technologies." In *Information and Communication Technologies: Visions and Realities*, ed. William Dutton. New York: Oxford University Press, 1996, 37–52.

Miles, Matthew, and Michael Huberman. *Qualitative Data Analysis: A Sourcebook of New Methods*. Beverly Hills: Sage Publications, 1984.

Millman, Gregory. *The Vandal's Crown: How Rebel Currency Traders Overthrew the World's Central Banks*. New York: The Free Press, 1995.

Minister of Human Resource Development. *Federal and Provincial Support to Post Secondary Education in Canada: A Report to Parliament 1993–94*. Ottawa, Ontario: Minister of Supply and Services Canada, 1995.

———. *Federal and Provincial Support to Post Secondary Education in Canada: A Report to Parliament 1994–95.* Ottawa, Ontario: Minister of Supply and Services Canada, 1996.

Ministry of Education, Skills and Training. *Charting a New Course.* Victoria, B.C.: Ministry of Education, Skills and Training, 1996.

Mintzberg, Henry. *Mintzberg on Management: Inside Our Strange World of Organizations.* New York: The Free Press, 1989.

———. *Power In and Around Organizations.* Englewood Cliffs, NJ: Prentice-Hall, Inc., 1983.

———. *The Structuring of Organizations—A Synthesis of Research.* Englewood Cliffs, NJ : Prentice-Hall, Inc., 1979.

Morgan, Gareth. *Images of Organization.* Thousand Oaks, CA: Sage Publications, 1997.

Morley, David, and Kevin Robins. *Spaces of Identity: Global Media, Electronic Landscapes and Cultural Boundaries.* New York: Routledge, 1995.

National Center for Educational Statistics. *Digest of Education Statistics.* U.S. G.P.O., 1994.

National Commission on Excellence in Education. *A Nation at Risk: The Imperative for Educational Reform.* Washington, D.C.: U.S. Department of Education, April 1983.

Nevitte, Neil, Miguel Basañez, and Ronald Inglehart. "Directions of Value Change in North America." In *North America Without Borders*, eds. Stephen Randall, Herman Konrad, and Sheldon Silverman. Calgary: The University of Calgary Press, 1992, 245–259.

Newson, Janice. "NAFTA and Higher Education in Canada." Unpublished Manuscript. York University, Toronto, Ontario, 1994.

O' Banion, Terry. *The Learning College for the 21st Century.* Phoenix, AZ.: American Council on Education and the Oryx Press, 1997.

———. "Teaching and Learning: A Mandate for the Nineties." In *Teaching and Learning in the Community College,* ed. Terry O'Banion. Washington, D.C.: The American Association of Community Colleges, 1995, 3–20.

———, and Associates. *Teaching and Learning in the Community College.* Washington, D.C.: Community College Press, 1995.

Owen, Starr. "An Interpretive Approach to Leadership: Developing a Theme from a Case Study." In *Educational Leadership: Challenge and Change,* eds. Erwin Miklos and Eùgene Ratsoy. Edmonton, Alberta: Department of Educational Administration, University of Alberta, 1992, 259–284.

———. "Organizational Culture and Community Colleges." In *Challenge and Opportunity,* ed. John Dennison. Vancouver, B.C.: The University of British Columbia Press, 1995, 141–168.

Palmer, Howard, and Tamari Palmer. *Alberta: A New History.* Edmonton: Hurtig Publishers, 1990.

Pascarella, Ernest, and Patrick Terenzini. "Studying College Students in the 21st Century: Meeting New Challenges." *The Review of Higher Education* 21, no. 2, (Winter 1998): 151–165.

Peters, Tom, and Robert Waterman. *In Search of Excellence.* New York: Warner Books, 1982.

Pfeffer, Jeffrey, and Gerald Salancik. *The External Control of Organizations: A Resource Dependence Perspective.* New York: Harper and Row, 1978.

Phillipe, Kent. *National Profile of Community Colleges: Trends and Statistics.* Washington, D.C.: American Association of Community Colleges, 1995.

Pincus, Fred. "How Critics View the Community College's Role in the Twenty-First Century." In *A Handbook on the Community College in America,* ed. George Baker III. Westport, CT: Greenwood Press, 1994, 624–636.

Pratt, Larry. "The Political Economy of Province Building: Alberta's Development Strategy, 1971–1981." In *Essays on the Political Economy of Alberta,* ed. David Leadbeater. Toronto: New Hogtown Press, 1984, 194–222.

Province of Alberta. "Framework for Technology Integration in Education. A Report of the MLA Implementation Team on Business Involvement and Technology Integration." Edmonton: Alberta Education Cataloguing in Publication Data, March, 1996.

———. *New Directions for Adult Learning in Alberta: Adult Learning Access through Innovation.* Edmonton: Alberta Advanced Education and Career Development, 1994.

Province of Alberta, Alberta Advanced Education and Career Development. "Encouraging Excellence and Rewarding Success in Alberta's Public Adult Learning System." Edmonton, Alberta: December 1996.

———. "Enhancing Alberta's Adult Learning System through Technology. Policy, Guidelines and Procedures for the Learning Enhancement Envelope." Edmonton, Alberta, undated.

———. "A Proposal for Performance-Based Funding. Promoting Excellence in Alberta's Public Adult Learning System." Edmonton, Alberta, November 1995.

———. "Vision for Change: A Concept Paper for the Development of a Virtual Learning System." Edmonton, Alberta, September 25, 1995.

Province of British Columbia, B.C. Human Resources Development Project. "Report of Steering Committee." Victoria, November 1992.

Province of British Columbia, British Columbia Labour Force Development Board. "Training for What?" Victoria: Ministry of Skills, Training, and Labour, 1995.

Province of British Columbia, Ministry of Education, Skills and Training. "Charting a New Course." Victoria, September 13, 1996.

Province of British Columbia, Ministry of Skills, Training and Labor. "Opportunities in Post Secondary Education and Training." Victoria, undated.

———. "The Report of the Post-Secondary Policy Forum on Distributed Learning Environments." Victoria, 1995.

Ralston Saul, John. *The Unconscious Civilization.* Concord, Ontario: House of Anansi Press, 1995.

Ratcliff, James. "Seven Streams in the Historical Development of the Modern Community College." In *A Handbook on the Community College in America,* ed. George Baker III. Westport, CT: Greenwood Press, 1994, 3–16.

Ravitch, Diane. "Multiculturalism." *The American Scholar* (Winter 1990): 337–354.
Reich, Robert. "Hire Education." *Rolling Stone* (October 20, 1994): 119–125.
———. *The Work of Nations*. New York: Vintage Books, 1992.
Report of the Commission on Innovation to the Board of Governors of the California Community Colleges. *Choosing the Future: An Action Agenda for Community Colleges*. Sacramento: Board of Governors, California Community Colleges, 1993.
Rhoades, Gary. *Managed Professionals: Unionized Faculty and Restructuring Academic Labor*. Albany: SUNY Press, 1998.
Rhoads, Robert, and James Valadez. *Democracy, Multiculturalism, and the Community College*. New York: Garland Publishing, 1996.
Rice, Richard, William Bullough, and Richard Orsi. *The Elusive Eden: A New History of California*. New York: Alfred Knopf, 1988.
Richardson, Richard. "Responsible Leadership: Tipping the Balance Toward Institutional Achievement." In *Community College Leadership for the '80s*, eds. John Roueche and George Baker III. Washington, D.C.: American Association of Community and Junior Colleges, 1983.
———, and Louis Bender. *Fostering Minority Access and Achievement in Higher Education*. San Francisco: Jossey-Bass Publishers, 1987.
———, Elizabeth Fisk, and Morris Okun. *Literacy in the Open-Access College*. San Francisco: Jossey-Bass Publishers, 1983.
Rifkin, Jeremy. *The End of Work*. New York: G.P. Putnam's Sons, 1995.
Ritzer, George. *The McDonaldization Thesis: Explorations and Extensions*. Thousand Oaks, CA: Sage Publications, 1998.
Robertson, Roland. *Globalization: Social Theory and Global Culture*. London: Sage Publications, 1992.
Robins, Kevin, and Frank Webster. *Times of Technoculture*. New York: Routledge, 1999.
Roe, Mary Ann. *Education and U.S. Competitiveness: The Community College Role*. Austin: IC2 Institute, University of Texas at Austin, 1989.
Roueche, John, and George A. Baker III. *Access and Excellence*. Washington, D.C.: The Community College Press, 1987.
———, George Baker III, and Robert Rose. *Shared Vision*. Washington, D.C.: The Community College Press, 1989.
———, and Suanne Roueche. *Between a Rock and a Hard Place*. Washington, D.C.: Community College Press, 1993.
———, Lynn Taber, and Suanne Roueche. *The Company We Keep: Collaboration in the Community College*. Washington, D.C.: American Association of Community Colleges, 1995.
Sale, Roger. *Seattle: Past to Present*. Seattle: University of Washington Press, 1976.
Sandelands, Lloyd, and Robert Drazin. "On the Language of Organizational Theory." *Organization Studies* 10, no. 4 (1989): 457–478.
Sassen, Saskia. *The Global City*. Princeton: Princeton University Press, 1991.
Schaffer, Edward. "The University in Service to Technocracy." *Education Theory* 30, no. 1 (Winter 1980): 47–52.

Schein, Edgar. *Organizational Culture and Leadership.* San Francisco: Jossey-Bass Publishers, 1985.

Schlager, Edella, and William Blomquist. "A Comparison of Three Emerging Theories of the Policy Process." *Political Research Quarterly* 49, no. 3 (1996): 651–672.

Schrag, Peter. *Paradise Lost: California's Experience, America's Future.* New York: New York Press, 1998.

Schugurensky, Daniel, and Kathy Higgins. "From Aid to Trade: New Trends in International Education in Canada" In *Dimensions of the Community College: International, Intercultural, and Multicultural,* eds. Rosalind Raby and Norma Tarrow. New York: Garland Publishing, 1996, 53–78.

Schuster, Jack, Daryl Smith, Kathleen Corak, and Myrtle Yamada. *Strategic Governance: How to Make Big Decisions Better.* Phoenix, AZ: American Council on Education and Oryx Press, 1994.

Schwantes, Carlos. *The Pacific Northwest: An Interpretive History.* Lincoln: University of Nebraska Press, 1996a.

———. "Wage Earners and Wealth Makers." In *The Oxford History of the American West,* eds. Clyde Milner, Carol O'Connor, and Martha Sandweiss. New York: Oxford University Press, 1996b, 431–467.

Seidman, Earl. *In the Words of the Faculty.* San Francisco: Jossey-Bass Publishers, 1985.

Shaw, Kathleen, Robert Rhoads, and James Valdez. "Community Colleges as Cultural Texts: A Conceptual Overview." In *Community Colleges as Cultural Texts,* eds. Kathleen Shaw, James Valdez, and Robert Rhoads. Albany: State University of New York Press, 1999.

Shires, Michael. *The Future of Public Undergraduate Education in California.* Santa Monica, CA: Rand, 1996.

Skocpol, Theyda. "Bring the State Back In: Strategies in Current Research." In *Bring the State Back In,* eds. Peter Evans, Deithrich Reuschemeyer, and Theyda Skocpol. New York: Cambridge University Press, 1985, 3–37.

Skolnik, Michael. "Higher Education in the 21st Century." *Futures* 30, no. 7(1998): 635–650.

Slaughter, Sheila. *The Higher Learning and High Technology.* Albany: State University of New York, 1990.

———. "Who Gets What and Why in Higher Education? Federal Policy and Supply-Side Institutional Resource Allocation." Presidential address, Association for the Study of Higher Education annual meeting, Memphis, TN, 1997.

———, and Larry Leslie. *Academic Capitalism, Politics, Policies, and the Entrepreneurial University.* Baltimore: The Johns Hopkins University Press, 1997.

Smith, Anthony. "Towards a Global Culture?" In *Global Culture: Nationalism, Globalization and Modernity,* ed. Mike Featherstone. Newbury Park, CA: Sage Publications, 1990, 171–191.

Smith, Ken. "Philosophical Problems in Thinking about Organization Change." In *Change in Organizations,* ed. Paul Goodman. San Francisco: Jossey-Bass Publishers, 1982, 316–374.

Smith, Peter. "A Province Just Like Any Other." In *The Provincial State*, e ' ˜ ´ ːhael Howlett and Keith Brownsley. Mississauga, Ontario: Copp Clark Pitman, 1992, 242–264.

Snyder, David. "High Tech and Higher Education: A Wave of Creative Destruction is Rolling Toward the Halls of Academe." *Horizon* 4, no. 5 (1996): 1–7.

Starr, Kevin. *Endangered Dreams: The Great Depression in California.* New York: Oxford University Press, 1996.

State of California, Commission on Innovation. "Choosing the Future: An Action Agenda for Community Colleges." Report of Commission on Innovation to the Board of Governors of the California Colleges. Sacramento, October 1993.

State of California, State Legislature. "Education Code and Government Code including AB 1497 Chap. 1214 of the Statutes of 1991 and SB 3512 Chap. 805 of the 1994 Statutes." Economic Development Program Codes and New Legislation, Revised, November 18 1996.

State of Hawaii. "Chapter 304, University of Hawaii." The Statues of the State of Hawaii, 1996. Honolulu, HI, 1996.

State of Hawaii, Governor Benjamin Cayento. "Restoring Hawaii's Economic Momentum." Governor's Report. Honolulu, 1996.

State of Washington. "Title 28B. RCW. Higher Education." 1998.

———. "Title 131 WAC. Community and Technical Colleges." 1993.

———. "Washington Laws, Chapter 238." 1991.

State of Washington, Higher Education Coordinating Board. "The Challenge for Higher Education: 1996 State of Washington Master Plan for Education." Olympia, WA, 1996.

State of Washington, State Board for Community College Education (SBCE)/ State of Washington Information Services and Enrollment Planning (SWSEP). "Academic year report 1992–93," Olympia, WA, 1993.

———. "Fall Enrollment & Staffing 1995." Olympia, WA, 1996.

State of Washington, Workforce Training and Education Board. "Workforce Training: Supply, Demand, and Gaps." Olympia, WA, 1996.

Statistics Canada. *Annual Demographic Statistics.* Catalogue no. 91–913, 1998.

———. *Annual Demographic Statistics.* Catalogue no. 91–213, 1993.

———. *Annual Demographic Statistics.* Catalogue no. 91–213, 1998.

———. "Operating Income of Community Colleges by Source of Funds and by Province, Fiscal Years Ending in 1991." Ottawa, Ontario, 1999.

———. "Operating Income of Community Colleges by Source of Funds and by Province, Fiscal Years Ending in 1997." Ottawa, Ontario, 1999.

———. *Profile of Higher Education in Canada.* Report 81–222. Canada, Department of the Secretary of State. Ottawa: Ministry of Supply and Services, 1991.

Strong-Boag, Veronica. "Society in the Twentieth Century." In *The Pacific Province*, ed. Hugh Johnstone. Vancouver: Douglas & McIntyre, 1996, 273–312.

Taber, Lynn. "Chapter and Verse: How We Came to Be Where We Are." In *The Company We Keep: Collaboration in the Community College*, eds. John Roueche,

Lynn Taber, and Suanne Roueche. Washington, D. C. : American Association of Community Colleges, 1995, 25–37.

Tapscott, Don. *The Digital Economy Promise and Peril in the Age of Networked Intelligence.* New York: McGraw-Hill, 1996.

2005 Task Force of the Chancellor's Consultation Council. Technical Papers, California Policy Analysis and Management Information Services Division. Sacramento, California: Chancellor's Office, 1997.

Taylor, Charles. "Social Imaginaries." Presentation at the biennial meeting of the Association for Canadian Studies in the United States, Pittsburgh, PA. November, 1999.

Teeple, Gary. *Globalization and the Rise of Social Reform.* New Jersey: Humanities Press, 1995.

"Telecommunications Infrastructure Model Master Plan and Guidelines Appendix A." ORSA Consulting Engineers, Inc., Fullerton, California, for The California State University, 1995.

Thomas, Robert, and Thomas Kochan. "Technology, Industrial Relations, and the Problem of Organizational Transformation. " In *Technology and the Future of Work,* ed. Paul Adler. New York: Oxford University Press, 1992, 210–231.

Thor, Linda, Carol Scarafiotti, and Laura Helminski. "Managing Change: A Case Study in Evolving Strategic Management." In *Organizational Change in the Community College: A Ripple or a Sea Change?,* ed. John Stewart Levin. San Francisco: Jossey-Bass Publishers, 1998, 55–65.

Tierney, William. *Building Communities of Difference: Higher Education in the 21st Century.* Westport, CT: Bergin and Garvey, 1993.

The University of Hawaii, Board of Regents. "Policy Section 4–2, Part D Distance Learning." June 19, 1998.

The University of Hawaii, The Board of Regents and Office of the President. "Mission." November, 1997.

The University of Hawaii Community Colleges. "Annual Report 1993–94." Honolulu: The Office of the Chancellor for Community Colleges, 1995.

———. "Facing the Future: On the Edge of a New Millennium, Annual Report 1994–1995." Honolulu: Office of the Chancellor for Community Colleges, 1996.

The University of Hawaii Community College 1990–95 Annual Reports. Honolulu: Office of the Chancellor for Community Colleges, undated.

The University of Hawaii Community Colleges Strategic Plan 1997–2007. Approved by the Board of Regents 1997. Honolulu: Office of Senior Vice President and Chancellor University of Hawaii Community Colleges, 1997.

U. S. Census Bureau. "Estimates of the Population of States: Annual Time Series, July 1, 1990 to July 1, 1998 and Demographic Components of Population Change." *Annual Time Series,* Block 1, 1998.

U. S. Bureau of the Census. "Estimates of the Population of Counties and Demographic Components of Population Change: Annual Time Series, July 1, 1990 to July 1, 1997." PE-62, CO 97–6, 1997.

———. "U.S. Counties." Censtats, 1996.
U. S. Department of Commerce. *Statistical Abstract of the United States.* Washington, D.C.: Bureau of the Census, 1981, 1985, 1986, 1987, 1989, 1990, 1991, 1992, 1993, 1994, 1995, 1996, 1998.
U.S. Department of Education. *Digest of Educational Statistics,* Table 223. Washington, D.C.: National Center for Educational Statistics, 1998.
———. *Digest of Educational Statistics,* Table 218. Washington, D.C.: National Center for Educational Statistics, 1996.
———. *Digest of Educational Statistics,* Table 210. Washington, D.C.: National Center for Educational Statistics, 1991.
———. *National Assessment of Vocational Education.* Washington, D.C.: Office of Education Research and Improvement, 1994.
———. National Center for Education Statistics, *Higher Education General Information Survey* (HEGIS), "Financial Statistics of Institutions of Higher Education," Table 54–1, 1998.
Vallas, Steven. *Power in the Workplace: The Politics of Production at AT&T.* Albany: State University of New York Press, 1993.
Vaughan, George. *The Community College Presidency.* New York: American Council on Education/Macmillan, 1986.
Washington State, Employment Security Department. "Washington Selected Economic Data." Office of Financial Management, 1998.
Waters, Malcolm. *Globalization.* New York: Routledge, 1996.
Weick, Karl. "Educational Organizations as Loosely Coupled Systems." *Administrative Science Quarterly* 21 (1976): 1–19.
Weis, Lois. *Between Two Worlds: Black Students in an Urban Community College.* Boston: Routledge and Kegan Paul, 1985.
Wheeler, Wendy. *A New Modernity? Change in Science, Literature and Politics.* London: Lawrence and Wishart, 1999.
Workforce and Career Development Act of 1996. Conference Report, H.R. 104–707, 104th Congress, 2nd session, 1996.
Workforce Training and Education Coordinating Board. "High Skills, High Wages: Washington's Comprehensive Plan for Workforce Training and Education." Progress report. Olympia, WA, 1995.
Yin, Robert. *Case Study Research.* Newbury Park, CA: Sage Publications, 1984.
Young, Jerry. Personal communication from Chief Executive Officer, Chaffey College. California, November 24, 1999.

INDEX

academic capitalism, x, xi
adaptation, 6, 7, 10, 83, 147, 193
applied degrees, 26, 37, 38, 45, 106, 109, 110, 126, 151

baccalaureate, baccalaureate degrees, 26, 27, 34, 35, 36, 51, 55, 58, 86, 110, 116, 126, 127, 128, 130, 131, 149, 150, 154, 162, 176
Badway, Norena, 70
Baker, George, 11
Bell, Denise, 70
Bragg, Debra, 70
Brawer, Florence, 65, 179–181
Brint, Steven, 11, 169, 176
buffered, buffering, 114, 133, 142–147
buffeted, 114
business culture, 64

Cameron, Kim, 10, 193
Carlyle, Thomas, vii
Carnoy, Martin, 111
case study, 6–7, 185
Castells, Manuel, 91
Chomsky, Noam, 63
City Center College, 21, 22, 32–34, 43, 44, 45, 47, 55, 56, 58, 60, 76, 77, 78, 114, 117, 141–145, 175
City South Community College, 21, 27–29, 38, 43, 44, 45, 46, 47, 48, 49, 50, 56, 66, 67, 68, 75, 76, 77, 93, 95, 96, 115–116, 132–137, 163, 174
Clowes, Darrel, 11, 176
Cohen, Arthur, 65, 119, 179–181
commercialism, 99
commodification, 40, 50–51, 56, 83, 87, 102, 126
communications, 15, 16, 57, 78, 79, 80, 94, 167, 168–169

Community Colleges as Cultural Texts, 20
contract training, 45, 70, 162, 166
contradictory college, 178
corporatism, corporate, 9, 25, 63, 64, 65, 66, 68, 69, 92, 164–165, 168
culture, xxi, 8, 9, 22, 31, 41, 164–165, 170

data analysis, 190–193
De Weert, Egbert, 100–101
Deming, 65
Dennison, John, xiii, 11, 119
Dickens, Charles, vii, xv
distance education, learning, 83, 86, 87, 88, 94, 95, 96, 106, 122, 123
diversity, 20, 71, 76, 77
domains of globalization, 41–42, 43
domains of globalization (cultural domain), 41, 42, 43, 63–80, 182
domains of globalization (economic domain), 41, 42–62, 182
domains of globalization (information domain), 41, 42, 43, 81–97
domains of globalization (politics), 41, 42, 43, 99–120
Dougherty, Kevin, 11, 112, 178
Drazin, Robert, 10
Dudley, Janice, 16

East Shoreline College, 21, 25–27, 43, 44, 45, 47, 49, 51–52, 55, 58, 61, 73–74, 94, 116, 117, 125–132, 168, 173
economic, economics, economy, xi, xviii, xx, xxiii, 1, 2, 3, 8, 13, 14, 16, 18, 23, 30, 31, 32, 33, 35, 36, 38, 39, 41, 43, 47, 52, 53, 54, 56, 58, 60, 62, 63, 67, 78, 82, 88, 91, 99, 100, 101, 105, 106, 107, 109, 111, 119, 120, 121, 133, 137, 150, 152, 155, 156, 160, 181–182
Eisenhardt, Kathleen, 184

electronic communication and information, 41, 102, 103, 108, 109, 110
electronic technology, 14, 15, 36, 37, 41, 54, 64, 81, 95, 122, 124, 151, 153, 154, 162, 167
employee participation, 167–168
entrepreneur, entrepreneurial(ism), 17, 25, 54, 58, 60, 61, 64, 68, 130, 138, 141, 179–181

facilitatory state, 101
Figure 3.1 (Globalization Behaviors), 42
Figure 3.2 (Domains of Globalization), 43
Figure 6.1 (Globalization Behaviors), 102
Figure A.1 (Globalization Categories), 191
Figure A.2 (Categories for Government Policy Document Analysis), 192
Figure A.3 (Organizational Adaptation Continuum), 193
Fisk, Elizabeth, 11, 19
Fretwell, Jr., E. K., 92
Frye, John, 22
functional processes, 5, 65

Galbraith, John, vii
Gallagher, Paul, 11, 65, 119
Gephart, Robert, Jr., 64
Gianini, Paul, 69
Glaser, Barney, 192
global, globalization, x, xi, xiii, xviii, xix, xxi, xxii, xxiii, 1, 2, 4, 6, 7–9, 11–18, 20, 28, 29, 38, 39–42, 43, 52, 63, 69, 70, 74, 77, 78, 79, 81, 86, 87, 88, 89, 91, 93, 99, 100, 102, 103, 108, 109, 111, 113, 116, 118, 119, 120121, 126, 131, 113, 136–137, 141, 145, 146, 150, 155, 156–157, 159, 171, 172, 180–182, 183, 186
globalization theory, 7, 190–193
globalized institution,.118, 179, 180
Goedegebuure, Leo, 100–101
Gordon, Robert, 69
governance, 23, 25, 26, 27, 32, 34, 59, 65, 75, 77, 78, 104, 110, 117–118, 126, 127, 131, 146, 150, 167–168
government, xix, xx, xxii, 1, 4, 7, 10, 14, 15, 17, 18, 23, 25, 26, 27, 29, 30, 32, 33, 35–36, 37, 38, 41, 44, 46, 52, 53, 54, 56, 57, 60, 62, 66, 67, 72, 82, 88, 94, 95, 96, 99–118, 119, 120, 127, 131, 134, 137, 142, 143, 146, 150, 151, 154, 155
Grubb, Norton, 55, 70, 179–180

Hardy, Cynthia, 92
Hardy, Thomas, xv
Hartmark, Leif, 113
Helminski, Laura, 69
Higgins, Kathy, 70
Hines, Edward, 113
homogenization, 40, 102
Huberman, Michael, 184, 191
Humber College, 69

immigration, immigrants, 14, 16, 23, 28, 29, 32, 3871, 72, 74, 75, 76, 122, 141, 143, 165
information technology, technologies, xxi, 38, 79, 81–89, 89–97, 122
institutional theory, 7, 9, 10
instruction, 18, 38, 40, 56, 62, 75, 77, 79, 80, 81–89, 95, 96–97, 109, 122, 124–125, 135, 139, 164, 167, 173
international(ism), 70, 73, 74, 75, 128, 141
internationalization, 40, 42–44, 73–74, 102, 103, 107, 108
interventionary state, 101, 113, 118
investigative strategy, 183–186, 187–188

Johnson, Steven, 70

Kaiser, Frans, 100–101
Karabel, Jerome, 11, 169, 176
Keller, George, 3

Larabee, David, 178
labor alterations, 41, 93, 102
labor relations, 2–3, 24, 27, 32, 59–60, 91–93, 114–115, 147
League for Innovation in the Community College, 163
learning college, 178–179
learning community, 77, 124
legislation, 96, 107–108, 110, 116, 117, 127, 131, 146
Leslie, David, 92
Leslie, Larry, x, xi, xiv, 11, 92
Levin, Bernard, 11, 176
Levin, John, 11

INDEX

Levin, Lee, xiii
Levy, Amir, 5, 159
liberal education, 39118, 181
liberal technological philosophy, 171
London, Howard, 19

Maassen, Peter, 100–101
MacDonaldization, 9, 63, 181
managerial culture, 64
managerialism, 92, 168
Marginson, Simon, 17
Maricopa Community College District, xvii, xviii, xx
Marketplace, xviii, xix, xx, 9, 17, 25, 26, 27, 31, 38, 39, 40, 44, 48, 50, 52, 53, 54, 69, 99, 106, 139, 140, 150, 154
marketization, 40, 41, 44–48, 79, 82, 87, 99, 102, 103, 105, 106, 107, 108, 109, 110
McGrath, Dennis, 19, 118, 170
McLuhan, Marshall, 181
Meier, Ken, 70
Merry, Uri, 5, 159
Miles, Matthew, 184, 191
Mintzberg, Henry, 64
"Mission and Structure," 183, 184
mission, 74, 88, 99, 118–119, 145, 154, 155, 159, 162–163, 170–177
multiculturalism, 40, 70, 72, 73–78, 102, 111, 112, 122, 134, 139, 163

neoliberal, neoliberalism, 35, 63, 64, 114,
neoconservative, 150
North Mountain College, 21, 36–38, 43, 44, 45, 46, 47, 55, 57, 60–61, 66, 68, 76, 79, 84–85, 93, 95, 117, 150–156, 163, 174, 177

O'Banion, 180
Okun, Morris, 11, 19
organization theory, 7, 193
organizational change, 5, 7, 10, 11, 38, 40, 69, 72, 131, 142, 159

Pacific Rim, 7, 185
Pacific Suburban Community College, 21, 30–32, 38, 4344, 45, 47, 49, 50, 51–52, 53, 55, 56, 75, 7, 78, 79, 86, 93, 94, 114–115, 137–141, 175
paradigm, 5, 39, 56, 70, 82, 160–162, 165

partnerships, 69
performance indicators, 36, 48, 51, 116, 117, 139
Peters, Tom, 64
Pfeffer, Jeffrey, 11
Policy; in Alberta, 109–110; in British Columbia, 110–111; in California, 104–105; in Canada, 108–109; in government, 99–100, 102–118, 126, 145, 154; in Hawaii, 105–106; in the United States, 102–104; in Washington, 106–108
policy theory, 7
politics, xxii, 8, 32
postmodern, postmodernism, 64, 156, 181
practitioner's culture, 35, 170
privatization, 12, 52, 126, 130, 146–147, 150
procedures; interviews and observations, 188–190; document collection, 190
productivity and efficiency, 41, 48–50, 82, 87, 88, 93, 95, 97, 99, 100, 102, 103, 105, 106, 107, 108, 109, 110, 123, 126, 151
Proposition 13, 23–24
purposeful sampling, 186

qualitative field research, 183

Ralston Saul, John, 16, 63, 64
Ratcliff, James, 170
Reich, Robert, 152, 176
remedial, remedialization, xii, 2, 3, 17, 24, 50, 55, 56, 69, 124–140, 166
restructuring, 40, 41, 50, 102, 103, 105, 106, 109, 110, 123, 124, 126, 134–135, 138, 139–141
Rhoades, Gary, xiv, 92, 96
Rhoads, Robert, 19
Richardson, Richard, Jr., 11, 19
Rio Salado College, 69
Ritzer, George, 16, 63
Roueche, John, 11
Rural Valley College, 21, 34–36, 43, 44, 45, 47, 52–53, 55, 58, 67, 68, 69, 85, 86, 94–96, 117, 145–150, 168, 176
Russman, Maxine, 70

Salancik, Gerald, 11

Sandelands, Lloyd, 10
Sarantos, Sandra, 69
Scarafiotti, Carol, 69
Schugurensky, Daniel, 70
Schuster, Jack, 92
Slaughter, Sheila, x, xi, xiv, 11, 92, 101
socialist, 114
Spear, Martin, 19, 118, 170
stakeholders, 195
state, 10, 11, 24
state intervention, 41, 51–52, 87, 102, 103, 107
Stewart, Lee, xiii
strategy, 57, 84, 85, 88, 123–125, 127–132, 134–136, 138–141, 144–145, 148–149, 152–156
Strauss, Anselm, 192
student learning, 17
Suburban Valley Community College, 21, 23, 25, 43, 44, 45, 46, 47, 48, 50, 51, 53, 54, 56, 57, 59–60, 69, 73, 75, 76, 77, 79, 83–84, 85–86, 95, 116, 121–125, 163, 168, 172, 173–174

Table 3.1 (Government Base Operating Grants as a Percentage of Total Revenues), 44
Table 3.2 (Contract Services as a Percentage of Total Revenues), 45
Table 3.3 (Tuition and Fees as a Percentage of Total Revenues), 47
Table 3.4 (Full-time and Part-time Faculty at U.S. Community Colleges), 49
Table 4.1 (Immigration to the United States, by Place of Birth, 1961–1990), 71
Table 4.2 (Immigration to Canada, by Origin, 1981, 1989, 1991, and 1993), 72
Table 4.3 (Immigration to Canada, by Origin, 1926–1991), 72
Table 4.4 (International Students, 1996), 74
Table 5.1 (Employment Distribution, Percentages by Industry, Canada and the U.S., 1920s–1990s), 90
Table 5.2 (Percentage of Employment in Information Handling in U.S. and Canada), 91
Table 6.1 (Themes of Globalizing Behaviors in Policy Documents), 103
Table 8.1 (Suburban Valley Community College), 172
Table 8.2 (East Shoreline College), 173
Table 8.3 (City South Community College), 174
Table 8.4 (Pacific Suburban Community College), 175
Table 8.5 (City Center College), 175
Table 8.6 (Rural Valley College), 176
Table 8.7 (North Mountain College), 177
technology, 7, 39, 96, 121, 163
Teeple, Gary, 63
Thor, Linda, 69
trajectories of change, 177–181
Truman Commission, 2

unions, unionization, collective bargaining, 2, 3, 24, 25, 26, 32, 33, 35, 52, 58, 59, 92, 95–97, 125, 142, 166–167
university-college, 146, 148–149

Valadez, James, 19
Valencia Community College, 69, 70
vocationalism, vocationalizing, 12, 17, 55, 99, 150, 174, 177

Waterman, Robert, 64
Weis, Lois, 19
Wheeler, Wendy, 118
Woodard, Doug, xiv

GPSR Compliance

The European Union's (EU) General Product Safety Regulation (GPSR) is a set of rules that requires consumer products to be safe and our obligations to ensure this.

If you have any concerns about our products, you can contact us on

ProductSafety@springernature.com

In case Publisher is established outside the EU, the EU authorized representative is:

Springer Nature Customer Service Center GmbH
Europaplatz 3
69115 Heidelberg, Germany

www.ingramcontent.com/pod-product-compliance
Lightning Source LLC
LaVergne TN
LVHW011809060526
838200LV00053B/3715